No Escape

NO ESCAPE

*The Future
of American Corrections*

JOHN J. DiIULIO, Jr.

BasicBooks

A Division of HarperCollins*Publishers*

The discussion of *Ruiz v. Estelle* in chapter 4 is a revised and updated version of my article "Prison Discipline and Prison Reform," *The Public Interest* (Fall 1987): 71–90; pages 180–202 in chapter 5 are an updated version of my article "What's Wrong with Private Prisons," *The Public Interest* (Summer 1988): 66–83, reprinted by permission.

Library of Congress Cataloging-in-Publication Data
DiIulio, John J.
  No escape : the future of American corrections/John J. DiIulio, Jr.
    p. cm.
  Includes bibliographical references and index.
  ISBN 0-465-05111-1
  1. Corrections—United States.   I. Title.
HV9469.D55   1991
365'.973—dc20   90-55596
                                                      CIP

To Rosalee Beth

Let us not declare an evil incurable, which others have found means to eradicate; let us not condemn the system of prisons; let us labour to reform them.

—Alexis de Tocqueville and Gustave de Beaumont,
On the Penitentiary System in the United States and France (1833)

Contents

Acknowledgments

MY PRINCIPAL DEBT is to the hundreds of federal, state, and local corrections practitioners around the country— commissioners, wardens, officers, counselors, probation and parole agents, and others—who, over the past decade, have allowed me to talk to them and to observe what they do. They perform a crucial but thankless public service, supervising people most of us would neither care nor dare to be around. They deserve our respect and appreciation; they have every bit of mine.

I would also like to thank academic colleagues who read and commented on all or part of this book as I drafted it: Professors Aaron Friedberg, Jameson W. Doig, Mark Alan Hughes, Ethan Nadelmann, Richard P. Nathan, and, last but by no means least, James Q. Wilson. I also thank my editor, Martin Kessler of Basic Books, for his helpful work on the manuscript. And I am grateful to the John M. Olin Foundation for giving me the resources to write this book, to the Brookings Institution for office space, and to Princeton University for the time off. None of these individuals or institutions, however, is responsible for the contents of this volume (except for whatever good parts are to be found in it). To borrow a bit of corrections slang, I will gladly take the rap for any problems.

A final acknowledgment is due to Alexis de Tocqueville, the unsurpassed genius who, with his friend Gustave de Beaumont, in the 1830s spent months interviewing American prison and jail officials and carefully observing operations "behind the walls." Most scholars have neglected their *On the Penitentiary System in the United States and France*; some have studied it, but mostly as only a window on ideas that Tocqueville expressed in his later and more celebrated writings. For me, however, this work has been a special source of inspiration: Tocqueville, too, was awed and engaged by the better corrections officials of his day and understood that the future of American corrections lay ultimately in their hands.

Introduction

NEARLY TEN YEARS AGO, I began studying America's prisons and jails. Since then, I have spent countless hours in scores of federal, state, and local institutions, observing operations and interviewing inmates and staff. My time behind bars has been spent as an academic researcher with an interest in finding ways to make prisons and jails more safe, civilized, and cost-effective. More recently, I have been exploring ways of supervising criminals in the community that protect the public (and its purse) more effectively than do conventional probation and parole programs. Among other activities, I have written books and articles, attended and organized conferences, lectured policy makers and administrators, served as a consultant, reviewed research funding proposals, written government reports, and granted interviews to print and broadcast journalists who invariably billed me as an expert on corrections.

The truth, however, is that there are no experts on corrections. As near as we come to such experts are the men and women who have spent their adult lives working with criminals: wardens, correctional officers, probation and parole agents, and so on. Most of what I know about the subject I have learned from them.

Like any large and diverse group of thoughtful people engaged in an important public task, corrections people are not all of one mind. But with only the rarest of exceptions, they share a perspective on the past, present, and future of corrections that is sober without being cynical, sanguine without being overly optimistic, and compassionate without making justice a hostage to mercy. To them, most offenders and would-be offenders are neither fallen saints nor remorseless demons; and these officials know that our nation's correctional systems are neither perfectly healthy nor terminally ill.

I cannot claim to speak for all or even most of the hundreds of corrections people I have come to know over the last decade, but I can claim to have been influenced by their balanced perspective. With them, I have become impatient with academic analysts, activists, judges, politicians, and media pundits who consistently paint a rosier or a bleaker picture of American corrections than is justified by the facts, and who propose policy changes without any apparent concern for how, if at all, those changes can be implemented.

Most of the acknowledged "experts" on corrections suggest that we can escape from the human, financial, and moral problems of managing an increasingly large population of convicted criminals; of course, their escape plans vary. Some see an escape simply by indiscriminately increasing the use of community-based alternatives to incarceration; others, simply by building more prisons and jails. Some advocate longer prison terms; others, early release.

Both call this "sentencing reform." Some seek salvation in the privatization of corrections; others, in a rebirth of old-fashioned rehabilitation programs; and still others, in a return to such "correctional" measures as corporal punishment and an unfettered use of the death penalty.

I wrote this book in the belief, bred by years of intimate discourse with corrections practitioners and informed by a prolonged stare at hundreds of relevant research monographs, that there is no escape from the problems that now beset American corrections. There are, however, better and worse ways of conceptualizing these problems, and better and worse ways of addressing them through public policies. While the future of corrections in this country looks bleak, a series of incremental improvements is possible. Before we can make these improvements, however, the intellectual and moral quackery of the "experts," and the fruitless political, legal, and academic controversies they engender, must be succeeded by a respect for certain unpleasant facts about American corrections that are well understood and freely acknowledged by most of those who work in its trenches.

First, over the next two decades there will be *no escape from the greatly increasing numbers of citizens in prison, in jail, on probation, and on parole.* In 1989, some 3.6 million citizens lived under some form of correctional supervision—roughly 1 in every 35 adult white males, 1 in every 9 adult black males, and 1 in every 4 black males between the ages of eighteen and thirty. About 675,000 of them were in prison, over 300,000 of them were in jail, and the rest—about three-quarters of the correctional population—were supervised in the community under various types of probation and parole programs. By the year 2000, even if a radical, sudden, and unexpected change takes place in both demographic trends and sentencing practices, the total number of citizens in the charge of corrections officials will easily surpass 4 million. The California Department of Corrections and the Federal Bureau of Prisons alone will house over 200,000 prisoners. Corrections will represent the largest single item in many state budgets; adjusted for inflation, corrections expenditures may total some $40 billion annually, roughly twenty times their cost in 1975.

Second, even with a continued increase in the use of alternatives to incarceration, there will be *no escape from the need for more prisons and jails*. In the 1980s, the national rate of incarceration approximately doubled, and the rate of community-based supervision nearly tripled. As a result, in many jurisdictions the caseload of the average field services (probation or parole) officer at any given time has risen to over 200. Overcrowding behind bars has not prevented overloading on the streets.

Nationally, only a small fraction of prisoners, and only a slightly larger fraction of jail inmates, would appear to be good candidates for alternative programs. Over 95 percent of prisoners are violent offenders, repeat offenders (having two or more felony convictions), or violent repeat offenders; under 5 percent of prisoners can be meaningfully characterized as minor, petty, or low-risk offenders. Nevertheless, we are funneling offenders of all sorts out of secure institutions as quickly as possible; even murderers now serve only a fraction of their sentences behind bars (an average of just over seven years), and in most states violent offenders are eligible for furloughs.

We are already working near the limits of our capacity

to manage offenders in the community. Thus, unless we begin to take more risks and to be less punitive than our current penal practices allow—and I do not think that likely—we will need to build, staff, administer, and fund hundreds of secure facilities over the next twenty years.

Third, even if prison and jail construction projects proceed apace, there will be *no escape from institutional overcrowding*. In virtually every state and at the federal level, billions of dollars are rushing through the pipeline to renovate old facilities and to construct new ones. But even when innovative, fast-track construction projects have been completed, the supply of beds has not kept pace with the demand for them. One result has been overcrowding, in many instances associated with a rise in individual and collective violence behind bars, as well as with deterioration in the quality and quantity of the educational and work opportunities available to inmates. In other cases, however, overcrowding has been managed without these consequences. Although the problem of overcrowding will not abate anytime soon, we may be able to learn how to mitigate its harmful effects.

Fourth, there will be *no escape from the need to discriminate carefully among community-based options*. One indirect and deleterious result of institutional overcrowding has been an overzealous use of community-based options: High-risk and hard-to-handle offenders have been furloughed or released early, sometimes with tragic results. The political fallout from these ill-fated efforts has made it more difficult for proponents of tested and well-administered community-based options to get a fair hearing.

Nevertheless, a political consensus, similar to the one that gave birth to work-based welfare-reform initiatives in the early 1980s, is gradually forming around certain innovative approaches to probation and parole supervision. These initiatives, known generally as intensive-supervision programs, seem promising—our last best hopes where alternatives to incarceration are concerned.

What unites the chapters in this book, however, is not so much that they examine distinct but related pieces of a single public policy puzzle. Rather, they are united by a perspective on these issues which, though leavened by academic researches, takes its cue mainly from those who must carry out whatever mix of correctional policies is concocted. I am convinced that nothing good can happen in this area unless those who manage the nation's offenders today, and who will manage them tomorrow, are ready, willing, and able to make it happen. Owing to the harsh realities of dealing with criminals in the cellblocks and on the streets, no program, however well conceived, and no reform, however widely supported, can make its way unless those who are responsible for implementing it accept its wisdom and covet its results. Whatever the "experts" say, write, or do, and whatever the public demands, the future of American corrections is in the hands of the practitioners.

What can the practitioners do to improve the quality of life behind bars in a cost-effective manner? Most of the academic literature on prisons and jails focuses on inmate society, not on penal administration. Over the last several years, however, a small but growing body of exploratory research on correctional management has emerged. Its preliminary findings are encouraging. Among other things, certain types of institutional policies and procedures may reduce cellblock violence, improve inmate work and educational opportunities, enhance staff morale, and trim costs. In at least some cases, these results may be achieved even in the face of problems ranging from overcrowding and dilapidated structures to underfunding and political pressures. Better prison and jail management is possible, as I explain in chapter 1.

Improving the quality of life behind bars does not obviate the need for sensible alternatives to incarceration. Just as there are better and worse ways of managing offenders who are locked up, so are there better and worse ways of managing offenders who are on the streets. But all alternatives to incarceration are not equal. Only some species of probation and parole programs work. In chapter 2, I discuss the pros and cons of traditional and new approaches to community-based corrections, highlighting those that are most promising and suggesting what administrative features they have in common.

An important criterion of success for any type of correctional supervision, institutional or community-based, is what, if anything, it does to reduce the probability that those who are subject to it will recidivate (commit new crimes) once the supervision ceases. In the 1960s and early 1970s, we witnessed the rise and fall of the rehabilitative ideal. Studies showed, or were interpreted to show, that participation in treatment programs ranging from psychological counseling to remedial education had little or no effect on convicts' postinstitutional behavior. Ignoring both the problems with these studies (which were many) and the cautions of their authors (which were clear), the idea that "nothing works" became a rallying cry for those who opposed rehabilitative efforts on ideological or moral grounds.

In chapter 3, I revisit the literature on rehabilitation, including studies that have been completed over the last several years, and take the reader on a tour of Maryland's Patuxent Institution, one of the few maximum-security prisons that reaffirmed the rehabilitative ideal when other prisons were abandoning it. Except for those who prefer to treat rehabilitation as a four-letter word from a bygone era, the news is heartening. I find through analysis what most corrections practitioners know through experience: Certain types of rehabilitative efforts do succeed.

Like most other contemporary public bureaucracies, corrections agencies operate in a complex political and legal environment. Gone are the days when corrections officials managed their charges with little or no outside interference. Over the last two decades, increased media scrutiny, heightened legislative oversight, proliferating correctional officer unions and prisoners' rights organizations, and related developments have had a significant impact on how, and how well, corrections agencies perform. But the single most significant change in the operating environment of corrections agencies has been the rise of judicial intervention.

In 1970, not a single prison system was operating under judicial orders to change and improve; today, over three dozen agencies operate under such orders. In chapter 4, I offer a close examination of the causes and consequences of judicial intervention in this area. Contrary to the lessons drawn by the friends and foes of judicial activism, the record on judicial intervention in this area is mixed. For every instance where a judge's involvement led to a clear improvement in conditions, there is one where it clearly made things worse. The intersection between courts and corrections has been the scene of both smooth traffic and tragic accidents. It is possible for judges, corrections officials, and others to learn from these experiences, and in chapter 4 I offer some tentative lessons for the future.

In the 1960s and early 1970s, one popular answer to the nation's correctional problems was to stop building secure institutions and simply to deinstitutionalize offenders—to "tear down the walls." In the 1980s, amid judicial tumult and an ongoing search for meaningful alternatives to incarceration, proposals have been made to give the private sector a significant role in the administration, finance, and construction of correctional facilities and programs—to "sell the walls." To date, the debate over private prisons has been little more than a crossfire of assertions. In chapter 5, I discuss the past and present record of private sector involvement in corrections, casting a critical but far from wholly unsympathetic eye on the promises of the privatizers. Rather than a privatization strategy, I suggest that a "nationalization" strategy—an enhanced federal role in state and local corrections directed from the executive branch rather than from the federal bench—may be both more feasible and more desirable.

In the United States, social scientists have had a pervasive if often unrecognized influence on the course of correctional policies and practices—but the quality of social science research in this area has been abysmal. Most of the ideas and proposals about corrections generated by social scientists over the last several decades have proven to be trivial, meaningless, or false. Most corrections practitioners have little confidence in academic Pied Pipers, and justifiably so.

But there is a type of policy-oriented social science research that minimizes methodological and ideological biases and often yields findings that are both intellectually interesting and practically useful. Known as "demonstration research," it has been applied with great success of late in the area of welfare reform. I see no reason why it cannot be applied with similar results in the area of penal reform, and in chapter 6 I try to rehabilitate the social science of corrections by introducing it to demonstration research.

In the concluding chapter, I briefly discuss the moral tensions that continue to be at the heart of American corrections. America's correctional system is a sharp reflection of its moral culture—at bottom, a Judeo-Christian culture whose ethic of punishment is satisfied neither by a mere slap on the wrist nor by routine use of cruel and unusual sanctions. It is an ethic of punishment in which revenge must be restrained by forgiveness and justice tempered by mercy. It is an ethic of punishment that forces Saint Francis and Draco into a mutual, never quite steady embrace.

With respect to handling criminals, the public mood in the United States shifts between "Get tough" and "Go easy," reflecting a moral tension that is never resolved—certainly not for corrections practitioners, the men and women who labor under it every working day. As one veteran corrections officer remarked to me when I began my research, "Corrections is like walking a tightrope. You keep your balance by leaning to punishment and hate one moment, reform and love the next." Whatever tangible progress is made, the future of American corrections offers no escape from this delicate moral balancing act; nor should we hope that it does.

1

Better Management Equals Better Prisons and Jails

MANY LIBERALS AND CIVIL LIBERTARIANS are fond of depicting prisons and jails as hellholes in which inmates inevitably suffer rape, abuse, and life-sapping idleness. Many conservatives, on the other hand, are fond of depicting prisons and jails as country clubs in which inmates enjoy tennis, counseling, and college courses at an exorbitant cost to the taxpayers. To the former, offenders are generally people from distressed life circumstances who just got a bad break or were victimized by the system; to the latter, offenders are generally remorseless demons who committed crimes strictly for fun and profit.

The fact is that few prisons and jails are either hellholes or country clubs. To be sure, such facilities exist, but most fall somewhere between these two extremes. What accounts for these variations, and how is it possible to improve the quality of life in prisons and jails where conditions are poor to wretched? How can prisons and jails, even good ones, be made more safe, civilized, and cost-effective?

The answer, I think, is to change where necessary the

11

ways in which these institutions are organized and managed. Other factors matter, but organization and management are the keys to more orderly and humane cellblocks. Here is my thesis, stated baldly: Poor prison and jail conditions are produced by poor prison and jail management; cruel and unusual conditions are the product of failed management. And the reverse is also true: Prisons and jails where inmates can "do time" without fearing for their lives, without being pressured by their peers for sex, drugs, or money, without being abused by their officers, and without being abandoned to their educational (or other basic life skills) deficiencies are the product of sound prison and jail management.

Here is my thesis out on a limb: No group of inmates is "unmanageable"; and no combination of political, social, budgetary, architectural, or other factors makes good management impossible. Difficult, yes; fatiguing, always; thankless, mostly; impossible, never. Even overcrowded maximum-security facilities can be improved simply by changing the ways in which they are organized and managed.

If there were a large body of systematic studies specifying the types of correctional organization and management associated with better prisons and jails, my task here would be simple. Unfortunately, few such studies exist, and most of them tell us more about the colorful world of inmates and their leaders than about the difficult task of correctional workers and their supervisors. Later in this chapter, I shall mention one or two of the few meaningful studies.

THE CASE FOR GOOD MANAGEMENT

A political science colleague of mine once half-jokingly observed that "the plural of anecdote is data." In collecting together anecdotes of the people behind the management at the California Men's Colony, New York City's Tombs and Rikers Island, the Federal Bureau of Prisons, and the Texas Department of Corrections, I offer "data" in the following sections intended to highlight the importance of organization and management to the quality of life behind bars.

The California Men's Colony

Warden Wayne Estelle of the California Men's Colony (CMC), a maximum-security prison located in San Luis Obispo, is a reflective man of simple tastes and no pretensions. He prefers the title "warden" to that of "superintendent" and thinks of himself as an "overpromoted guard." A descendant of the first warden of California's infamous San Quentin prison (who was twice fired for official misconduct), and the brother of a former director of the Texas Department of Corrections (who resigned his post after publicly battling a federal judge over orders to change the way that state ran its prisons), Estelle has quietly carved out his own niche in correctional history: He is known as the best warden in California, and many of his peers across the country think he is the best warden west of the Rockies. They elected him president of the Western and Central Wardens and Superintendents Association.

13

When I studied CMC in the mid-1980s, the prison was overcrowded and operating at about 120 percent of its rated capacity. Over 80 percent of its inmates were violent offenders, and virtually all of them were repeat offenders. In corrections lingo, CMC had its share of "heavies" and "hard-asses." In fact, it had more than its share. About 25 percent of its more than 2,000 inmates were highly incorrigible felons who, according to their official security classification, should have been housed in one of the state's two highest-security prisons (San Quentin and Folsom); but these facilities were overflowing, too.

When I encountered Warden Estelle again in early 1989, the population density at CMC had increased dramatically. Indeed, Estelle had spent the last several years managing over 6,500 inmates (up to 7,000 at one point) and hence one of the most heavily populated prisons in the free world. CMC's share of hard-core and hard-to-handle offenders had increased as well.

But CMC remained what it had been for years: the safest, cleanest, most program-oriented, most cost-effective maximum-security prison in California, and one of the best such prisons in the nation. Rates of inmate-on-inmate assaults remained low, as did rates of inmate assaults on staff; in fact, rates of violence actually *decreased* as the prison became more crowded. Meanwhile, cellblocks continued to sparkle and prison industry programs hummed. Inmate participation in all sorts of educational and vocational programs grew, recreational facilities were expanded and improved, and the already far above average institutional meals were diversified and enriched. All these improvements were achieved while CMC had the highest inmate-to-staff ratios and the lowest annual per inmate expenditures of any maximum-security prison in California. But how?

The Tombs and Rikers Island, New York City

To most citizens (including, unfortunately, many journalists who report on corrections), *jail* and *prison* are interchangeable words, but there is a simple and clear distinction between them: A jail is a local correctional facility that holds people who are awaiting trial or serving sentences of a year or less; a prison is a state or federal facility that holds sentenced felons for a year or more. For instance, Attica is a prison run by New York State officials under the command of the governor; the Manhattan Tombs is a jail run by New York City officials under the command of the mayor. There are exceptions: For example, Hawaii and a few other states have no jails, and the Federal Bureau of Prisons has both prisons and "metropolitan correctional centers" (the Bureau's term for jails).

For the most part, however, the distinction holds. It is true that today's prisons and jails share many of the same problems, including overcrowding. But these problems pose rather different administrative dilemmas for prison and jail administrators. Believe it or not, corrections practitioners are divided on the question of whether, on balance, it is harder to run a maximum-security prison or a typical jail.

The New York City Board of Corrections oversees the New York City Department of Corrections. As a consultant to the Board, I have seen firsthand one of the largest,

15

most complicated, and most politicized jail systems in the country. In 1988, most of the city's over 15,000 jail inmates (some 11,000 of them pretrial detainees) were housed on Rikers Island. "Rikers" is not one jail but a complex of many jails for many different types of inmates. On Rikers and throughout the system, overcrowding has been a serious problem, compounding the violence, unsanitary conditions, inadequate medical services, and other problems that have plagued New York City jails for decades.

In the mid-1970s, Morris E. Lasker, a federal district court judge, placed the jails under his supervision. He oversaw the building and administration of the new Manhattan Tombs jail. The old Tombs, which the city had closed in the face of Lasker's 1974 order to improve it, was a filthy, dilapidated, riot-torn facility that would have made a medieval dungeon look good. By comparison, the new Tombs is a slick high-rise building with all the modern correctional conveniences (save high-speed elevators) and a security-conscious design (few "blind spots"). Rates of disorder at the new Tombs are extremely low (months have passed without a serious assault), good remedial reading and other programs are in place, and spring and summer recreation includes occasional staff-run barbecues for inmates and their visitors.

Architecture is fate, and some observers attribute the relative success of the new Tombs to its superior physical plant. Others, however, including many veteran New York City corrections officers, believe that while the plant has helped, it is by no means the whole story. For one thing, other new jails, including some with even more state-of-the-art designs than the Tombs, have been plagued by escapes and other major disorders. For another, Judge Lasker not only rebuilt the jail, he engineered a fundamental change in its management.

As early as 1971, the National Institute of Corrections, a small-budget research and training arm of the federal prison system, recommended that the New York City Department of Corrections adopt "unit management." In essence, unit management is an approach to correctional administration in which a team of uniformed security staff and counselors work together in a given cellblock or wing of an institution under the direction of a unit manager, a sort of mini-warden. Each team is held responsible for managing the inmates in its unit, including everything from counting, locking, frisking, and cell searching to monitoring inmates' disciplinary records, keeping track of their program activities and release dates, maintaining sanitation, and so on.

In the early 1970s, the Federal Bureau of Prisons adopted unit management, and everything from inmate-staff relations to rates of violence and cost-effectiveness seemed to improve. Many other systems followed suit. Though the results have been mixed, in most places unit management has worked rather well.

When Judge Lasker mandated unit management for the new Tombs, many veteran officers were at first skeptical (to put it mildly). One officer remembered predicting, "Either we'll get too close to the inmates, in which case you'll have fraternization and other headaches; or we'll come to despise them, in which case you'll have 'head beaters' [physically abusive officers] and such." Others worried about the possible boredom of being confined to one unit. Still others simply saw no need to change the way things had always been done, least of all at the behest of a "know-nothing judge."

But, as most officers now readily admit, they were wrong. Unit management was institutionalized with relative ease, and with clear gains, at the new jail. But what about the jails on Rikers? As late as 1986, many officers persisted in the belief that although unit management might work in Manhattan, it would never work "on the Island." Though their reasons varied, most assumed that, were city officials ever silly enough to try exporting it there, the greater crowding and "heavier" populations on Rikers would make unit management fail; one Tombs captain who had spent most of his career on Rikers, however, was more sanguine: "It works here, and with nips and tucks to fit the particular jail, it'll work on Rikers."

It appears that the captain was right. Because the fiscal start-up costs are significant and the savings long-term, and because any change of this sort could upset labor-management relations and cause a political row (New York City has one of the nation's strongest and most militant correctional officers unions), the responsible city officials were understandably reluctant to implement unit management anywhere on Rikers. But helped along by the advice of a few well-placed insiders (echoed later in a 1987 *New York Times* editorial), it was tried in a Rikers jail.

It took several months for officers to understand fully and to work within the unit management concept. The department "brass" were patient and allowed for these growing pains. They consciously sold the measure to field staff as a way of making the job of handling inmates more rewarding and less dangerous, and they believed in what

18

they were selling. As indicated in a 1988 memo from then City Corrections Commissioner Richard J. Koehler to then First Deputy Mayor Stanley Breznoff, the results of unit management on Rikers Island were much the same as they had been at the new Manhattan Tombs: a 28 percent overall decline in the rate of violent infractions over an eight-month period, compared with the same eight-month period in the previous year; even greater reductions in the rate of major violent incidents (assaults and stabbings); better inmate-staff relations, reflected in a nearly 50 percent reduction in the use of force; a marked improvement in officer morale, reflected in a reduction in absence rates and transfer requests; and so on.

Still, many observers doubt that this success can last, and few believe that it can be extended throughout the system. Can it? And some officers (a minority of those I talked to about it) think the positive experiences with unit management represent "freakin' flukes" (one such officer's neat phrase for statistical outliers). Are they right?

The Federal Bureau of Prisons

On May 14, 1930, President Herbert Hoover signed the Act of Congress that created the Federal Bureau of Prisons (BOP). The signing was accompanied by little fanfare, not much controversy, and modest hopes for the future.

Until the 1890s, most federal prisoners were housed in state facilities. The U.S. Marshalls found beds for them and paid for their keep with funds supplied by the Attorney General. Along with other inmates, the federal prisoners were leased out to farmers and private businessmen.

Most "contract" inmates performed menial labor under brutal conditions. In 1887 Congress passed a law that prohibited state officials from leasing out federal prisoners. Some states responded by refusing to accept any more federal prisoners; others began charging exorbitant boarding fees. Meanwhile, the number of federal prisoners rose steadily, growing from a few hundred in the mid-1840s to over 15,000 as the 1880s came to a close.

In 1891, Congress passed the Three Prisons Act; and for the first time, the federal government assumed direct charge of its prisoners. U.S. penitentiaries were opened in Leavenworth, Kansas (1895), Atlanta, Georgia (1902), and McNeil Island, Washington (1907).* In theory, these prisons, and the federal reformatories that followed, operated under the direction of a Superintendent of Prisons in the Department of Justice. In practice, each warden ran his prison (or, in the case of the Institution for Women in Alderson, West Virginia, her prison) in an independent, autocratic fashion, taking little or no direction from Washington. Each prison was funded separately by Congress. Wardens obtained their jobs through political patronage. In time, each prison became the fiefdom of the warden and his or her cronies.

The results were not good. In the 1920s, federal prisoners were beaten mercilessly for minor rule violations. They ate rotten food served from buckets. Baths were a luxury. Recreation, work, education, and other opportunities for inmate self-betterment were virtually nil. Meanwhile, enforcement of the Eighteenth Amendment

---

*Leavenworth and Atlanta were built as federal penitentiaries. McNeil was opened as a territorial prison, but in 1907 it was redesignated as a federal penitentiary.

(Prohibition) had swelled the corridors of these already crowded prisons.

An aggressive and flamboyant assistant attorney general named Mabel Walker Willebrandt had worked for years to improve the quality of life inside federal prisons. In 1929, she helped recruit Sanford Bates, known nationally as the reform-minded director of the Massachusetts Department of Corrections, as Superintendent of Prisons. In the same year, the congressionally sponsored report of the Cooper Commission was circulated far and wide. It documented the horrors of the existing system, and contained the seeds of the legislative proposals that gave birth to the Federal Bureau of Prisons in the following year.

Not unexpectedly, Bates became the Bureau's first director. A skilled administrator and prisons man, Bates and those who worked with him on the reorganization legislation knew that even a top-notch corrections executive could be rendered ineffective if his post was weak statutorily. The example of California was too fresh for anyone to ignore. In 1929, the California Department of Penology was created to centralize administrative controls over the state's abuse- and corruption-ridden penal facilities. Within the year, however, it became clear that the state's Director of Penology would fail; his formal powers went no farther than calling a meeting of five division deputies once a month.

Bates and his colleagues avoided this mistake. From the beginning, the Bureau director's position had real teeth. Among other things, the director was vested with complete authority to hire and fire wardens and division heads. By the time Bates resigned as director of the federal prison system in 1937 (he eventually went on to the bigger and better job of directing New Jersey's prisons), federal prisons had begun to improve. Among other things, officer brutality had become less commonplace (no mean achievement for the day), and the idea of a professional officer corps dedicated to the individualized care and custody of inmates had started to take hold.

Most of the improvements, however, lay ahead. They occurred under Bates's successor, James V. Bennett, who directed the agency from 1937 to 1964. A lowly attorney-clerk in the Bureau of Efficiency (forerunner of the Bureau of the Budget and hence the Office of Management and Budget), Bennett managed to get himself on the team that investigated conditions inside the federal prisons, and to write most of the Cooper Commission's report to Congress. In 1930, he became assistant director of the agency and proceeded immediately (and without Bates's urging) to make two major administrative innovations, one mainly technical, the other largely political. First, he guided the development of a prisoner classification system intended to rationalize inmate management and promote rehabilitation; second, he laid the political groundwork on which Federal Prison Industries (a multimillion-dollar-a-year enterprise known since 1978 as UNICOR) was built. He achieved both innovations within four years and continued implementing changes at about the same pace for the next three decades.[1]

From the outset, Bennett was the agency's public face and chief spokesperson. He fought pitched battles with bureaucratic rivals (often besting the likes of the Federal Bureau of Investigation's J. Edgar Hoover); he developed and maintained alliances with key congressional representatives, judges, attorneys general, journalists, prison reform activists, and academic opinion makers; and he wrote, lectured, and made public appearances to cultivate a positive image of the agency within the broader Washington community and beyond.

Meanwhile, he kept a tight personal grip on life inside the prisons. He developed a selective recruitment and training program for agency workers, sponsored awards for outstanding officers, and remained sensitive to a wide range of staff needs—all in the hope that, somehow, some way, prisons would someday succeed in rehabilitating many offenders, unlocking "the treasure" that he believed lay buried in the heart of even the most callous criminal.[2]

When Bennett stepped down as director, he was praised mightily for his outstanding public service by liberal and conservative representatives in both parties. The founding father of the Federal Bureau of Prisons maintained an office in the agency's Washington headquarters for several years after his retirement and still answered a few letters and phone calls from VIPs. Ex-prisoners who found themselves down on their luck were still welcome to come by Bennett's office for advice and, if need be, a little cash drawn from the royalties on his writings (or, in later years, straight from his own pocket).

Bennett was succeeded by Myrl Alexander, who was director from 1964 to 1970. He consolidated many of Bennett's last initiatives and made a few of his own, but Alexander was no Bennett. An intelligent man with impressive academic credentials and years of experience in Bennett's shadow, he lacked the extraordinary political and administrative skills that had enabled Bennett to transform federal prisons from a national disgrace in 1930 to a source of national pride thirty-four years later.

Bennett often spoke like a "bleeding heart" who embraced rehabilitation as the only legitimate goal of imprisonment. But more often he spoke about the need to balance the multiple and competing ends of imprisonment, and he was adamant that inmates who violated the rules be punished fairly but firmly. Alexander, on the other hand, seemed to make a headlong rush toward the medical model of corrections, based on the theory that prisoners can be "cured." His line staff (uniformed corrections officers) tended to find him too pro-prisoner, and certain of the Bureau's once-unshakable political allies viewed him as something of a loose cannon. Yet the Federal Bureau of Prisons not only survived but improved under Alexander. Indeed, federal prisons have improved in every decade since the agency was created.

Alexander's successor, Norman A. Carlson, served from 1970 to 1987. Arguably, Carlson, who had served as Alexander's executive aide, was every bit as talented a bureau chief as Bennett; indeed, some (myself included) might even rank him higher in certain respects. But Carlson was of a different executive species, unlike Bennett in everything from physique to management style.

A hulking six feet, five inches, favoring a crew cut, Carlson began his career as a corrections officer in Iowa. He joined the BOP as a parole officer at Leavenworth. In 1961, he launched a multiyear project that eventuated in the Bureau's Halfway House program. Four years later, he spent a year in a federal executive education program at Princeton's Woodrow Wilson School. He then served as Alexander's executive assistant until becoming director. Throughout his tenure as director, Carlson was a tough-minded, pragmatic administrator who got the job done and won acclaim on Capitol Hill, but without the high-visibility antics of Bennett and without being identified with any particular correctional ideology, as was Alexander.[3]

The two most popular explanations for the Bureau's historic success are false or misleading. The first is what may be termed the Club Fed explanation: The Bureau, it is said, simply has gotten a better class of criminals. Historically, however, the agency has never held only white-collar offenders; in mid-1988, for example, 46 percent of its prisoners had a history of violence, and each year the states transfer many of their too-hard-to-handle cases to "the Feds."

In fact, from its inception, the Bureau has handled everything from the most violent felons to politicians convicted of official corruption. For example, the U.S. Penitentiary in Marion, Illinois, is the Bureau's super-maximum-security prison, replacing Alcatraz. All but a few of the inmates in Marion have a history of violence or escape attempts. In the mid-1980s, following a spate of major disorders that resulted in the murder of several staff members, the Bureau tightened security at the prison and the rate of serious disorders dropped almost to zero. Contrary to popular accounts, this was achieved without completely curtailing inmates' movement or resorting to "warehousing" measures that allow no room for work or other activities.[4] At the other end of the spectrum, the Bureau has over a dozen prison camps where security is suitably lax. For example, at Allenwood prison camp in Pennsylvania, inmates go about their daily chores and recreational activities virtually unsupervised.

Staff transfers within the Bureau are frequent and have

been a sine qua non for promotion beyond the rank of lieutenant (or its non-uniformed equivalent); on average, those who make associate warden have moved seven or eight times in twenty years. An officer may work with the "heavies" in Marion one month and with the "light-weights" at Allenwood the next. Bureau staff are trained and expected to work well in penitentiaries, camps, and regular Federal Correctional Institutions (FCIs); some-how, most do.

The second popular explanation for the Bureau's success is that it simply spends more money than any other prison system. In truth, it spends almost exactly at the national per-prisoner-per-year median, and has (so far as raw statistics permit one to tell) for most of the last fifty years.

So what does explain the historic success of federal prisons? And given that Carlson's successor as director, J. Michael Quinlan, will likely preside over a doubling in the number of agency prisons (from 50 to 100) and in the number of agency employees (from 13,000 to 26,000) by 1995, can we expect to see this success continue? Will federal prisoners at all levels of security continue to live in progressively safe and humane facilities?

The Texas Department of Corrections

Unfortunately, the successors of George Beto, director of the Texas Department of Corrections from 1962 to 1972, did not continue to mount successes the way the successors of James V. Bennett did. The story of what happened to Texas prisons after George Beto resigned as director has been analyzed in many published accounts from as many points of view.[5] On one point, however, all accounts agree: Whatever the flaws of Beto's administration, they were magnified by his successors.[6]

Beto was an ordained Lutheran minister from Illinois with a doctorate in education. He assumed the helm of the agency after O. B. Ellis, who had founded the agency in 1947 after years atop the Tennessee prison system, died at a Texas Board of Corrections meeting in 1961. Beto was greeted with doubts about his toughness. Wardens who "liked the way Mr. Ellis had done things" bucked his efforts to reform the system. But Beto soon "showed them the light." Inmates came to know him as "the preacher man with a baseball bat in one hand and a Bible in the other." Wardens and division heads came to respect (and fear) "Dr. Beto," as they called him, and he earned the nickname Walking George for his habit of showing up (always unannounced) at the prison gates for a surprise inspection or, as he put it, "look-see."

Beto instituted what came to be known as the control model of correctional administration, which entailed a rigorous, paramilitary system of prison governance that emphasized inmate obedience, work, and education, roughly in that order. In the space of a decade, Beto created prison industries, developed a massive agribusiness complex, and made the prison system almost self-supporting financially. He opened the first fully accredited prison educational system in the country, and required all inmates to attain basic literacy skills. He worked to see that the prisons were models of cleanliness. And, last but not least, he made sure that control was maintained. Under Beto, the Texas inmate population increased by about

50 percent, became more racially diverse, and contained a higher proportion of violent offenders than it had under Ellis. Yet few inmates were seriously assaulted or murdered during Beto's tenure (the homicide rate dropped to one-third of what it had been in the Ellis years, and the assault rate dropped as well, though not significantly), earning Beto and the Texas Department of Corrections the respect of numerous prison officials at home and abroad.

Beto, like Bennett, cultivated strong alliances with key political leaders. He also opened the prisons to journalists and academics. Most observers went away impressed, and the preacher thereby made several converts to his control philosophy.

Beto believed that inmates were bound to choose leaders, and that these leaders would typify the worst criminal traits. Better, he supposed, for prison officials to select these leaders themselves, give them quasi-official status, and, in return for their help in watching the officers' backs and providing information, reward them with extra food, better work assignments, and so forth. He knew, too, that while he could not select (in the preacher's words) "pansies" as leaders, neither could he select the type of convict who "would rape a snake through a brick wall." So he carefully selected tough customers who were capable of following official orders. Known as building tenders, these inmates were monitored carefully to assure that they were not abusing their status or running the very "con-boss" racket this system of quasi-official selection was intended to forestall. (In the con-boss system, officers use selected inmates to intimidate and abuse other inmates.)

Under Beto's handpicked successor, W. J. Estelle,

brother of the California warden Wayne Estelle, the building tender system ran amok. Though talented in many ways, Estelle, who directed the department from 1972 to 1983, was no Beto. Somehow, Beto had managed to resolve the contradiction between the highly formalized and bureaucratized paramilitary controls, on the one hand, and the quasi-official building tender system with its irreducibly discretionary elements, on the other. In this regard, Beto's roving, charismatic, hands-on leadership was essential to keeping the building tenders on a short leash, and to making sure that staff did not become overly dependent on (and possibly corrupted by) them.

But Estelle was an officebound executive, and by 1980 he had to contend with twice as many facilities as Beto had run. Gradually, the building tender system became a con-boss system, spreading like an administrative cancer and weakening but not destroying the other parts of Beto's control regime. Despite these problems, throughout Estelle's tenure rates of institutional violence remained low, and levels of inmate participation in meaningful work, education, and other programs remained high.

It was not until Estelle was replaced by Raymond Procunier, a maverick former California prison chief with no ties to Beto, that the formal elements of the control regime were abolished along with the building tender system. As a veteran officer observed sadly, "We throwed the baby out with the dirty bathwater." Staff morale sagged as the once-proud department fell increasingly under the direction of a federal district judge, William Wayne Justice. Procunier and Justice combined to sweep away the last traces of Beto's control model, leaving in its place administrative turmoil and confusion.

The results were tragic for all concerned. In 1984 and 1985, a total of fifty-two Texas prisoners were murdered by other prisoners; rates of inmate-on-inmate and inmate-on-staff violence quadrupled at most prisons; predatory inmate gangs organized along racial and ethnic lines emerged to rule the cellblocks; rape became commonplace. Most staff, including veteran officers who only a few years earlier had proudly boasted of the department's accomplishments and their role in bringing them about, now knowingly kept their backs to the walls, ignoring most rule violations (save escape attempts) and hoping only to survive "until the next paycheck or until I can find me another job."

Between 1986 and the end of 1989, while Judge Justice threatened to hold Texas prison officials in contempt every time the state's prisons neared the population limit he had divined, Procunier's two successors struggled to bring some semblance of control to Texas prisons. Things improved, but no citizen confined in a Texas prison could count on living in a safe or humane setting. The days when Texas prison officials worked assiduously to protect and guide those in their custody were past glories, not present realities or even future hopes. Dr. George Beto mourned the death of his control model as "an old friend who died of unnatural and unnecessary causes."

THE EFFICACY OF INSTITUTIONAL MANAGEMENT

Consider the following examples of the determinative influence of prison and jail management on the quality of institutional life.

William Leeke, a humble man who led the South Carolina prison system from 1968 to 1988, implemented reforms that led to an end of abuse and discriminatory practices in that state's prisons.

Warden Frank Wood made correctional management history at two Minnesota prisons. First, he turned around Stillwater, a maximum-security prison so violent and troubled that it was slated to be replaced. Indeed, he did such an outstanding job that plans for Oak Park Heights, its replacement, were almost scrapped. In 1981, Wood became warden at Oak Park Heights, a high-tech facility with a superb security-conscious design. Observers who were unfamiliar with Wood's special management abilities have attributed the remarkably high quality of life at Oak Park Heights to its architecture; but a maximum-security prison in Virginia with a physical plant almost identical to that of Oak Park Heights has been racked by violence and other problems.

Raymond Procunier, the salty director of California's prisons from 1967 to 1975, presided over scores of inmate murders and unfettered gang activity in that system, and had much the same record in other states (including Texas, Virginia, and New Mexico) where he served.

Anna Kross, who, like Walking George Beto in Texas, made surprise visits to the jails in her jurisdiction (arriving by helicopter to inspect conditions at Rikers Island) made major reforms in New York City jails.

Joseph Ragen, for decades the nationally known tough-as-nails warden of Stateville Penitentiary in Illinois, is credited (even by many radical and liberal analysts) with making the Big House more safe and humane, despite his iron-fisted, no-nonsense practices. (Beto considered both Ragen and Bennett his mentors.)

William Fauver, as of 1990 the nation's longest-reigning corrections director (in office since 1973), recruited talented staff who made significant improvements in such seemingly hopeless maximum-security facilities as Trenton State and Rahway.

A string of New Mexico prison directors and wardens in the 1970s did nothing to institute basic security measures or to provide basic amenities at the Penitentiary of New Mexico; in 1980, thirty-three inmates were murdered at this prison (many after being raped and mutilated with torches), staff hostages were beaten, and millions of dollars' worth of property was destroyed.

Warden Dennis Luther of the federal medium-security prison in Danbury, Connecticut, in 1984 inherited a facility where (at least by Bureau of Prisons standards) sanitation was poor, rule infractions were high, staff morale was low, and labor-management relations were abysmal. By the end of 1988, Luther and his executive staff had turned the prison into one of the system's model facilities.

But neither these examples, nor the scores of others I would gladly offer if I did not fear taxing my reader's patience, would suffice to persuade a confirmed skeptic that whether prisons and jails are safe and civilized, on the one hand, or riotous and wretched, on the other, depends mainly on how they are organized and managed—on what corrections officials at all levels think and do, and on how (and how well) they coordinate their activities around the fundamental task of handling incarcerated citizens.

Neither my own research and experience, nor the research findings reported by others, offers any support for the idea that buckets of money, uncrowded cellblocks, surplus staff, new buildings, or angelic inmates are necessary to improving the quality of life behind bars; nor have I found any reason to believe that such conditions lead automatically, inevitably, or inexorably to better prisons and jails. Facilities have been safe and humane—or deadly and hellish—where such conditions have obtained as well as where they have not. Instead, I have found that differences in the character of organization and management explain most (in some cases all) of the variance in prison and jail conditions. Levels of crowding, rates of expenditure, and other contextual factors matter, but they are generally of secondary importance to the quality of life behind bars.[7]

At least with respect to prison riots, similar conclusions have been reached by the sociologists Bert Useem and Peter Kimball. In their study of major prison riots in the United States from 1971 to 1986, they found that variables related to prison organization and management were the single most important determinants of the riots.[8] In prisons whose security procedures had broken down, inmates were not frisked, crowds were not dispersed, cells were not searched, doors were not locked, and contraband was not controlled with requisite intensity. In some cases, overcrowding, underfunding, racial animosities among inmates, and court intervention were factors in the disorder; in other cases, they were not. In every instance, however, the riot plagued an administration that had already been suffering from a host of organizational and management problems, including leadership instability, declining staff morale, and political and public relations failures (the last of which Useem and Kimball measure cleverly with indices that include the quality and content of the department's annual reports).

Similarly, studies of the relationship between overcrowding and prison violence published over the last few years have poked holes in the notion, broadcast in literally hundreds of earlier studies and consonant with popular intuitions, that overcrowding causes disruption behind bars. In 1986, for example, the statistician Christopher A. Innes reported the results of his analysis of over 180,000 housing units at 694 state prisons.[9] The most overcrowded maximum-security prisons, he found, had a rate of homicide lower than that of moderately crowded prisons and about the same as that of prisons that were not overcrowded. He concluded that there was little evidence that crowding levels were directly related to the incidence of homicide, assault, or major disorders. In closing, he noted that some correctional systems respond to population pressures by increasing levels of supervision; others do not. Several recent studies reinforce Innes's findings and dispute the notion that overcrowding produces other harms.[10]

PREJUDICES AGAINST THE IDEA THAT "MANAGEMENT MATTERS"

I could summarize the roster of other monographs that bear on my claims about the efficacy of correctional organization and management, but that would be no more helpful than multiplying relevant anecdotes. For meaningful and systematic studies of this kind are few and inconclusive (I hope that may change); and, besides, in my innocent and unsophisticated view of the subject, I have few unflagging allies, even among my friends in the corrections community. Popular, scholarly, and professional prejudices to the contrary are strong, perhaps invincible.

Popular prejudice is fed by journalists who normally report on prisons and jails only when something has gone wrong, and who discuss riots and disturbances in terms of "complex and underlying" factors that create "powderkeg" conditions. There are occasional "human interest" stories about hospitals that excel in treating burn victims, fire companies that save lives, and police departments that have improved their ties to the local community or enhanced their crime-fighting technologies. But when did you last read a story about a prison or a jail that did not focus on its internal troubles? And when has the memoir of an ex-warden made the best-seller list alongside the sensationalistic one by an ex-convict?

Scholarly prejudice is borne mostly by sociologists who, for most of the last five decades, have analyzed prisons and jails mainly in terms of the language, leaders, laws, rites, and rituals of inmates, treating administrators (if they treat them at all) as pawns of inmate society or captives of broader sociopolitical forces. Political scientists

35

and students of public administration have done little to correct this imbalance, as few of them have trained their attention on correctional policies and institutions.

For their part, policy analysts from a variety of disciplines have been much concerned with such things as statistical explorations of interjurisdictional variations in imprisonment rates; but they have shown little interest in exploring interjurisdictional, intrajurisdictional, or historical variations in how, and with what impact on the quality of institutional life, prisons and jails have actually been organized and managed. From an academic point of view, one can hardly blame them: The former studies are methodologically tidy and can be performed from the quiet of the computer room; the latter are methodologically messy and require extended on-site visits to unappealing (indeed, sometimes dangerous) places.

Professional prejudice takes two forms, one among activists and the other among corrections practitioners themselves. Today, most penal reform activists are champions of alternatives to incarceration (see chapter 2). While nobody has shouted "Tear down the walls!" lately, many activists have an ideological bias against incarceration; they see a contradiction between calling for good alternatives and searching for ways to improve secure facilities.

For example, in a 1988 essay written in honor of the late sociologist Donald R. Cressey, the activist/penologist John Irwin, an influential author and former inmate at California's Soledad prison, wrote:

> To his credit, Cressy was not involved in ["how-to-manage-prisons" studies]. . . . Cressey had concluded that prisons are

a dumb idea we are still stuck with. As his student, I agree, but I cannot leave it at that. . . . Moreover, I think it would be a tragedy if we did succeed in managing so many prisoners, many of which [*sic*] are serving excessive long [*sic*] sentences. . . . What are needed from criminologists right now are not how-to-manage-prisons studies but studies that reveal how to get by with less prisoners [*sic*] and shorter sentences.[11]

The leading private foundations that fund in this area share Irwin's views. (Fortunately, I have never had any difficulty finding sources to fund my research.) They devote practically none of their resources to serious studies of how to improve the administration of prisons and jails; most of these foundations, and the criminal justice research centers and corporations they support, lean heavily toward investigating alternatives to incarceration. On the other hand, staunchly pro-prison activists (there are few of these) are not much help, either; they seem not to care what happens inside prisons and jails, or why it happens, so long as nobody escapes and costs are not too high. Both groups have an influence over correctional policy out of all proportion to their size.

For their part, when the results are good, corrections practitioners naturally do not mind when responsibility for what happens behind bars is attributed to organizational and management practices. But when the results are mixed or bad, some hide behind such hidden causes of failure as overcrowding, underfunding, faulty architecture, incorrigible felons, and so on. As one Michigan prison official told me: "If they blame the budget, blame the programs, blame the overcrowding, and blame the inmates, they won't blame me." Another official remarked candidly: "Nobody wants to say in public that they screwed up the prisons. It's best to say that the prisons are just screwed up."

IMPROVING INSTITUTIONAL MANAGEMENT

Most corrections practitioners understand that the quality of inmate care and custody is mainly a reflection of the quality of their organizational and management practices; and, at least in private, a majority of them acknowledge that while overcrowding and other problems may make safe and humane cellblocks more difficult to achieve, they do not make them impossible. Most prison and jail staff are eager, in some cases desperate, for advice about how to improve prisons and jails by improving their operations.

What little advice I have to give them is general and derives from my comparison of their own experiences. But "experience," as Publius observed, "is the oracle of truth." After sifting through the experiences they shared with me in federal, state, and local correctional institutions, I have found that, allowing for obvious differences related to levels of security, the best institutions are organized and managed in much the same way and in much the same spirit. Administratively, the ways of success seem uniform, the ways of failure various. The following sections focus on the behavioral norms of successful correctional executives (commissioners and directors), managers (wardens, associate wardens, and senior officers), and line workers (correctional officers and counselors).

Correctional Leadership and Organizational Culture

Beto, Bennett, Carlson, and other successful leaders of correctional agencies have differed in many ways, from their penological credos to their personal styles. In certain crucial respects, however, they and the organizations they led were the same.

One important trait they share is devotion to building or maintaining an organizational culture. James Q. Wilson has defined *organizational culture* as "a persistent, patterned way of thinking about the central tasks of and human relationships within an organization. Culture is to organization what personality is to an individual. Like human culture generally, it is passed on from one generation to the next." As Wilson has observed, unlike students of business administration, students of public administration have not puzzled much over "creating the right organizational culture," and little is known about how government executives "define tasks and motivate workers to perform those tasks."[12]

While the literature includes nothing of note about the relationship between correctional leadership and organizational culture, certain interlocking patterns are clear.

1. *The successful leaders focus, and inspire their subordinates to focus, on results rather than process, on performance rather than procedures, on ends rather than means.* Managers are re-

warded (or not) according to whether the cellblocks are clean, the inmates safe, the classes orderly, the industries productive, the staff turnover rate low, the escape rate zero, and so on. A warden who fails to deliver these goods cannot excuse himself by reciting budget woes, crowding problems, red tape, too many "heavies," or anything else.*

Some of the successful leaders have concentrated more or less exclusively on results, but all of them have stressed results in accordance with their sense of the organization's mission and primary objectives. In Beto's case, the mission was promulgated as "obedience, work, and education." In the case of Bennett and Carlson, the mission was "safety, humanity, and opportunity." But in each case, a clear mission statement existed and the institutions were organized and managed around it.

2. *Organizational culture is custodial at core.* Doctors, nurses, secretaries, counselors, accountants, and other non-uniformed institutional staff are trained to think as correctional officers first, and the primary responsibility of every employee is to protect the inmates and to keep them from escaping. Leaders have made institutional safety and security their top priority and have worked hard to see to it that the organization's formal and informal (peer group) incentive structure mirrored this emphasis.

In the Federal Bureau of Prisons, for example, all staff members have undergone the same basic training. They

---

*I recognize, of course, that the distinction between means and ends, process and performance, activities and results, is by no means entirely clear-cut. For example, one could say of Beto's Texas Department of Corrections what Alexis de Tocqueville said about the Roman Catholic Church: "the doctrine and the form are . . . so closely united as to form one point of belief."[13] Compared to Beto, Bennett and Carlson were more exclusively oriented toward results, allowing most staff significant discretionary authority.

have been required to take target practice and are expected to join shoulders with uniformed officers in the event of a major disturbance. The spectacle of middle-aged secretaries in skirts toting guns on the perimeter of a prison amazed (and distressed) some on-site observers of the 1987 hostage incident at the Bureau's Atlanta Penitentiary—but it was an example of the kind of management that has made the Bureau a close-knit family organization with high esprit de corps and little of the workaday tension between treatment and custodial personnel that has harmed other corrections agencies. Similarly, a Michigan prisons research analyst was amused when he telephoned his counterpart in the Texas Department of Corrections and was told that the fellow was out hunting down escapees. Such practices accounted for the once-healthy staff morale and good relations among Texas prison workers at all levels.

As Wilson points out, public organizations that have strong management and a concomitantly strong sense of mission sometimes suffer from resistance to needed administrative changes, slowness in adapting to new political circumstances, and other problems.[14] The net effect, however, is almost always positive, and correctional organizations that have been led in ways that promote a strong custodial culture have everywhere been more safe and humane than those that have not.

3. *Leaders of successful institutions follow the MBWA principle: Management By Walking Around.* In this regard, Walking George Beto takes the prize, but his successful peers come in close seconds.

New Jersey's William Fauver, for example, began his practice of "feet-on" leadership when he was the warden of Trenton State Prison. As he later recalled: "When I first came to Trenton, a warden walking around without a bodyguard was unheard of. I felt it was necessary—a symbolic thing that says you're in charge." He has continued this practice as commissioner, making regular visits (not "tours" or "inspections") to each of his facilities.

The same was true for Bennett, Carlson, and other successful leaders. None was a stranger to the cellblocks he directed; each knew the facilities almost as well as he knew his own home and was always on the scene (often in the center of things) when major trouble erupted. MBWA kept them from becoming hostages to (often distorted or incomplete) reports from the field, and helped them escape the iron bars of paperwork. Moreover, it gave the staff greater personal respect for their chief and enhanced his reputation among the inmates as well.

In prison and jail settings, one's personal reputation is crucial: Inmates who lie about their criminal exploits or "punk-out" when challenged physically by their peers are not respected; and officers who are easily intimidated, break their word, or do not act in a "firm but fair" manner are not taken seriously. Everyone "looks through" the uniform to the person inside it. Of senior officers who have weak personal reputations, one often hears comments such as, "He's just a paper captain," or "His bars aren't for real," or (from inmates) "He's Major No-Balls."

Correctional leaders who have not practiced MBWA have not made a reputation; instead, staff and inmates have made one for them. In most cases, the reputation they fastened to the director was not flattering ("removed," "chickenshit," "out of touch," "head up his ass," and so on). Leaders who have practiced MBWA have not always done so successfully (Procunier is one example), but most have. An inmate once told Fauver: "You try to be accommodating without force if you can, but we know if you have to, you'll shoot us." A veteran officer remarked of Fauver: "I've seen him everywhere I've worked. He talks to you. He's quiet and nice, but he has guts. . . . He doesn't let the inmates run the joint, but he doesn't let staff do whatever they want either. He's not Almighty God and he doesn't act that way. . . . You get the feeling he knows your job almost as well as you do. And I think he could do my job, too! So usually I'm willing to go along with his ideas and to go the extra mile here if I have to."

4. *Successful leaders make significant alliances with key politicians, judges, journalists, reformers, and other outsiders with the ability to affect the organization's fiscal health, statutory authority, and public image.* Among the strategies they employed were throwing parties for key outsiders (in some cases at the executive's personal expense), responding quickly and cordially to legislative requests for information (Carlson required of his Washington staff a one-day turnaround time on letters from senators and representatives), lecturing in public, attending conferences, freely granting interviews, publishing articles and essays (including, in Bennett's case, reviews of books that promoted ideas in keeping with agency objectives and interests), and developing good personal relationships with top officials in other law enforcement agencies or, when that failed, creating interagency procedures to "force" and routinize cooperation.

Above all else, important outsiders were invited into the facilities to see for themselves what conditions were like and how things operated. Often, events were staged;

for example, an inmate college graduation ceremony. As often, however, the outsiders (including judges) were invited to take a long, hard look at what was going on. Sometimes they liked what they saw; other times they did not. In some instances, the resultant political fallout, press coverage, and public attention were favorable; in other cases, it caused fresh headaches for the director and his staff.

But successful correctional leaders followed a policy of openness and alliance building, and in the long run they fared better than leaders who did not. Leaders who tried to keep the outsiders out, or who simply ignored them, were more likely to wind up fired, burned out, or forced to resign, even when their institutions did not fare as badly as those of other systems where leaders were more open. And leaders who merely followed the global strategy of improving the general public's understanding and appreciation for what their institution did often met the same sad fate as those who "prison-walled" the outsiders. Nevertheless, the global strategy of making broad appeals to the general public remains popular in corrections circles; it is the prescription one hears over and over again at conferences of corrections officials.

Successful leaders, however, have taken it as axiomatic that the general public can neither know nor care enough about correctional staff (or the unpopular people they supervise) to furnish anything like sturdy political support for their institutions. Instead, they have made such broad appeals only one component, and by no means the largest one, of their strategy for handling outside "coaches, customers, and critics."[15] They have consciously managed their agency's external relations with as much zeal as they have managed its cellblocks.

5. *Successful leaders rarely innovate, but their innovations are far-reaching and the reasons for them are made known in advance to both inmates and staff.* Changes are made slowly, allowing staff and inmates plenty of time to learn the new ways and "get on board." For the most part, the innovations address a current or potential problem that most of those who live and work in the facilities already acknowledge as serious. As often as not, the innovation represents a fundamentally new way of achieving an old mission, rather than being a new mission itself. And in most cases, the old practices are abolished without any implication that they (and hence those who followed and believed in them) failed or were misguided; rather, they are presented as necessary or unavoidable responses to changed circumstances and "sold" to inmates and staff accordingly.

For example, starting in 1973, Carlson began to regionalize the Federal Bureau of Prisons. Gradually, he and his executive staff carved out five regions, each with its own headquarters and regional director. Rather than looking to Washington, wardens would now send much of their paperwork, route many of their requests, and receive most of their policy directives via the regional offices.

On the surface, one might suppose that regionalization represented some sort of decentralization of administrative authority, and, initially, that is what some field staff thought. Most of them, however, understood (or were quickly made to understand) that regionalization was meant to strengthen Washington's ability to oversee the prisons. At this time, new prisons were coming on line, and the Bureau, like other corrections agencies, was facing heightened scrutiny from judges and other outsiders. Regionalization was one of Carlson's responses to this situation.

Like unit management, which he introduced around the same time, regionalization was intended to create more dexterous administrative appendages, not semi-autonomous centers of policy-making authority. At the same time, however, Carlson used regionalization as a way of involving wardens and other field staff more fully in the planning and implementation process (which most of them liked), while wardens used unit management in much the same way within the institutions vis-à-vis line staff. Whatever opposition there was to both initiatives was overcome without recriminations, and the positive results soon spoke for themselves.

In these and other innovations, Carlson was successful. By the time he resigned in 1987, however, the field staff was starting to feel that the Bureau had not done much for them lately. In particular, as one officer remarked, they felt that "all the changes were to make us work better and harder so the inmates could live better and softer."

Correctional line staff are notoriously sensitive to what their leaders "do for the inmates" versus "what they do for us." Signs of appreciation, tangible and symbolic, for the public service that line staff perform tend to be few and to come from within the organization. As one warden stated, at times it is almost as though there were a sibling rivalry between inmates and line officers. Thus, to give inmates a new athletic facility without making a commensurate gesture toward line staff, or to enhance inmates' eligibility for college and vocational courses without improving (or at least attempting to improve) the educational benefits of staff, can erode staff loyalty to "the brass," harm labor-management relations in other areas, and cost a director much of whatever personal and professional capital with line workers he may have accumulated over the years.

Thus, many "innovations" in correctional settings are in actuality attempts to correct this sort of real or perceived imbalance. For example, soon after taking office in 1987, Carlson's successor, J. Michael Quinlan, attempted to do just that through a host of innovations aimed at improving working conditions, pay, and fringe benefits for staff. Seventeen years earlier, Carlson had done the same to correct the perception of line staff that the agency's top officials had grown too pro-prisoner and were taking them for granted.

6. *Successful leaders are in office long enough to understand and, as necessary, to modify the organization's internal operations and external relations.* Most of them served for at least six consecutive years; some for over a decade. With respect to length of service, there have been four kinds of corrections leaders, which I classify (with shameless alliteration) as flies, fatalists, footsoldiers, and founders.

Over the last two decades, corrections directors have served an average of only three years before quitting, getting fired, or moving on to another agency; several have stayed in office less than a year. These flies of summer have either come and gone unnoticed or have attempted

47

to reform the agency in one fell swoop. The former flies were inconsequential; the latter buzzed loudly and were a nuisance until they were swatted down by reality.

The fatalists served similarly brief terms that began and ended with their complaining about the futility of incarceration and the hopelessness of institutional reform. Often, they had little or no previous experience managing correctional institutions. In some cases, they were talented and energetic people who convinced key decision makers that their institutions were beyond repair; several brought about deinstitutionalization schemes of one sort or another. Whatever the results of these schemes (usually the results have been poor to mixed), the fatalists did nothing to achieve institutional reform but did succeed in abolishing some institutions.

Compared to the flies and most of the fatalists, the footsoldiers served long terms. Whether they inherited their job from a fly, a fatalist, or a founder, they worked in the trenches to make whatever incremental improvements they could, usually in a pragmatic spirit unleavened by a commitment to any particular penological theory. When what they inherited was good, they tried to preserve as much of it as they could and to consolidate new administrative measures around old routines. W.J. Estelle in Texas, Steve Bablitch in Wisconsin, and Orville Pung in Minnesota would rank among the footsoldiers.

The founders were those who created an agency or reorganized it in major and positive ways. Generally, like Bennett, Beto, Carlson, Fauver, and Leeke, they served long terms.

Not every leader who served a long term has done good things organizationally. And some leaders (for example,

Alexander) are hard to classify meaningfully. But the record suggests that footsoldiers and founders are a boon to the quality of institutional life; indeed, if I were forced to choose between one mediocre leader for ten years and a succession of four talented ones over the same period, I would probably entrust the institutions to the former.

Correctional Managers

In terms of their tenure and the other characteristics discussed in the preceding section, wardens, associate wardens, and senior officers who have run good prisons and jails have reflected the practices of the successful directors; indeed, as I hinted with respect to Fauver, the successful leaders often began these practices while they were coming up the ranks. Even where dominated formally by weak or ineffective leaders, or enmeshed in a system rife with violence, cost overruns, and other problems, such correctional managers have made a positive difference.

Again, Warden Estelle of California is a prime example. Estelle has engaged in MBWA with a twist. He has been fond of walking *and* talking around the prison, seeing for himself what staff and inmates are doing, asking questions, and answering them. He has stressed results: His staff knows that "excuse mongering" does not win his heart, and that he does not like to deal with the same inmate problem (or see the same cigarette butt on the industry plant floor) twice. They know as well that, as much as he values inmate participation in work programs and educational activities, security and control come first.

That is understood by freshman counselors—and goes as much for them as it does for grizzled uniformed veterans. Innovations at the California Men's Colony have been rare; as Estelle remarked, "I don't know why it works, and I'm not inclined to tinker." But when the prison's population tripled, several administrative innovations were necessary and he made them without breaking CMC's basic managerial mold. His three basic rules—"no dirt, no graffiti, no bad behavior"—were enforced as always. Meanwhile, as a member of the local Rotary Club and other community organizations, he has cultivated positive relations with San Luis Obispo officials, offering the services of inmate volunteers to assist in certain forestry and fire-fighting activities. Finally, he has been at CMC for most of his career, working for years as associate warden before occupying the warden's chair.

Other California maximum-security prisons have been managed differently by wardens or superintendents who are more hidebound, inexperienced, process-oriented, and hermitlike in their dealings with the surrounding community. These prisons have been less safe, humane, and cost-effective than CMC.

Neither would they compare favorably to the Bureau of Prisons' facilities where Estelle's basic management practices, which are idiosyncratic for his system, are largely institutionalized. For example, like Estelle, Warden Pat Keohane of the United States Penitentiary in Lewisburg, Pennsylvania, gets out into his massive institution on a regular basis—usually daily—and lines up with his deputies in the dining hall to hear inmates' requests, to address inmates' problems, and to answer inmates' questions. By training policy (which encourages such communications), and more so by organizational custom, such lining up also occurs at other Bureau penitentiaries and at virtually all of its other facilities.

Correctional Line Workers

Whatever leaders and managers do, it is the line workers who make or break a correctional operation; what is more, they know it. For it is they—the lowest-level correctional officers, counselors, and others—who do the nitty-gritty work of handling incarcerated citizens in prisons and jails.

Over the last decade, several good scholarly studies of correctional line workers have been published, focusing mainly on uniformed security officers.[16] These studies, though rich in detail and capable of transporting their readers into the guard's world, do not easily lend themselves to generalizations about the types of line worker behavior and characteristics that have been associated with better prisons and jails. In the quest for such generalizations, my own research and experiences with line staff provide me with little advantage. Three facts, however, are worth noting here.

1. Most line staff are living rebuttals to the popular stereotypes of prison workers as sadistic, mean-spirited, racist, and uneducated. If anything, they are more, not less, likely than most blue-collar Americans to believe that inmates can be reformed or rehabilitated.
2. Corrections workers have more formal education than their blue-collar counterparts in many other industries;

51

in several systems, over half the officers have some formal education beyond high school, and a significant fraction have bachelor's degrees. But the relationship between formal schooling and job performance is unclear. In terms of the kinds of judgmental and verbal skills that make for success in dealing with largely underclass and working-class incarcerated felons, persons with military experience or with backgrounds in law enforcement (such as ex-cops), but with no advanced formal education, seem to do just as well as their more educated peers.

3. Line staff who survive and make a career in corrections are capable of "separating the criminal from the crime," dealing with their charges in terms of how they behave inside the institution, not what they did on the outside.[17] The line staff harbors a sober view of convict nature that leads them to distrust most convicts most of the time, to be deeply suspicious of them, and always to stay alert and slightly on edge (but never edgy or jumpy) while on duty.

CAN INSTITUTIONAL MANAGEMENT BE IMPROVED?

I have offered six ideas about correctional leadership and organizational culture:

1. Focus on results
2. Infuse the organization with a custodial ethic
3. Manage by walking around
4. Form alliances with and remain open to outsiders

5. Innovate on an incremental basis
6. Stay in one place long enough to cast two presidential ballots while there.

This list could easily be extended to include other lessons, general and specific, from the practices of successful institutions: immerse staff in organizational history; adopt new hardware (for example, electronic locking devices and monitors) slowly but surely, and always after a thorough analysis of the potential impact of the hardware on everything from escape risks to informal staff relations; take pains to court even those key outsiders who have publicly opposed agency positions (and even agency existence); and so on. And what I have said in this vein about correctional managers and line workers can easily be extended as well.

But extending these prescriptions, or further multiplying the examples and studies that support them, would add nothing to my main argument: Management and organization are of crucial importance. The major implications of this argument are hopeful: Prisons and jails can be improved by changing the ways they are organized and managed, even without such improvements as more money, fewer inmates, and better physical plants.

But the argument also implies that the quality of institutional life is contingent on a highly variable commodity—namely, who runs prisons and jails, and how much skill, prudence, and persistence they run them with.

At CMC, Estelle and his staff have acted wisely for quite some time with remarkable results. But whether he and his staff can continue to do the right things with the same results remains to be seen.

The New York City jail system has successfully adopted unit management in selected jails. But whether this success can be sustained or repeated elsewhere in the system must depend on how the concept is implemented.

George Beto made significant improvements in Texas prisons, but he depended heavily on his own charismatic leadership abilities and failed to institutionalize fully his control model. In his wake, there arose administrative pathologies and problems from which the system has yet to recover fully.

James V. Bennett did institutionalize most of his organizational and management practices, leaving behind something on which his successors (including at least one of lesser talent) could build, as well as the personal legacy of being the father of one of the world's finest prison systems. Whether J. Michael Quinlan can continue this success amid a rapid doubling in the agency's size depends on what he and his staff at all levels do; so far the signs are encouraging.

But there is no one theory of organizational leadership among these examples, and certainly no management formula that guarantees success. Still, in these and countless other cases—cases widely separated by time, place, political circumstances, and penological beliefs—leaders, managers, and correctional workers who have done things a certain way have succeeded more often, and more grandly, than their peers who have not. I can thus infer that those who manage jails and prisons in the ways I have discussed will stand a better chance of succeeding than those who do not.

Of course, this is a very large inference. For example, perhaps the patterns I think I have discovered among the successful leaders are illusory reflections of a more basic and underlying similarity among them: namely, that they were blessed with certain unique administrative talents. Perhaps these skills can be admired and studied by others who do not possess them. But can they really be learned, if *learning* means the acquisition of a new or enhanced practical ability to translate such lessons into particular administrative actions on a day-to-day basis?

Taking this perspective to an extreme, one would say that successful correctional leaders, managers, and line workers are born, not made, and that good correctional administration is an art, or craft, that can be aped but not imitated or mastered. I have heard this opinion voiced by scores of practitioners—successful, mediocre, and poor. But we do not need to go to this extreme in order to throw cold water on the possibility that the prescriptions I have offered (supposing, for the moment, that they are valid) can do anything to improve the quality of institutional organization and management, and hence the quality of institutional life.

For there is another big supposition in my argument that better management makes for better prisons and jails: namely, that it is possible to analyze differences in organizational performance and to trace them systematically (if not always scientifically) to organization and management. That the "public management variable" can be isolated and assessed in this way is by no means certain. My belief that it can be so examined is deepened by the progress made by certain scholars who have studied schools, armies, and police departments.[18]

But here, too, no sooner do we satisfy ourselves that we have produced passably systematic knowledge about what works than we are confronted again with the thorny problem of whether the generalizations that make up such "knowledge" can be put into practice—and, alas, whether putting them into practice in untried and disparate settings will produce good consequences, bad consequences, unintended consequences (good and bad), or no consequences worth noting.

Perhaps future scholarship will get us over these and related intellectual humps. That it will, and that we may someday be able to specify with confidence and precision the types of organizational structures and management regimes that work best, and under what conditions, is an article of my scholarly faith.[19]

THE FUTURE OF PRISON AND JAIL MANAGEMENT

In the meantime, however, even skeptics must recognize the influence of organization and management on the safety, humaneness, and cost-effectiveness of our prisons and jails.

When it comes to other public policy issues and public management problems, Americans are every inch the "administrative determinists." Let me pluck just three examples from our recent history to illustrate this national trait.

Within weeks of the explosion of the space shuttle Challenger in January 1986, the search for the cause of the disaster was on. Only a crank would have dared to say, "It was inevitable," and let it go at that; and only a fool would have ignored the possibility that the management decisions and organizational routines of NASA officials had something to do with the tragedy (as, indeed, they did).

Soon after the Iran-contra affair had boiled over, and official Washington resumed its normal calm, a commission was appointed to study the event. Nobody thought it odd that the Tower Commission spent lots of time and effort in 1987 analyzing the organizational and management practices that made it possible for the Iran-contra business to be transacted under the auspices of the National Security Council. And, though people disagreed about the Commission's recommendations for institutional reforms, nobody balked at the idea that institutional reforms were necessary to reduce the probability that something like this could happen again.

In October 1987, when the stock market crashed, instant theories to explain what had happened were offered by experts on the evening news. Some blamed the words of a high-ranking official; others anthropomorphized the market, which they characterized as having been "nervous" and headed for "a big breakdown" for quite some time; still others pointed to organizational developments related to computerized program trading. In its government-sponsored report, the Brady Commission highlighted a number of institutional reforms that might help to avert a plunge of this magnitude in the future. Again, "experts" disagreed about the recommendations, but not about the idea that some such institutional reforms were necessary.

Following the 1971 riot at Attica prison in New York State in which forty-one people were killed, the McKay Commission issued a report containing this line: "Attica is every prison; every prison is Attica." It also contained a fair amount of bogus but high-toned organizational analysis and prescriptions for management reform. Yet nobody much questioned the report's integrity or its intelligence.

But imagine if the commission that examined NASA had concluded: "Every space shuttle is Challenger; Challenger is every space shuttle." Or imagine the Tower Commission writing: "Every covert operation is Iran-contra; Iran-contra is every covert operation." Or imagine the Brady Commission advising: "Every day is Black Monday; Black Monday is every day."

Our assumption that changes in organization and management can improve the performance of institutions and give us more of the things we want (public safety, well-educated children, secure national borders, cleaner oceans, and so forth), often without spending more than we have been spending for these things, may be unfounded. But this assumption informs everything from acts of corporate restructuring to (probably too frequent) reorganizations of public agencies. It is a part of our public philosophy, and deeply rooted in our national history: The men who met at the Constitutional Convention were nothing if not believers in the absolute importance of institutional arrangements to the quality of government and hence to the public welfare.

Yet when it comes to prisons and jails, our willingness to make this assumption has been weak and fleeting. The greatest enemy of better prisons and jails is the idea that they are not possible with our current human and financial resources. Unless this idea changes, the future of American prisons and jails will be bleaker in every respect than is necessary: More energy will be wasted, more money will be spent, and more lives of inmates and staff will be lost.

2

Promising Alternatives to Incarceration

IN 1988, MONTHS BEFORE the presidential race between Vice-President George Bush and Massachusetts governor Michael Dukakis was under way, the governor of California, George Deukmejian, was asked about his views on supervising convicted criminals in the community instead of behind bars. He responded that the state would start using alternatives to incarceration when criminals started using alternatives to crime.

At the height (some might say rock-bottom) of the presidential race, several television ads for Bush focused on Dukakis's alleged use and abuse of one such alternative, prison furloughs. A furlough is a leave from confinement monitored by regular or random checks on the inmate's whereabouts and behavior. In one ad, scruffy-looking characters exited prison through a revolving door. In another ad, the mug shot of Willie Horton, a convicted murderer and Massachusetts prisoner, filled the screen as the voiceover told of how Horton had committed a sexual assault in Maryland during an unsupervised prison furlough. The Dukakis campaign attempted to strike back by pointing out that serious crimes had also been committed by furloughed prisoners in California when President Reagan was governor there.

A few weeks before the election, I appeared on NBC's "Today Show" to discuss the furlough issue. Time was short, but I tried (without great success) to make a few basic points. First, in the previous year, over 200,000 furloughs had been granted to some 50,000 inmates around the country. Second, some 99 percent of those furloughed neither violated the terms of their release nor committed new crimes while on the outside. Third, overall, the program that furloughed Willie Horton was even more successful than those in most other jurisdictions. But Horton, who was serving a life sentence without the possibility of parole, would have been eligible for a furlough in only one other state, North Carolina. Fourth, the federal system grants furloughs to murderers, as do most state systems. (Unfortunately, I did not have time to add that prisoners furloughed by the federal system would not have been convicted of murder in the first degree, and that they are selected carefully, are generally supervised without incident, and are within months of their official release date when furloughed.) Fifth, many systems have been tightening furlough eligibility requirements (some formally, others de facto) and using furloughs more sparingly, in the wake of the political pressures generated by the publicity over the Horton incident. And sixth, the furlough issue is legitimate, but it should be discussed more thoughtfully than it was in the campaign.

The responses startled me. Newspapers picked up the "story" about how widely furloughs were being used. My telephone rang off the hook for days—everyone from my

61

academic friends (few of whom study criminal justice professionally) to my old friends in South Philadelphia (some of whom have practiced criminal justice professionally) seemed a bit disturbed to know that so many furloughs were being granted to so many criminals, even violent ones. My referring to the 99 percent success rates did not seem to make many converts. I explained that most experts believed that, other things being equal, a prisoner who receives a furlough is statistically less likely to recidivate; if he does recidivate, the chances are that he will commit a less serious crime than an otherwise comparable prisoner who does not receive a furlough. But that did not seem to put them at rest.

I wondered how they would have reacted had I added the following six observations to my recitation on alternatives to incarceration.

1. Furloughs are just one of dozens of ways that convicted criminals are supervised on the streets. Some three-quarters of the persons under correctional supervision in conjunction with a criminal sentence imposed by a court of law are *never* behind bars but serve their entire sentences (probation) or the remainder of their sentences (parole) in the community, many without supervision, most without meaningful supervision (see table 2.1) At the time Governor Deukmejian made his remark about being opposed to alternatives, California had over 200,000 probationers and over 35,000 parolees, many of them placed in the community during his tenure.

2. Over the last several years, the rate at which we have been putting convicted criminals on the streets

has exceeded the rate at which we have been putting them behind bars. While prison populations increased 32.7 percent between 1983 and 1987, parole populations increased by 47 percent; over the same period, jail populations rose by 32.6 percent while probation populations increased by 41.6 percent (see table 2.1)

3. Most convicted criminals do not serve even half of their sentences in confinement. For example, violent offenders—murderers, rapists, robbers, and others guilty of nonproperty crimes—serve about 50 percent of their sentences in the community; drug traffickers serve under 40 percent of their sentences behind bars (see table 2.2).

4. While we have been overcrowding prisons and jails, we have been overloading the streets. In many jurisdictions, the average probation or parole agent simply cannot provide more than token supervision to those in his or her charge. In Los Angeles, for example, probation worker caseloads range as high as 1,000; in New Jersey, a parole officer "supervises" as many as 200 offenders at one time.

5. Because a significant fraction of community-based convicted criminals are violent, and because probation and parole caseloads have grown so large, field services workers face enormous job pressures, including victimization by their charges.[1] Field service workers thus have every incentive to "avoid trouble" by developing a reputation as "competent" agents who do not designate too many of their clients as "dangerous men."[2] Under current circumstances, one can understand the

63

TABLE 2.1

Correctional Populations, 1983 to 1987

| | 1983 | | 1984 | | 1985 | | 1986 | | 1987 | | Percent increase in correctional populations 1983–87 |
	Number	Percent of adult population	Number	Percent of adult population	Number	Percent of adult population	Number	Percent of adult population	Number	Percent of adult population	
Correctional populations											
total	2,475,100	1.44%	2,684,222	1.55%	3,011,494	1.71%	3,239,631	1.82%	3,460,960	1.92%	38.8%
Probation	1,582,947		1,740,948		1,968,712		2,114,821		2,242,053		41.6
Parole	246,440		266,992		300,203		325,638		362,192		47.0
Jail[a]	221,815		233,018		254,986		272,736		294,092		32.6
Prison	423,898		448,264		487,593		526,436		562,623		32.7

Source: Adapted from Bureau of Justice Statistics, *Probation and Parole, 1987* (Washington, D.C.: November 1988), p. 4.
Note: The following are estimates of the U.S. resident population age 18 and older on July 1. 1983: 171,332,000; 1984: 173,469,000; 1985: 175,727,000; 1986: 177,807,000; and 1987: 179,856,000. Population counts for probation, parole, and prison custody are for December 31, and jail counts are for June 30. Every year some states update their report; this table uses the corrected counts.
[a]Estimates of jail populations include convicted and unconvicted adult inmates.

TABLE 2.2
Time Served in Confinement, 1984

	Average Sentence length[a] (in months)	Percentage of sentence served in confinement (jail and prison)
All offenses	64.7	45.4%
Violent offenses	92.2	50.5
Murder	244.8	42.2
Manslaughter	95.4	50.2
Kidnapping	106.5	51.8
Rape	113.1	50.7
Other sexual assault	86.5	43.6
Robbery	96.3	52.4
Assault	59.8	51.4
Other violent offenses	65.7	46.7
Property offenses	53.2	44.0
Burglary	60.5	44.2
Larceny/theft	46.8	43.4
Motor vehicle theft	36.5	55.3
Arson	80.0	39.7
Fraud	46.2	42.5
Stolen property	45.1	41.5
Other property	46.2	46.8
Drug offenses	55.2	38.8
Possession	44.2	39.2
Trafficking	54.4	38.7
Other drug offenses	63.0	38.7
Public-order offenses	35.4	39.5
Weapons	47.3	48.9
Other public-order offenses	31.4	35.7
Other offenses	51.4	50.6

Source: Adapted from Bureau of Justice Statistics, *Time Served in Prison and On Parole* (Washington, D.C.: United States Department of Justice, December 1987), p. 3.
Note: Data on sentence length were reported for all first releases with sentences of more than a year for which the most serious offense and sentence length were reported. Time served in prison only was based on first releases with data on most serious offense and time served in prison. Time served in jail and prison was based on those cases with known conviction offenses where both jail time credited to prison sentence and time served in prison were reported. The percentage of sentence served is calculated for those cases where both sentence length and time served in jail and prison were reported.
[a]Excludes persons sentenced to death or life in prison.

propensity of field services workers to (as one Michigan official remarked to me) "just get by" and train their energies only on the "most volatile cases."

6. The members of the law-abiding public who almost certainly are at greatest risk of criminal victimization at the hands of unsupervised convicted criminals are minority citizens who live in so-called underclass neighborhoods; the next greatest risk is probably to citizens who live in the poor and working-class neighborhoods that border these ghettos. For example, in 1980, 43 percent of New Jersey's prisoners came from ghetto areas in and around Newark. When released back to their communities, many of these deviant persons returned to prey on their disadvantaged neighbors.[3] It has been my personal observation that many of the loudest and most strident advocates of alternatives to incarceration are middle- and upper-class activists who themselves live far from ghetto areas.

Had I recited these points to my friends and colleagues, my guess is that they would have thought I had unwittingly made their Horton-inspired case against alternatives to incarceration for them. And so would most Americans: Historically, alternatives to incarceration have not been favored by anything approaching a majority of the American public. On the contrary, dozens of surveys demonstrate the public's support for incarceration and its opposition to alternative measures. For example, a 1987 survey revealed that a prison or jail term was the preferred punishment of a majority of those surveyed for every offense except property theft of under ten dollars that occurs outside the home; and over 90 percent of the respondents favored incarceration for certain types of robbery and rape.[4] So far as I can discern, there is virtually no public support for radical alternative programs that hasten the return to the streets of twice-convicted criminals; yet such programs exist and are supported by the National Center on Institutions and Alternatives in Virginia and similar organizations.

Even studies designed to minimize the public's support for incarceration have recorded little mass support for alternative sanctions. A typical example is the 1988 report prepared by John Doble and his associates for the Edna McConnell Clark Foundation, one of the nation's leading financial backers of research and programs that advance the use of alternatives to incarceration.[5] A pretest questionnaire on twenty-three hypothetical criminal cases was administered to a scientifically selected sample of Alabama citizens. The cases ranged from first offenders who had committed petty crimes, stealing under a few hundred dollars' worth of property without physically injuring (or threatening to injure) anyone, to armed robbers and other violent offenders. The respondents were asked to declare which of two sentencing options—imprisonment or probation—they would impose in each case. After filling out the questionnaires, they were bombarded with information about prison overcrowding and various alternatives to incarceration via a twenty-minute film and small group discussions that argued for and against alternative sanctions. They were then asked to complete a posttest questionnaire on the same twenty-three cases they had read earlier. This time, however, they could choose between incarceration and five alternative sanctions.

This survey technique can surely be called into question, but despite all the propaganda, fully 60 percent of the respondents (down from the pretest figure of 77 percent) believed that *"most* offenders should serve at least some time in prison." And a solid majority still thought that all violent offenders, and several types of nonviolent offenders, should be incarcerated.

THE PEOPLE VERSUS THE EXPERTS

Most Americans think that criminal sanctions that make little or no use of incarceration fail to protect the public adequately, to deter would-be criminals, and to prevent convicted offenders from finding new victims. Furthermore, they simply do not feel that alternatives to incarceration are an adequate moral response to the pain and suffering imposed upon innocent victims by often calculating and remorseless victimizers. Also, in part because the average citizen owns less property (and has less ability to replace it) than the typical penal reformer, the former's belief in the efficacy and desirability of incarceration as opposed to community-based measures does not melt where nonviolent offenders (or "mere" property crimes) are concerned. And since, unlike the reformers, average citizens neither purchase (except as taxpayers via government-funded reports) nor consume (except by occasional newspaper accounts) research on the subject, they have little opportunity to change their views.

Clark Foundation officials and other leading proponents of alternative sanctions know they are at odds with the average citizen, but they seem convinced that the public needs "educating" by elite penal reformers to bring it (and the officials it elects) closer to their views. The following examples illustrate this tendency among those who champion alternatives to incarceration.

In 1979, William G. Nagel, executive vice-president of The American Foundation and author of *The New Red Barn*, an influential and widely publicized critique of American prisons, addressed a group of state legislators on "Alternatives to New Prison Construction." Invoking Alexis de Tocqueville's warnings about the "tyranny of the masses," Nagel characterized convicted criminals as a despised minority and urged lawmakers "to stand firm as oaks against the winds of tyranny arising out of the majority's fear or hatred . . . against the fear and hatred of those who would build even more prisons. There are other ways."[6] In other words, he implored the legislators to turn a deaf ear to the voices of a clear and persistent majority of their constituents, the better to follow the alternative strategies proposed by well-intentioned reformers like himself.

A more recent example is the speech given by Perry M. Johnson at the 1987 meeting of the American Correctional Association (ACA).[7] The ACA is the nation's largest and most influential organization of corrections professionals, and Johnson, a past president and award-winning member of the body, directed Michigan's violent and troubled prison system from 1972 to 1987.[8] In his speech, Johnson stated that the public, "exploited on occasion by demagogues" (by which he meant people who echoed the public's own ostensibly faulty views), has "become frustrated by the absence of a rational corrections policy to deal with violent crime." He lamented as "bad news" the demise of early prison release programs, and attributed

69

this development to exaggerated public fears about the incidence of predatory street crime.

Unfortunately, he did not mention that public reactions to documented excesses in the administration of revolving-prison-door programs, such as have occurred in his agency, were also responsible for this development.[9] He concluded by suggesting, in effect, experimenting with ways of "managing the risk of criminal behavior in the community" that the public itself would not support and wondered aloud whether even "some offenders who have committed violent offenses" should, in accordance with the inclinations and judgments of experts like himself, be placed not behind bars but under community-based correctional supervision.[10]

A final illustration can be found in the perspective articulated by a number of leading corrections analysts at a May 1990 conference convened in Berkeley, California, to discuss the report of California's Blue Ribbon Commission on Inmate Population Management. Several speakers blamed the growth of prison and jail populations in California and nationally on politicians who had adopted "get tough" policies in deference to the will of their constituents. These experts chastised the politicians for their "overreliance" on incarceration as a penal sanction and called for "rational" corrections policies, meaning policies that eventuate in less use of prisons and jails and more use of "intermediate" or community-based sanctions.

There is, to be sure, truth in the assertion that some elected leaders are mere political weathervanes on correctional and other issues. But this all-too-common expert rhetoric about inmate population growth leaves much to be desired. For if the experts are small "d" democrats, then the sensitivity of politicians to the will of a persistent majority of their constituents should be a cause for celebration, not lamentation. And if, as their remarks imply, they are instead small "r" republicans, then they have all the more reason to celebrate, for those who make the nation's corrections policies are clearly *not* merely registering the public's will but refining it.

In most jurisdictions, the public has been ready, willing, and able to put its tax dollars, and the land it owns, where its preferences are: namely, into building more prisons and jails. But as I have indicated, today some 75 percent of all convicted criminals are not behind bars, and the average convict serves less than half of his sentence in confinement. The general public does not cheer for the policies that have led to these results. The politicians who nonetheless support these policies are clearly weighing factors that refine the popular will, including in many cases the pro-alternatives views of the experts themselves.

WHY ALTERNATIVES HAVE FLOURISHED

It is by no means self-evident why alternatives to incarceration have flourished despite proven public resistance to policies that put convicted criminals on the streets. There are at least four explanations that are worth considering: costs, overcrowding, social control, and lobbying.

The cost of corrections, most of it centered on the building, renovation, and administration of prisons and jails, has been rising steadily. In 1988, Americans spent an estimated $20 billion on convicted criminals; adjusted for inflation, that is roughly ten times what they spent just a decade ago. According to a report by the National Conference of State Legislatures, between fiscal year 1987 and fiscal year 1988, corrections spending nationwide increased by 10 percent, surpassing the rate of increase in spending for education for the second consecutive year. Half the states increased spending by more than 10 percent; only three states cut corrections spending. Indeed, it grew faster than general fund spending in thirty-six states.[11]

It is widely believed that alternatives to incarceration are less expensive than incarceration; later in this chapter, I shall examine these and related claims with reference to three promising alternative programs. But only the most unreasonable proponents of alternatives doubt that keeping someone behind bars makes him less likely to commit new crimes (at least while he is incarcerated) than placing him on the streets under any kind of community-based supervision. And since incapacitating criminals in secure facilities keeps them from doing crimes they might do if they were on the streets (supervised or not), there is room for debate over the cost-effectiveness of incarceration not only relative to alternative programs but relative to non-incarceration as well.

There have been several salvos in this debate. First, in a widely circulated 1987 report for the National Institute of Justice, the economist Edwin Zedlewski offered the findings of a benefit-cost analysis of incarceration. By surveying cost data from several systems, he estimated that the total cost of one year's imprisonment is $25,000 per offender. And using crime and criminal victimization data, he estimated that the typical offender commits 187 crimes per year and that the typical crime exacts $2,300 in property losses and/or physical injuries and suffering. Multiplying these two figures, he calculated that the typical incarcerated convict is responsible for $430,100 in social costs per year. Thus, he concluded that incarceration has a "benefit-cost ratio" of just over 17 (430,100 divided by 25,000).[12] This ratio can be expressed in many ways. For example: Putting 1,000 felons behind bars costs society $25 million per year; but *not* putting them behind bars costs us about $430 million per year (187,000 felonies times $2,300 per felony)!

Zedlewski's findings are incredible; I do not know of any other government activity that would yield such a high benefit-cost ratio. Inevitably, several challenges were made to his pro-incarceration results. One of the most cogent was published in 1988 by two noted penologists, Franklin E. Zimring and Gordon Hawkins. In "The New Mathematics of Imprisonment," Zimring and Hawkins argued essentially that Zedlewski had inflated the incarceration benefit-cost ratio by inflating the numerator and deflating the denominator. They cited several good studies to prove their point, including one indicating that the typical offender commits fewer than 20 (as opposed to 187) crimes per year.[13]

They did not, however, use their insights into Zedlewski's measurement errors to recalculate the incarceration benefit-cost ratio. Instead, they asserted that such measures are inherently arbitrary; if that is the case, one wonders why they bothered to criticize Zedlewski's exercise. Nor, alas, did they suggest that one who did not agree with this assertion (and many social scientists would not), and who recalculated the figures accordingly, would see Zedlewski's ratio of 17 shrink to 1 or below. Rather, they simply concluded by decrying the fact that many people continue to support imprisonment and to demand more prisons.

Given their own analysis, however, it is unclear why people should not continue to favor incarceration as a socially necessary and cost-effective way of handling felons. Zedlewski's study was recast in a 1989 essay by U.S. Assistant Attorney General Richard B. Abell. With minor modifications, Abell popularized Zedlewski's analysis and echoed its findings. He added several anecdotes to put flesh on the reality behind the numbers, and to illustrate the costs of not incarcerating felons. For example:

> Wayne Lamarr Harvey participated in the brutal shotgun killing of two people in a Detroit bar in December 1975. A plea-bargain reduced his two first-degree murder charges to second degree, and he was given a 20-40–year prison sentence. On the day he entered prison, he was automatically granted nine and a half years of "good-time" credits, which he was allowed to keep despite 24 major prison rule violations during his incarceration. His minimum sentence was further reduced by two years under Michigan's "Prison Overcrowding Emergency Act." . . . Harvey was paroled to a halfway house in July 1984 after serving eight and a half years of his original minimum sentence. On October 25, 1984, Harvey and a female halfway house escapee killed a 41-year-old East Lansing police officer and father of six, then proceeded to a nearby home where Harvey shot and killed a 33-year-old woman as she opened the front door.[14]

Abell's widely circulated essay, which was reprinted in part as a featured op-ed piece in the *Wall Street Journal*, was denounced by many so-called experts as sensationalistic. The article did contain some misleading material, including a grossly oversimplified depiction of the relationship between crime rates and imprisonment rates. And Abell made no effort to correct for the methodological mistakes that marred Zedlewski's analysis. Instead, he broadcast Zedlewski's finding as settled fact.

What the essay's critics failed to note was that the "sensational" Harvey anecdote was a completely factual tale of a released felon who actually had served *more* time in prison than most murderers now do. They failed to cite evidence of the thousands upon thousands of cases each year in which prisoners released early commit violent and brutal crimes. And they failed, à la Zimring and Hawkins, to improve upon Zedlewski's benefit-cost analysis by bringing to bear sounder methodological assumptions, or more sophisticated statistical techniques, or more recent and solid empirical data on crimes per offender, the costs of incarceration, and the social costs of crime.[15] (Even if one reduces Zedlewski's 187 crimes per year to 11, the ratio is still greater than 1.)

One reason the experts have such an easy time lambasting an essay like Abell's is that the field's respected academic and quasi-academic journals seem to have placed a virtual embargo against any work, regardless of its quality, that supports strong incarceration policies, seriously challenges alternatives to incarceration, or highlights the human and financial toll exacted by released felons on their old and new (post-release) victims. Indeed, the only publications that make a staple of such articles are popular ones that the experts, especially the academics and penologist-practitioners among them, feel free to reject out of hand or to ignore as wholly beneath serious notice.[16] Having visited these forbidden literary lands, I can report that they are indeed populated in the main by intellectual lightweights, crackpots, and rank ideologues. But some of what appears in the field's respectable academic journals and other outlets can be found guilty of the same charge.

The existing evidence, such as it is, simply does not permit an honest analyst to embrace or to deny the notion that incarceration has become too expensive. The rhetorical power of that notion, however, remains great, and it has made state and local political leaders, and groups such as the National Governors Association, more receptive to the expert alternatives hucksters, and more deaf to the voters, than they might otherwise be.

A second explanation for the proliferation of alternative programs is the fact that many of the nation's prisons and jails are overcrowded. The causes and consequences of institutional crowding are less clear than most analysts suppose (see chapter 1), and standard definitions of *overcrowding* tend to overstate the problem. Most jurisdictions define an institution as overcrowded if it holds more inmates than it was originally designed and intended to hold ("rated capacity").

One has only to visit almost any city jail or state prison to see that crowding presents a real challenge to institutional managers. Essentially, there are three solutions: More prisons and jails can be built and staffed as necessary; prison and jail managers can learn to cope more effectively with bulging cellblocks and detention rooms; alternatives to incarceration can be used more extensively.

Even if the new construction and staffing option did not present itself with such a huge tax bill up front, it would be nearly impossible to build our way out of the problem. In California, in the Federal Bureau of Prisons, and in other agencies, aggressive and well-oiled expansion plans have failed to keep pace with the rising numbers. So-called fast-track construction projects and the use of prefabricated building materials have worked well in many jurisdictions; in lots of others, however, they have resulted in physical plants that give every evidence of the haste with which they were constructed: faulty plumbing, unusable electronic locking systems, and dozens of security-jeopardizing features.

Even if it were possible to build more, faster, and better than we have been building, it would not be possible to staff the new facilities as well: There is no such thing as fast-track staffing and management. There simply are not enough trained middle managers, experienced institution heads, and top corrections executives to run three or four times as many prisons and jails as we now have. It is hard enough to manage prisons and jails well under present circumstances; it is ridiculous to think that they can be managed well under trying conditions by inexperienced people.

A sensible variant on the "better institutional management" strategy has often been proposed: Get a better handle on the flow of inmates via enhanced coordination among police officers, prosecutors, judges, and corrections officials (both institutional and field services). In certain cases, such a strategy might work. But as every self-respecting criminal justice junkie knows all too well, the criminal justice system is a loose confederation of agencies; just about everywhere, the system is too fragmented or too politicized, or both, to effect this sort of coordination in the first instance, or to sustain it where it already exists.

Thus, an increasing number of elected officials have embraced alternative programs as the most realistic way of responding to the overcrowding problem. But, as I shall illustrate, some alternatives are more workable and promising than others.

A third explanation for the increase in community-based corrections looks beneath arguments about rising costs and overcrowding to the motivations and interests of middle- and working-class Americans and their political representatives. Proffered mainly by radical criminologists and so-called critical theorists, the idea is that the rise of alternative measures is an effort to expand the net of social control over society's least popular citizens, especially impoverished welfare-dependent minority males. In this view, the distance between average citizens, who tend to favor incarceration, and leading penal reformers, who tend to favor alternatives, is more apparent than real. Both groups are working to the same end, the former half-knowingly, the latter unwittingly.

Many leading advocates of this provocative view draw their inspiration in part from the work of the late French social theorist Michel Foucault. In his widely acclaimed *Discipline and Punish*, Foucault argued that bourgeois societies have successively replaced one apparently self-serving, but ultimately self-destructive, system of "power/

knowledge" with another; thus, the hooded executioner gave way to the prison warden, and now the prison warden is giving way to house arrest via electronic monitoring "ankel bracelets" (discussed later in this chapter) and other seemingly more humane, and less liberty-threatening, alternatives to incarceration.[17]

Along with others who have worried about the hidden consequences for politics and society of technological progress and the spread of rational, scientific thinking, Foucault suggested that each system of power/knowledge was much less conspicuous, but far more degrading and dangerous to freedom, than the previous one. In effect, each system in its turn concentrated more coercive capability in fewer "progressive" hands, making it easier for government officials to categorize and monitor citizens, and to profess publicly and sincerely that the method of coercion being employed against these citizens was as mild as humanly possible and in the interests of both the criminals and the society.

Foucault's theory and the ideas that radical criminologists and others have spun from it may be fascinating intellectual constructs, sweeping but bogus indictments of capitalist civilizations, heartfelt intuitions about the destructive but unseen potentialities of scientifically organized societies, or symptoms of psychological aberration; to my thinking, they are all of the above.

But one thing is clear: They do not explain the rapid rise in community-based corrections in the United States over the last decade or so. For that matter, they do not account for the checkered patterns of historical difference in punishment practices within the United States and Europe over the last two centuries, for the differences in punishment practices that exist between the United States and most European countries today, or for the differences that exist from jurisdiction to jurisdiction within the United States today. Among other problems, the subtle and deeply rooted processes that supposedly give rise to new systems of power/knowledge out of the ruins of the previous ones have not operated in any consistent or predictable fashion—or at least not in any fashion that jibes with my unrepentantly "bourgeois" and "positivistic" conceptions of empirical causality (for example, things that happened at time T cannot be causes of things that happened at time $T - 1$).

The Alternatives Lobby

Another, more reasonable attempt to explain the expanded use of alternative measures, like the explanations offered by some of my radical colleagues, emphasizes both material factors related to costs and crowding trends and ideas about how to respond to these trends from a politically influential and well-motivated group of citizens.

As every political science study of corrections policy-making has shown, corrections is one place on the American political landscape where pluralism—the clash among numerous societal and governmental groups organized to affect domestic policy—is not a force.[18] Instead, corrections policy-making is best characterized as a relatively closed, government-centered process in which a small network of influential people in the elected executives' offices, in the legislatures, in the corrections bureaucracies, and in the leading penal reform lobbies decides which policies to pursue and how to pursue them.

In corrections, as in other policy areas where such "subgovernments" exist, the probability that official policies will be at odds with mass public opinion is higher than average. Nevertheless, such subgovernments sometimes work well and have shown themselves to be capable of changing over time. They do not always produce a gap between majority preferences and public policies.

Since the middle of the nineteenth century, most Americans, including most penal reformers, have equated punishment with incarceration. The penitentiary was an American invention; by the 1960s most widely respected penal reformers thought of it as the American invention that failed.

During the revolutionary period, the Jacksonian era, the Civil War, the Progressive Era, and the New Deal, elected officials and other leading citizens made penal reform central to their broader agendas for social and political change. In each of these periods, the dungeonlike quality of many of the country's prisons and jails was brought to light in books, journalistic exposés, government reports, and public speeches.

But, however deplorable the institutional conditions they documented, most reformers began by reminding their audiences (and themselves) that, against the backdrop of world—or simply seventeenth- and eighteenth-century American—history, the mere deprivation of liberty was a recent and humane advance in the handling of criminals. Jails and prisons in the United States no longer used branding, whipping, or most other forms of corporal punishment against criminals; exile and banishment existed only insofar as convicted criminals were kept locked up in institutions within a day's journey (or less) from their friends and relatives.

For the most part, the penal reformers of these periods celebrated the ideal of incarceration even as they damned practices that fell far short of it. In their efforts to close the gap between the civilized conditions they worked toward and the unspeakable reality of prison life, they bring to mind Blake McKelvey's apt description of the history of U.S. prison reform as "a history of good intentions."[19] As David J. Rothman and other historians have argued persuasively, these good intentions often paved the road to hell, resulting in institutional reforms that made prison and jail conditions worse rather than better, and created new and more oppressive instruments of social control.[20]

But, as the story of the Bureau of Prisons and other corrections agencies suggests (see chapter 1), the reformers had bona fide successes to complement their failures. In the 1960s, however, a new generation of penal reformers broadcast the failures and ignored or trivialized the successes. Drawing from that era's bountiful well of countercultural assumptions, they saw America's prisons and jails as reflections of its ostensibly racist, oppressive, class-based, bourgeois society. Some shouted, "Tear down the walls!" Others worked within the system to campaign for moratoria on prison construction.*

---

*The aforementioned Nagel is perhaps the best example. His *The New Red Barn* was so influential in part because its author was himself a former corrections official. Nagel and his associates differed from most other new-style reformers in their willingness to concede that most contemporary corrections workers were "good and dedicated people," and that the "new red barn"—the contemporary prison—was more safe and humane than the old one.[21]

Whatever their approach, these new-style reformers had in common a deep distrust of any effort to improve the quality of life behind bars. As one noted contemporary reformer scolded me: "If you are truly a penal reformer, you don't waste your energies on improving prisons and jails any more than you oppose the death penalty by re-wiring the electric chair."

By the same token, to today's network of anti-incarceration penal reformers, a major purpose of the litigation to improve prison and jail conditions, and the sweeping judicial intervention that often results from it, is to gather negative media attention and escalate the costs of confinement, thereby creating political pressures favoring a greater use of alternative sanctions. The effectiveness of these interventions in improving the quality of institutional life is an important but wholly secondary concern to these lobbyists. The political and judicial pressures resulting from their litigation and lobbying efforts have been legitimized and lionized by the books, articles, and pamphlets of researchers affiliated with, and often funded by, the penal reform organizations themselves.

To judge whether this strategy has been effective, one need only recall that some three-quarters of all convicted criminals, including tens of thousands of violent and repeat offenders, are not now incarcerated.

THREE PROMISING ALTERNATIVES

Should all, some, or none of the nation's over 2.5 million community-based criminals be incarcerated? Are today's penal reformers correct in characterizing the public's support for incarceration, and wariness about alternative programs, as uninformed and overly emotional? Do some, all, or none of the many alternative measures currently in use protect the public (and its purse) better than incarceration?

My examination of probation and parole programs confirms what most experienced corrections practitioners know: Some of these community-based programs work, but most of them do not. And those that do work, like the institutional practices that are successful (see chapter 1), have in common that they are highly structured, intensively managed, and embody an unblinking recognition of the fact that their clients are people who, if left to their own devices, might well break the law.

There are three such promising alternatives to incarceration: house arrest with electronic monitoring, community service sentences, and intensive-supervision probation and parole programs.

House Arrest with Electronic Monitoring

Of the many different types of house arrest programs, I refer here to community-based correctional supervision programs with the following basic features:

1. The typical charge is a person convicted as an adult of three or fewer property crimes, and who has been convicted of not more than one crime of violence whether as a juvenile or as an adult.
2. The offender is required to stay in or around his or her home for all but court-approved activities, such as work.

3. The offender must meet curfews and other restrictions.
4. The offender is subjected to constant electronic surveillance as well as regular direct contacts (in person or by telephone) with field services agents.
5. The offender is incarcerated swiftly and certainly for any violations.

House arrest programs of this type are no picnic for the offender (which may be good) and involve more investment up front than less intrusive programs (which is bad). Especially costly are the electronic monitoring devices—ankle bracelets and other computerized "prison jewelry" that enable corrections officials to know an offender's whereabouts any time of the day. In New Mexico, for instance, nearly $100,000 was spent for two dozen such bracelets.

Moreover, the electronic systems have proven far from infallible. Utah officials, for example, went crazy responding to false alarms and, when making their face-to-face rounds, they found that many offenders were "out of bounds" though the system registered them "in bounds."

Largely because of the heftier initial investment and the fear of technical problems, in 1988 only about 10 percent of the 10,000 or so offenders under house arrest in the country were monitored by ankle bracelets and placed under the sort of highly structured house arrest regime outlined here. By early 1989, however, New York City and several other jurisdictions had decided to join the twenty states that have tried house arrest programs, and most of the newcomers seemed to be opting for electronic monitoring and tighter controls.

They are wise to do so. The less restrictive house arrest

programs simply do not work: Offenders tend to ignore the terms of their release and to miss court appearances. They find it easy to return to their criminal lifestyles and associates. Meanwhile, their supervisors are swamped with too many cases and become demoralized and burned out. Furthermore, judges are loath to permit many types of offenders, even lightweights, to return to their old neighborhoods without the promise of significant supervision.

Thus far, the most forthright experiment with house arrest has been made in Florida. It started in 1983 with 5,000 offenders, most of them petty criminals but many of them felons. Known as the Community Control Program, it was responsible for some 10,000 offenders in its first five years. Among its key features have been random, computer-generated calls to offenders; shockproof, tamper-resistant bracelets; payment by offenders of monthly fees to defray the costs of their supervision; and face-to-face contacts by field agents with the offender and the offender's relatives, employers, neighbors, and (where appropriate) social workers.

Florida officials themselves estimate that about six or seven of every ten house arrestees would have been sent to prison if the Community Control Program had not existed. On average, it costs nearly $30 per day to keep somebody locked up in one of Florida's overcrowded prisons. It costs under $5 per day to keep the same person in a house arrest program. Moreover, under 20 percent of the offenders in the program have had their house arrest sentences revoked for violating the rules.

Florida's house arrest program has inspired similar ones in California, Michigan, and other states. New York City has begun to use house arrest for a small number of its pretrial detainees (in early 1989 about 200). As one veteran field services worker remarked of these programs: "Finally, we're doing the job in a way that makes it doable." While much remains to be done before house arrest programs can be used routinely, and while the very success of these efforts will feed the temptation to place too many offenders, and offenders of serious crimes, on the streets (or "in their own backyards"), they represent one alternative to incarceration that makes sense.

Community Service Sentences

Another promising alternative to incarceration involves placing offenders in the community under close supervision and requiring them to perform a variety of socially useful tasks, to pay restitution to their victims, and to defray the costs of their supervision. A few dozen jurisdictions have tried various types of community service sentences. The most extensive, and the only well-studied, community service program was the one administered by the nonprofit Vera Institute of Justice in New York City. In a superb book entitled *Punishment Without Walls*, Douglas C. McDonald, formerly with the Vera Institute and currently a member of Abt Associates, a Boston-based consulting firm, described and evaluated this program.[22]

The program began in the Bronx in 1979, and was extended to Brooklyn in 1980 and to Manhattan in 1981. By the end of 1983, some 2,400 offenders, most of them nonviolent property offenders, were in the program. Most of them would have been sentenced to jail if the program had not existed—about 50 percent in the Bronx, 55 percent in Brooklyn, and over 65 percent in Manhattan.

Each offender was required to perform at least seventy hours of community service, including cleaning nursing homes, painting buildings, cleaning vacant lots, and so on. The offenders worked in small groups supervised directly by a Vera Institute staff member. Other project staff assisted offenders with housing, transportation, day care, and other needs.

The results of the program were mixed. For example, of 494 program participants tracked for six months after sentencing, 212 of them were rearrested 310 times. McDonald estimated that 33 percent of these rearrests were for crimes committed when, had the program not existed, the offender would have been in jail. In comparing the recidivism rates of program participants with those of otherwise comparable offenders who were sent to jail, he found no meaningful differences. And perhaps most damning of all, he found that most participants declined to describe the program as a "punishment"; indeed, they felt it was much less punitive and far more desirable than jail or conventional probation.

On the bright side, however, the cost of administering the program was about $920 per offender per year—a far cry from the $40,000 per year it costs to jail each inmate on Rikers Island. McDonald estimated that the project saved nearly 260 jail-years overall in its first three years of operation. Moreover, while his study did not make explicit comparisons to conventional probation programs, few observers would doubt that the community service sentences were a better bargain for the city, and more of a boon to public protection, that the unsupervised, unstructured, and socially unproductive alternatives.

Granted, the mixed results of this effort, and the unhappy news that most participants thought they were getting off easy, may make community service sentences a less promising alternative than house arrest with electronic monitoring. But the Vera Institute's experiment was just one way of carrying out community service sentences. As McDonald has noted, the program could have been administered differently, possibly with better results. At a minimum, we should wait to see what other (especially other more supervision-intensive) community service programs yield before putting this alternative to incarceration in a league with Hortonesque prison furloughs.

Intensive-Supervision Programs

Intensive-supervision probation and parole programs (ISPs) are probably the single most promising alternative to incarceration. Whereas conventional probation and parole is unstructured and undersupervised, ISPs are tightly organized programs to handle convicted criminals on the streets. Whereas conventional programs are poorly managed, undermanaged, or not managed at all, ISPs coordinate the offender's every move to ensure that he is behaving in accordance with the terms of his community-based sentence.

Among other requirements, participants in ISPs must submit to

Mandatory work and educational activities
Random drug and alcohol tests

Residence in a program center, which has no guns or bars but does have strict rules governing chores, curfews, and interactions with other offenders and program staff (or, where there is no center, regular face-to-face contacts with program officers)

Weekly checks of arrest records

Restitution payments to victims

Community service

Deductions from wages to defray the costs of supervision

Swift and certain confinement for any violations.

ISPs of one type or another have been tried in over twenty jurisdictions, with encouraging results. Three of the more notable experiments have occurred in Georgia, New Jersey, and Wisconsin.

Georgia

Originating in 1982, the Georgia ISP for probationers requires offenders to have face-to-face contacts with officers five times a week (reduced to twice a week as they progress through the program), to work 132 hours, and to submit to frequent drug and alcohol tests. One probation officer and one surveillance officer supervise twenty-five offenders. By the end of 1985, the program was responsible for over 2,300 offenders, persons who, had the program not existed, would have gone to prison. A small number of them had entered the program from prison (parolees).

Billie S. Erwin, a program analyst with the Georgia Department of Corrections, did an eighteen-month follow-up study that showed the rate of recidivism for the Georgia ISP offenders to be higher than that for offenders under conventional probation. Such a result was to be expected, however, since the average ISP offender was a "prison-bound" criminal, while the typical probationer had a less severe record. In the more relevant comparison of ISP offenders and prisoners with similar records, Erwin found that recidivism rates were significantly lower among the former: around 25 percent compared with over 40 percent for the state's prisoners.[23]

Moreover, the ISP was far more cost-effective than prison. In Georgia, the per-inmate-per-year cost of a prison bed has run about $14,000. By contrast, through taxes on their wages, room and board fees, and child support payments, the ISP participants typically contribute over 90 percent of the costs of their supervision (about $6,000 per inmate per year). Thus, through the ISP Georgia taxpayers have saved an estimated $145 million over the last several years. The program's success was recognized when Georgia won one of the Ford Foundation's ten Innovations in Government awards for 1987. It has since been expanded, apparently without any reductions in its overall effectiveness.

New Jersey

The New Jersey ISP selectively accepts prisoner-applicants, requiring that they serve at least two months in prison prior to entering the program. Its total active caseload cannot exceed 500 offenders. There must be regular face-to-face contacts between officers and offenders, and offenders who violate the rules are immediately dropped from the program. Participants are required to pay fines and restitution, to work, to provide community service, to undergo special counseling, and to meet with community sponsors and offender support groups.

Frank S. Pearson, a Research Associate of the Institute for Criminological Research at Rutgers University, has studied and evaluated this program. He found that the New Jersey ISP saved about $7,000 per offender compared to incarceration, and that ISP offenders did community service work worth about $200,000 a year and made good on some $225,000 in fines and restitution. Recidivism rates for ISP offenders were about 10 percent lower than those for otherwise comparable offenders who did not participate in the program.[24]

Wisconsin

Anyone familiar with the history of American corrections knows that some of the most innovative experiments with alternative programs have been launched in Wisconsin, easily the most progressive jurisdiction in the country when it comes to corrections (and other important areas of public policy as well). In 1989, about 80 percent of Wisconsin's convicted criminals were on the streets under various types of community-based supervision. In the late 1980s, led first by Walter J. Dickey and then by Stephen E. Bablitch, Wisconsin's corrections agency searched for ways to handle effectively an even higher percentage of offenders in the community. In many other jurisdictions, such efforts would have resulted in half-baked, ill-executed programs that victimized the public and its purse. But trading on its progressive organizational traditions, and blessed with outstanding and dedicated central office and field services leadership and management, Wisconsin's corrections agency has met with success.

Wisconsin pioneered the development of an ISP for high-risk offenders, centered in Milwaukee. There is no solid research to demonstrate this program's effectiveness. But most of the relevant departmental records, and my interviews with departmental personnel (some of whom initially opposed the initiative), indicate that the high-risk ISP offenders do no worse in terms of recidivism than otherwise comparable Wisconsin offenders who are kept behind bars. And, as in the cases of Georgia and New Jersey, keeping these Wisconsin offenders on the streets, even under extraordinary supervision, is less costly to the taxpayers than keeping them behind bars.*

Wisconsin's approach to intensive supervision has been anything but harsh and unforgiving to offenders. As one Wisconsin official stated: "Our program is intensive in more ways than one. There's intensive supervision of the offender's behavior. But there's also intensive attention given to the offender's needs, to developing options that

---

*In a preliminary report presented at the 1989 American Probation and Parole Association Institute meeting in Milwaukee, an ISP administered by the Milwaukee corrections authorities received a critical evaluation. This evaluation was based on preliminary findings from a demonstration research project (see chapter 6 in this book) conducted by the RAND Corporation in Santa Monica, California. Four points must be noted. First, the research project did not focus on Wisconsin's ISP for high-risk offenders. Second, the Milwaukee sample, and the samples from other jurisdictions, were quite small. Third, the Wisconsin officials responsible for administering the program were prohibited from making changes that they deemed appropriate but that RAND's research team feared would contaminate the study. Fourth, the Wisconsin officials shared with me a written statement to RAND that challenges the preliminary RAND report's conclusions about the Milwaukee program; to me, the statement was rather compelling. The knowledge gained via the "failed" program has been used by Wisconsin officials in other alternative programs, including electronic surveillance and ISPs for drug offenders.

might help to keep him on the street: drug therapy, a job, literacy training, and more. That's true in a sense for all of our community-based programs. They're all 'intensive' in the latter sense, if not the former as well." My own research and observations bear out this remark. So does a 1988 report by the former Wisconsin corrections chief Walter J. Dickey.

Entitled *From the Bottom Up: Probation Supervision in a Small Wisconsin Community*, Dickey's report describes community corrections as practiced by Ed Ross, a field services agent in Grant, Wisconsin. Ross does not handle a "caseload." Rather, he handles offenders on a case-by-case basis. As Dickey recounts:

> Ed Ross has frequent direct contacts with clients, particularly at the beginning of the supervisory relationship. . . . Over time, it does become clear that one result of the frequency and nature of the contact is that they reflect and communicate to the clients a true concern about their welfare. . . . To insure that a client took Antabuse every day [Ross] personally dispensed it and watched him ingest it daily for several weeks, lending support to him in his struggle with alcohol by the daily expression of interest and concern and by the effort expended. . . . [Never] did a client leave a meeting with the vague understanding that he would look for a job. Rather, the client knew where he was to look, when, and that the agent would be back in touch on an appointed day for a report on how things went. . . . The client knew why whatever was being required was important.[25]

In addition to Ross's intensive relationship with clients, Dickey documented other threads in "the fabric of supervision" that made the program successful, including the involvement of the offender's family, the involvement of the local community, and the support of the state corrections department. No reader of his report, and no honest observer of Wisconsin's accomplishments in the area of alternative programs, can fail to be impressed with the potentialities of intense, well-administered "punishment without walls."

Betting on ISPs

Where, as in Georgia, New Jersey, and Wisconsin, ISPs have been successful, they have been planned and implemented with great care. Moreover, they have managed the offenders in their charge with exactly the same tough, energetic, but compassionate spirit that has characterized the management of safe and humane prisons and jails.

Georgia, for example, has never been a state to coddle criminals, and many observers were shocked when the correctional system that perfected the chain gang started to perfect this alternative to incarceration. But that shock turned to admiration by 1987, when Harvard University evaluators nominated Georgia's ISP for a Ford Foundation award. And that award brought the program plenty of fresh attention from journalists and scholars.

Observers of the program have come away with the impression that the program works because it is managed in a caring, no-nonsense fashion. Wisconsin's Ed Ross has his peers in Georgia, New Jersey, and other jurisdictions. Journalist Neal Pierce has reported on Georgia's ISP; the following describes conditions at a program center there.

"We have no bars or guns here," said James Fletcher, the tough, 38-year-old probation officer who runs the facility. But, he added, "we have discipline—there are 62 rules here, determining a man's day from waking to sleep." Each resident knows that if he breaks the rules, or walks out through the unlocked doors, he's finished. . . . The regimen Fletcher imposes is no picnic. Each man must get up at 5:30, eat breakfast and leave his bunk and living area spotless. . . . Immediately after work, he's back, gets supper and then must take evening classes on subjects ranging from alcohol or drug abuse control to high school equivalency. . . . Ask Fletcher if it's a good idea to take a risk with convicted criminals, saving them the agony of confinement behind bars, and you get an emphatic "yes." Most of his charges, he tells you, are "confused young men.". . . "Many rebel at first," Fletcher said. "But after a while, they get a little more air in the chest, look you in the eye, get a better perspective on themselves. This is often the first time they have ever successfully completed something they had responsibility for."[26]

Pierce's description is echoed in virtually every other journalistic and scholarly account of the program's administrative character. So too, for the most part, are his impressions of the program: "A certain paternalism is visible in the approach. But who's to say that's bad— especially when contrasted with degrading, violent and now AIDS-infected prisons on the one side and carelessly bestowed probation on the other."[27]

To date, none of the ISPs have undertaken to manage the kinds of violent and hard-core convicts who do time in high-security prisons and jails. (Wisconsin's high-risk ISP handled offenders who were not quite maximum-security material.) Young felony offenders are one thing; young and not-so-young experienced street thugs are quite another. But from my perspective, it is a testimony to the wisdom of the ISP administrators that violent and chronic offenders have not been their typical charges.

There have yet to be any meaningful demonstration studies of ISPs that employ random assignment and other scientific controls. Unless such studies are done, it will be impossible to argue unreservedly that ISPs have proven themselves as an alternative to incarceration; the same, of course, can be said about the value of virtually every other correctional policy and practice (see chapter 6). But, as revealed here, the preliminary reports have been uniformly encouraging. And, just as was true of work-based welfare-reform measures, a political consensus has begun to form around ISPs on the strength of their early successes and in advance of any hard-nosed social science evaluations. As Georgia ISP manager Fletcher commented: "We can tell the conservatives we're law and order, providing true punishment and cost saving. . . . And we can tell the liberals there's true rehabilitation taking place."[28] And, as a Wisconsin official has observed: "There's a balance in our approach—administrative, budgetary, philosophical, and, yes, political, too." A New Jersey official experienced with ISPs noted: "It's common sense. We don't slap their wrist, and we don't let 'em rot in prison either. Everybody wins."

Of course, everybody does not really win. Inevitably, innocent citizens are going to be victimized by ISP offenders who, had they been jailed or imprisoned, would not have been free to commit new crimes against persons or property; Georgia, New Jersey, and every other jurisdiction have had their share of problems in that area. No alternative to incarceration is going to be foolproof.

But neither, for that matter, is incarceration foolproof. Those who demand this impossible standard of alternative measures had better ask themselves what it implies for incarceration. Only compassionless fools would want to execute every convicted felon on the grounds that even if the felon were incarcerated for life, he could still harm other inmates and correctional staff and, if ever released from custody, could still commit new crimes. By the same token, only intellectually, fiscally, and morally myopic morons would maintain that every felon should be incarcerated (or incarcerated for life), regardless of his prior criminal record or the severity of his latest crime of conviction.

In any case, the fact is that we are already making extensive use of alternative measures, and ISPs look like the most promising of the lot. Given that we are intent on developing punishment without walls, ISPs offer the best available administrative brick and mortar.

ALTERNATIVES: CONS AND PROS

Only a negligible fraction of the millions of offenders on the streets today are in any one of the three types of highly structured and intensively managed programs discussed in this chapter. In evaluating these alternatives to incarceration, the truth lies somewhere between the beliefs of average citizens and those of elite penal reformers, albeit much closer to the former than to the latter. While reformers may whine about the prospect of these get-tough alternative programs widening the net of social control, average citizens are paying for the lack of these programs in the currency of repeat victimization by these criminals, especially in the inner-city neighborhoods that a high percentage of predatory street criminals call home.[29]

But one group of average citizens, correctional workers, recognizes the germs of truth in the pleas of the pro-alternatives reformers. Corrections workers are uniquely positioned to understand issues that the rest of us would do well to heed.

First, they understand that conventional probation and parole programs are a farce, and that prison furlough and early release programs, though highly successful overall, needlessly put back on the streets many convicts who are time bombs capable of new crimes that not only devastate their victims but undermine political support for sensible alternatives sensibly administered. As one of my old correctional officer friends in Massachusetts put it: "We saw the Willie Horton thing coming; we were administering this thing on the edge for years. But the damn provisions on furloughs didn't let us have our way and use our professional judgment. . . . Now the liberal politicians and the never-satisfied big-mouth reformers are sorry . . . so are the officers and inmates who make furloughs work without tragedies."

Second, corrections workers understand that, while sophisticated studies designed to help judges and paroling authorities predict which offenders require incarceration are often worthwhile, and while it would be good to reserve prison and jail beds only for those offenders who are expected to commit new crimes against property or persons if released, the implications of such "selective in-capacitation" research and supersophisticated classification schemes are easier to contemplate in theory than to act upon in practice.[30] Any corrections administrator knows better than ten academic analysts that prison and jail space is a scarce resource that needs to be allocated rationally; but what is rational in a statistical exercise is often unworkable in the real world of administrative, le-gal, budgetary, and political constraints—not to mention legitimate moral disagreements about which offenders deserve which sanctions.

Third, and following from the previous point, correc-tions workers understand that alternative measures em-body all sorts of hard-to-resolve, and perhaps unresolvable, moral problems. For example, a longtime California prison camp administrator, a self-proclaimed proponent of alternatives to incarceration "both when it is and when it ain't fashionable," posed one little-discussed moral is-sue surrounding alternative measures. He noted that most white-collar offenders are well educated and white, while a disproportionate number of predatory street criminals are poor and black. For the most part, the former enjoyed a privileged, pampered, and protected existence; some even studied or practiced the law before breaking it. Such persons, he asserted, have less material reason to commit crimes for money than do ghetto street kids who have enjoyed none of life's advantages. But the former crimi-nals can commit their crimes by tinkering with their com-puters or arranging insider investment deals (or good old-fashioned bank frauds), mugging their victims without laying a hand on them. But in the course of stealing less than their white-collar counterparts, the ghetto kids may behave violently against living, breathing, victims. Yet the first is considered a nonviolent offender who does not require incarceration; the second is a violent offender who does. Which one really deserves the more punitive sanction?

In my view it would be the violent kid, but I thought the camp administrator raised a point that could not be easily dismissed. The same was true of the remarks made to me by a Michigan corrections official who, in blunt language, pointed out that the moral rationale for alternatives does not prohibit an outcome in which "your average Joe gets locked up, but people who haven't had to scratch and climb don't do time." He noted in frustration that when John Zaccaro, Jr., son of former vice-presidential candidate Geraldine Ferraro, was busted for drug dealing, he "did time" in a cozy Vermont apartment with the amenities of a high-priced health club. "Christ," the official said, "I've seen poor black kids rot in crowded jails for selling less. . . . True, most of the black kids are going to have juvenile records, and there's going to be smut [violence or other assault crimes] in their jackets [official criminal records]. I'm no sweetheart. But the fact that the Zaccaro kid had everything in life handed to him says to me that *he* should have been locked up before them; he deserved it more."

I can see ways around these moral objections to alternative measures, but they raise to consciousness a delicious irony: Many of the same people who in the 1960s were complaining that "the rich get richer and the poor get prison" are now supporting an approach to corrections in which "the poor criminals get prison and the well-off criminals get alternatives."

Fourth and finally, corrections workers have a profound understanding of the fact that the future of American corrections must involve *both* aggressive efforts to build and staff new prisons and jails *and* careful efforts to expand the use of ISPs and kindred alternative programs, ending the insanity of alternatives that permit offenders to do what they please and to find new victims at will.

They know that the choice is not between more incarceration and more use of alternatives. They know we must do more of both, and that, even with the wisest of efforts and the best of luck, it will not be easy or inexpensive to do so. In short, they know that, however astute the institutional management and however agile the administration of good alternative programs, the future of American corrections will be tough sledding. And from that reality, there can be no escape.

3

Rehabilitation Revisited

WHETHER BEHIND BARS OR ON THE STREETS, convicted criminals in most jurisdictions can participate in many types of correctional programs: remedial education classes, vocational training, substance-abuse counseling, mental health services, work opportunities, and so on. There are at least three different perspectives on such programs.

First, we can think of them as instruments of *offender rehabilitation*. In this conception, the question to ask is, How, if at all, do the programs reduce the probability that offenders who participate in them will recidivate? Second, we can think about correctional programs as tools of *institutional management*. In this conception, we would ask, How, if at all, do the programs facilitate or impede the operation of safe, cost-effective prisons and jails? Third, we can think about correctional programs in relation to our sense of what constitutes *humane custody*. In this conception, the question becomes, Is it morally possible to characterize as "decent," "civilized," or "humane" those forms of custody that do not make such programs readily available to persons under correctional supervision?

REHABILITATION: "SOMETHING WORKS"

For most of this century, corrections analysts, activists, and practitioners have thought about correctional programs mainly as instruments of rehabilitation. Conceptually, programs and rehabilitation have been correctional Siamese twins. In the medical model of corrections, which had its heyday between 1940 and 1975, criminality was viewed as a sickness to be cured. It is a curious vestige of this discredited model that, even today, most corrections cognoscenti cannot utter three consecutive sentences about programs without at some point mentioning recidivism rates or rehabilitation, or otherwise relating programs to inmates' postinstitutional or postsupervision behavior. Roughly speaking, since the end of World War II, there have been three models for examining the programs-rehabilitation nexus.

First, from 1940 to 1975, in the belief that "everything works," most observers thought correctional programs were effective instruments of rehabilitation. During this period, academic penologists joined with progressive practitioners in trumpeting a belief in the rehabilitative efficacy of these so-called treatment programs. This belief grew out of a fascinating and potent mix of social ideal-

The ideas for this section of this chapter were first tested at the Conference on Issues in Corrections sponsored by the U.S. Department of Justice, Federal Bureau of Prisons, and held in Washington, D.C., on June 9, 1989. I benefited greatly from the response of the practitioners present.

ism, practical experience, and preliminary research findings, all of it underwritten by a gutsy willingness to break with tradition and experiment in a field that was proudly conservative and backward-looking.

Between 1975 and 1985, many researchers doubted or flatly denied that programs were effective instruments of rehabilitation. No article was more of a nail in the coffin of rehabilitation than Robert Martinson's "What Works—Questions and Answers About Prison Reform," published in the spring 1974 edition of the influential neoconservative policy journal *The Public Interest*. Martinson's essay summarized the results of a review of 231 studies of rehabilitation published between 1945 and 1967. The review had been conducted by Martinson and two colleagues, and was published as a book in 1975.[1] Martinson concluded that, "with few and isolated exceptions, the rehabilitative efforts that have been reported so far have had no appreciable effect on recidivism."[2]

As might be expected, reaction to this damning academic study was fast and furious. Critics charged Martinson and his colleagues with everything from scholarly malfeasance to sheer stupidity. But in 1979 a panel of the National Academy of Science reviewed the same studies with much the same conclusion. "Martinson and his colleagues," the panel wrote, "were essentially correct. There is no body of evidence for any treatment or intervention with criminal offenders that can be relied upon to produce a decrease in recidivism."[3]*

Read correctly, however, neither the Martinson et al.

---

*Oddly enough, however, in the same year that the Academy's report was issued, Martinson recanted his earlier position.[4]

study nor the Academy's suggested that there was absolutely no relationship, or absolutely no positive relationship, between participation in given types of programs and recidivism rates. What each study found was that, in most of the 1945–1967 studies (many of them credible but methodologically flawed), the relationship between programs and rehabilitation appeared to be ambiguous. Both studies merely concluded that, statistically, the evidence was inconclusive, and that the available data did not permit one to generalize confidently one way or the other; thus one could not say for certain whether the relationship between participation in given programs and the likelihood of recidivism was direct, inverse, or non-existent.

But neither the Martinson et al. study nor the Academy report was read correctly by most commentators and critics, perhaps in part due to the often pithy language of Martinson's widely publicized 1974 article. For whatever reason, Martinson's article, the book from which it was loosely drawn, and numerous follow-up studies by others were interpreted far and wide as proof that, other things being equal, convicted offenders who participated in programs were no less likely to recidivate than convicted offenders who did not. Thus dawned the decade of "nothing works," a period when those opposed to correctional programs on ideological or other grounds could wrap themselves in the cloak of scientific respectability and confidently pronounce rehabilitation as a four-letter word from the bygone era of failed social experimentation behind bars.

Between 1985 and 1990, however, the inevitable intellectual counteroffensive against the idea that "nothing works" picked up speed. It began when Martinson's article was published and spawned some interesting studies as early as 1979, including one by Martinson himself.[5] But it was not until the mid-1980s that studies with a significant and contrary bearing on the efficacy of programs as rehabilitation devices appeared. Having tried "everything works" and screeched into "nothing works," we enter the 1990s in the spirit that "something works." Fifteen years ago, the academic chic was to deep-six rehabilitation; today, the academic chic is to jump-start it.

Most corrections practitioners welcome this return to pro-rehabilitation studies. They do so neither because they have read the latest analyses, nor because they have any naive faith in their ability to transform most of their charges into productive, law-abiding creatures via programs or other means. Instead, their receptivity to the emerging "something works" school on rehabilitation is rooted in their own common sense and experiences. Their common sense tells them that exposing offenders to life-enhancing, skills-imparting programs is likely to help keep at least some of them on the straight and narrow. And their experiences confirm that, under certain conditions, some types of programs do improve the post-release life prospects of some of the offenders who participate in them.

While there are many researchers whose work reinforces the practitioners' sober but hopeful views on rehabilitation, no one has contributed more fully to the literature on the revivification of rehabilitation than Paul Gendreau.[6] Director of research at Centracare Saint John Inc. in New Brunswick, Canada, Gendreau has reported on the results of original research by himself and others in a series of co-authored articles that should cause any open-minded observer to recognize that certain types of programs are effective vehicles for rehabilitating certain types of criminals. While Gendreau and his colleagues "do not claim that correctional rehabilitation is without problems or that it offers a panacea to the crime problem," they argue persuasively that a "growing body of data suggests not only that many interventions are successful but also that it is becoming increasingly possible to decipher the principles of effective treatment."[7]

As they emerge from the work of Gendreau and others, the "principles of effective treatment"—the basic strategic and organizational elements of correctional programs that have in many cases proven effective in reducing recidivism—include efforts to provide the offender with noncriminal role models that are within his reach (such as employed people who are making it, not sports celebrities); to enhance the offender's basic problem-solving skills, including the basic cognitive ability to relate actions to their consequences; to make use of whatever human and financial resources are available in the community to aid the program; to build interpersonal relationships that strengthen empathic impulses; to establish respect for legitimate authority; and to put in place relevant postprogram support services.

In essence, these principles of effective treatment amount to what one veteran corrections practitioner, vaguely familiar with the latest academic work on rehabilitation, phrased "staying with the man and getting him to stay with himself":

> Take it down to the core, what these guys [researchers] are finding is what any responsible person out in the field has

always known; namely, that to make a program work on its own terms—that is, just to get the guys [offender-participants] to come on a regular basis and make an effort, and then to make it work in terms of giving him what he needs to stay out of trouble—you need several things. You need to teach the guy to stop and think before he acts, which most of them [criminals] don't do. . . . Try to teach him empathy; use moral exhortation; but also stress that, hey, crime doesn't always pay. . . . Then you need to get his respect by showing him that you mean to help—and that just takes time. . . . You need to tap the good will and resources of people in the community where that's appropriate. And you really have to get him to know who is boss without pushing and shoving—it's the old "firm but fair," or [showing] that you'll be tough on him if he can't be tough on himself. But most of all, you have to make him really want to lead a straight life, equip him with the basic skills he needs to do that, and get him to believe that he really can succeed on those terms.

One of Gendreau's co-authors, Robert R. Ross of the University of Ottawa, explained the principles of effective treatment before a group consisting in part of corrections practitioners. As Ross presented them, the elements of correctional programs that succeed in keeping offenders from recidivating strongly parallel the elements of substance abuse programs that keep abusers from repeat or relapse drinking, shooting, smoking, or snorting. Ross made an explicit comparison to Alcoholics Anonymous (AA) and its famous "twelve steps" program, characterizing the typical criminal's basic "cognitive problem" as what AA leaders call "stinking thinking."[8]

Based on the recent work of Gendreau and others, the empirical evidence that certain types of correctional programs may succeed in rehabilitating certain types of criminals is too strong to allow the "nothing works" idea to breathe freely in the 1990s. This is especially true for certain types of prison-based programs for drug offenders. Marcia R. Chaiken has examined four such programs that seem to work. According to Chaiken, among the features these programs have in common are the following:

1. Clear statements of the program rules and the consequences of breaking them.
2. Obvious concern by program staff about the welfare of participants.
3. Participant regard for staff members as persons worth imitating.
4. Preparation of participants for future problems, including family and job problems.
5. Utilization of community resources.

Rates of recidivism for offenders in these programs were lower than for otherwise comparable offenders who did not receive such treatment; indeed, Chaiken reports that "the programs dealt with previously serious offenders, but their recidivism rates after participation were as low as 16 percent" (well below the average for untreated offenders).[9] The drug programs she analyzed were run in ways that are consistent with the general principles of effective treatment articulated by Gendreau and his colleagues.

Just the same, however, there are several points to consider before rushing to embrace the idea that "something works."

First, despite the heartening findings of Gendreau and others, the fact remains that mainly low-level offenders treated in the community are the ones who show any significant susceptibility to programs designed to rehabilitate. There is little in the latest studies to give one hope that violent, repeat (two or more felony convictions), or violent repeat offenders can be rehabilitated. And, concomitantly, there is virtually nothing in these studies to enhance one's confidence in the rehabilitative efficacy of most prison- or jail-based programs. So far as the relationship between institutional programs and recidivism goes, the best bet—and the bulk of the existing evidence—remains squarely on the side of "nothing works."

Second, the empirical evidence that "something works," if only with relatively low-level community-based offenders, is not terribly deep, not yet anyway. While an armful of rehabilitation studies on the experimental model of demonstration research with random assignment have been done (see chapter 6), much of the evidence for the idea that "something works" derives from *meta-analyses*. Essentially, a meta-analysis is a complicated statistical technique used to standardize the findings of disparate studies in a way that makes replication of the objective findings of literature surveys possible. Meta-analysis is not immune to data selection biases and related problems; moreover, the main statistic produced by meta-analysis— "effect size"—is itself problematic. The proper perspective on meta-analysis was captured in the remark of a corrections practitioner who, after hearing that the seemingly remarkable rehabilitative effects of a given type of prison-based rehabilitation program were calculated via such convoluted statistical gymnastics, said, "I guess that professor never met a meta-analysis he didn't like."

Third, there is what Gendreau has referred to as *therapeutic integrity*, meaning essentially the extent to which treatment personnel actually adhere to the theoretical principles and employ the techniques of the treatment they purport to provide. "To what extent are treatment staff competent? How hard do they work?"[10] Another way of couching this issue is in terms of the arguments about correctional management offered in the previous chapters: *No correctional program can succeed in rehabilitating offenders unless it is organized and managed appropriately.*

A good program—one that embodies the key strategic principles of effective treatment—will fail if it is ill managed, undermanaged, or not managed at all. Failure to factor in the management variable is another reason why meta-analysis and related research techniques often pull up lame. For example, in a 1989 paper Gendreau and D. A. Andrews highlight a forthcoming study indicating that, in conducting programs for juveniles, such factors as "therapist characteristics, location of intervention sessions, and techniques for breaking down family resistance are crucial to program effectiveness."[11] "Effect size" computations do not allow room for the importance of these factors, but the people who conduct such programs for juveniles know how vital they are.

More fundamentally, to the extent that the success of programs as rehabilitative tools depends crucially on the particulars of how, by whom, and possibly even where they are conducted, generalizations about their efficacy (or at least their "exportability") will be fraught with the same dangers that plague all generalizations that downplay the irreducible elements of contingency involved in any complex act of administration—among them the unique talents of a program's leader.

Fourth, there is clearly a temptation to oversell the idea that "something works." There is the same hint of intellectual hubris in many new-school rehabilitation thinkers that was exhibited among the proponents of the "nothing works" school.[12] This is unfortunate if only because corrections practitioners are in no mood to suffer academic fools gladly. At a minimum, they are inclined to laugh in the faces (literally, at some conferences) of those who tell them that major discoveries about how to rehabilitate are on the way. Worse, however, they are thereby inclined to tune out good, well-grounded ideas along with poor, hastily chosen ones. It is important, therefore, to continue to make necessary qualifications alongside enthusiastic assertions about the return of rehabilitation.

Fifth and finally, ideas about the revival of rehabilitation tend to crowd out other useful perspectives on the value of correctional programs, especially those in prisons and jails. In particular, while it may remain true that relatively little can be done to rehabilitate convicted criminals who are in the community, and virtually nothing can be done to rehabilitate chronic and predatory offenders who are behind bars, correctional programs do have an institutional value independent of their capacity to affect positively the post-release behavior of offenders.

"REHABILITATION" PROGRAMS VIEWED
FROM THE INSIDE

Most prison and jail administrators view correctional programs from what I have dubbed an *institutional* perspective. They evaluate programs not mainly in terms of what they do to reduce the likelihood of recidivism or otherwise affect inmates' post-release behavior but as institutional management tools. With rare exceptions, they strongly believe that making a wide range of meaningful program opportunities available to inmates is a necessary but insufficient condition for running prisons and jails in an orderly, cost-effective fashion.

Just how strongly most prison and jail administrators believe in the efficacy of education, work, substance abuse programs, and other initiatives as institutional management tools can be gleaned by examining the response of corrections agencies throughout the country to legislative changes aimed at gutting these programs. In the mid-1970s, legislatures in a number of jurisdictions mandated a severe reduction in authority and funding for correctional programs behind bars. In most cases, the legislatures were responding mainly to a perceived get-tough shift in public attitudes and, in a few cases, to the sting of lobbying efforts by newly formed victims' rights organizations as well. At the same time, the widely publicized "nothing works" findings of leading researchers made it difficult for defenders of the programs effectively to characterize program-gutting initiatives merely as the product of "lock 'em up and throw away the key" hysteria.

For example, in California, where the rehabilitative ideal had risen in the 1940s and taken shape in dozens of new programs, in the late 1970s the legislature changed the department of corrections' mandate to "punishment" plain and simple; Martinson was on the lips of many who testified in favor of ending or dramatically curtailing prison-based programs.

What corrections administrators in California and most other jurisdictions did in response to such new statutes was most revealing; namely, they did little or nothing. Few agencies actually cut back on programs at all; some even added new programs and expanded existing ones. Through an examination of departmental annual reports and interviews with present and former corrections officials around the country, I have searched for evidence of actual program retrenchment at the state level and within the Federal Bureau of Prisons during the period from 1975 to 1985 and found little or none. I have, however, found evidence that corrections officials, using techniques ranging in bureaucratic sophistication from obvious foot dragging and outright defiance, to exploitation of the sometimes vague language of the new statutes in order to "reinvent" old programs under new names, simply continued to staff and operate institutional programs. Just why they did so is summarized nicely in the colorful words of a veteran prison administrator who, as he recalled, "fought this stupid battle in two states":

I was around in the days when all the convicts did was sit on their asses, in their cells or on the tiers, all f——king day. . . . That got you two things. Either you [staff] went nuts with boredom and felt like you were working in a human warehouse. Or the bastards [inmates] had all the time in the world to sit and think up ways to make trouble. . . . When programs started in the fifties, then [got] bigger in the sixties, it seemed like a fad that would pass, and it was a real pain in the ass moving the bastards from the cellblock, to the ed center, to the shrink's cave, back to the ed center, over to shop [prison industry]. . . . But after a while, I liked, everybody liked it. It kept the convicts busy. It helped every third one grow up and act more mature. And it was interesting for staff. It nixed the boredom. . . . With the programs, you could become a white-collar by moving out of security and into counseling or what have you. . . . Now, I don't see how the hell you could run a joint without programs. Without them, staff would get fed up, and the convicts would probably be more trouble to themselves and everybody else. . . . There was no way we were going to f——k up everything just because some asshole legislator or double-asshole professor decided that rehabilitation was dead. *Rehabilitation* isn't in the vocabulary, never was. [Programs] are like custody, like food service. . . . They are part of what it takes to run a good joint, period.

A more recent and pointed example of how much prison and jail administrators value programs as institutional management tools is the response of the Federal Bureau of Prisons to congressional initiatives that would effectively destroy its prison industry program. Founded in 1934, the BOP's prison industry program has been known since 1978 as UNICOR, Inc. UNICOR makes a wide range of products, from high-quality office furniture to combat helmets, which it sells to other government agencies. In 1985, UNICOR's gross sales topped $250 million. Not only has UNICOR actively employed nearly half of all eligible inmates in its remarkable chain of plants at over three dozen BOP institutions, it has also generated funds used to support a wide range of other BOP programs, including inmate educational and vocational training programs.

In 1989, however, the BOP found itself battling a congressional measure that would have dramatically restricted UNICOR's capacity to produce and sell its products. The agency won this battle but it is almost certain that the same or a similar fight will occur in the next Congress, and it is by no means clear that the agency will once again prevail. The merits of the initiative to gut UNICOR to one side (in my judgment, one of the stupidest measures introduced in the 101st Congress), the BOP's struggle to save UNICOR was based on the institutional perspective on correctional programs shared by its leaders, managers, and veteran line workers.

Make no mistake, UNICOR has always been an administrative headache for BOP leaders and staff. It was founded in the swirl of enormous political opposition, and over the decades it has created terrific strains and conflicts within the agency.[13] And it would be wrong to assume that BOP personnel somehow benefit in direct and tangible ways (bigger salaries, plusher offices) from UNICOR's survival and prosperity; they do not. The reason the agency's employees at all levels feel so positively about UNICOR is simply that they know prison industries and related programs are essential to running their institutions safely and cost effectively. "UNICOR," said one veteran BOP officer, "makes it possible for us to run our institutions with a minimum of disorders, and it keeps inmates occupied and staff involved in something beyond turning keys." A high-ranking BOP official stated:

117

I can't believe they'd take UNICOR away from us or force it into a weak and sickly condition. There are problems with our prison industry operations, but they pale by comparison to the problems we'd have without it. Maybe it's just that the centrality of UNICOR and other programs to keeping the institutions from deteriorating is invisible to people who aren't as intimately familiar with them as [we are]. . . . No, you can't sell UNICOR or any other program as a rehabilitation mechanism, because they're probably just not. It's what the programs do for the operation of the institution that should count.

There is no body of empirical research to prove or refute what BOP and most other prison and jail administrators believe about the efficacy of programs as institutional management tools. But most of the existing evidence, such as it is, tends to support the practitioners' view that, other things being equal, the more programmatic an institution, the safer and less costly it is to operate. Let me, therefore, briefly summarize what I take to be the practitioners' three main propositions about programs and state the case for each of them.

Programs are valuable as incentives for good inmate behavior. Few inmates would prefer sitting in a cramped cell to working in an industrial plant, doing landscaping, attending classes, or receiving vocational instruction. Except in the case of legally mandated health services and the like, program participation is a privilege that administrators can extend to inmates or withhold from them in accordance with behavioral criteria that inmates can learn through formal orientations, official handbooks, the inmate grapevine, and informal communication with staff.

Where parole can still be had on such terms, inmates have an incentive to participate in relevant programs; but to participate in programs, they must first refrain from illicit and predatory behaviors that may render them ineligible.

In pondering this proposition, the BOP's experience with the Federal Correction Institution at Butner in North Carolina may be instructive. Butner was opened in 1976 as an experimental institution. Its population consisted of some of the most hard-to-handle inmates in the federal system. The inmates at Butner were purposely handled with a minimum of coercive measures, and within the context of institutional rules that made it possible for inmates to move about and interact rather freely.

A crucial feature of Butner's management process was its rich menu of self-help programs, offered to inmates but not required of them. An independent research team was hired by the BOP to study the effects of this regime on the recidivism of Butner inmates. (The team's studies were based on an experimental research design that was flawed in the execution, though by no means fatally so.) Finding that participation in Butner's programs had no discernible effect on inmates' post-release criminal activity or on their employment status, the studies did show that the programs had a major and positive effect on the quality of life *inside* Butner. A 1987 evaluation report concluded: "When inmates were allowed to volunteer for programs, they not only participated in more programs, but they also completed more programs. *There were fewer disciplinary problems and fewer assaults*"[14] (emphasis added).

Of course, even if one were to defer to the practitioners' wisdom on this matter, buoyed as it is by this and similar research findings, the case for programs as institutional

management tools would be far from clinched. For start-
ers, institutional safety is one thing, and cost-effectiveness
is another. I know of no competent cost-benefit analysis
of correctional programs, but, as most practitioners seem
to believe, it is possible that by lowering the incidence of
inmate violence and other institutional problems, programs may more than pay for themselves over time.

*Programs facilitate good inmate-staff and intrastaff relations
and communications.* The administration of programs rou-
tinizes personal interaction among and between inmates
and staff. Running programs successfully—indeed, running them at all—requires vertical and horizontal cooperation among otherwise disparate elements of the staff:
uniformed security staff and counselors, department
"brass" and line workers, for example. Programs get inmates and staff talking to one another and interacting on
a nonconfrontational basis. While no guarantee of peace
behind bars, an institution with a full complement of programs is more likely to achieve this positive state of affairs
than either a no-frills warehousing operation or a spartan,
paramilitary regime with relatively few program opportunities.

When I first heard this proposition expressed by practitioners, including many a grizzled old guard, I was
surprised. After all, conventional prison sociology taught
(and by and large still teaches) that there is an irreducible
and almost wholly unproductive tension between "treatment" and "custody."[15] But upon reflection, it occurred
to me that this disheartening idea grew out of studies
based largely on the experiences of the late 1940s, the
1950s, and the early 1960s. These studies were tales of
cataclysmic violence and administrative turmoil wrought

when uniformed security staff, long the sole sovereigns of the cellblocks, were suddenly forced into working with, and around, invading hordes of teachers, psychologists, nurses, and so on.

The leading analysts of the day were quick to infer that, administratively, the Big House would remain a house divided. Neither they nor their intellectual successors allowed for the possibility of administrative evolution and adaptation among and between so-called treatment and custody staff. In effect, they were blind to the possibility that, over time, programs could actually make *all* staff members more responsive to inmates' needs, could foster respect and cooperation among and between inmates and staff and enhance staff morale, esprit de corps, and sense of professional mission—all of which might translate over time into less staff turnover and burnout, less use of disability leave, less staff abuse of inmates, less litigation, and less of each problem that raises the human and financial toll of administering prisons and jails.

Most corrections administrators now believe that this is precisely what programs have done. There is little systematic evidence with which to validate or void this bit of their wisdom on the subject, at least not of the sort that would pass muster with any social scientist. But if one is willing to admit as evidence the testimony of hundreds of persons who have spent years running prisons and jails with and without programs, and if one is willing to cast a broad net over the "natural experiments" with programs that they have lived through and conducted, then the proposition that programs are a boon to institutional management seems a much better bet than its opposite number.

121

*Programs facilitate staff recruitment, training, and develop-
ment, and are a force for the professionalization of corrections.*
There may be some people who enjoy spending their time
doing nothing but counting, frisking, shaking down cells,
forcibly moving inmates, and so on. Every corrections institution has, and probably needs, a core of workers for
whom "lock psychosis" is a preferred mental state, and
who like nothing better than the camaraderie that comes
with such nitty-gritty, line-level work. But most people,
including the kinds of people one must attract if one is
to fill the middle and upper rungs of a large, complex
public bureaucracy, enjoy exercising a wider range of
mental and other skills, and will want readily identifiable
on-the-job outlets for personal and career growth over
time. For these people, what institutional corrections has
to offer is programs, or, more precisely, the chance to
have professional, or quasi-professional, employment opportunities within correctional settings.

As was true for the two preceding practitioner propositions about the utility of programs as management tools,
I know of no systematic body of evidence to document or
doom this view. But there is, again, the broad and deep
consensus among practitioners themselves and piles of an-
ecdotal material to support it.

For example, for years the Federal Bureau of Prisons
was able to attract and hold on to dedicated workers all
around the country. Clearly, this was due in part to the
fact that, in most jurisdictions, the BOP paid higher salaries than its state and local counterparts. But it was also
due to the fact that, because of its programmatic emphasis, the BOP gave its typical employee the chance for a
more challenging and diversified career. Indeed, when

in the 1980s the BOP lost its salary edge in most places—for example, entry-level corrections workers in many states could earn almost twice what an entry-level BOP worker could earn; typical upper-level managers in these states took home over $15,000 a year more than their BOP cousins—the agency continued to have a good deal of success in personnel recruitment and retention at all levels.

One BOP worker spoke for many when he maintained that, while they were aware of their relative financial deprivation (including, in many cases, in the area of pension plans), "the programs, the variety of challenges they present, the chance to work in many different capacities, has always made the federal system a more interesting place to work." Another worker, one who had left a higher-paying job in a state corrections department for a post with the BOP, stated: "With the programs, you get a sense of professionalism and being a professional. You have to know custody, and custody is the most important thing. But it's not the only thing. Programs are what makes corrections corrections."

CORRECTIONAL PROGRAMS AND HUMANE CUSTODY

Even among prison and jail administrators who take an institutional view on programs, there is no little disagreement over whether all, some, or no inmates really "deserve" access to education, work, substance abuse programs, and other services. Within the practitioner community, as within the ranks of corrections analysts,

activists, and the public at large, there are those who harbor extreme views on the moral issue of whether programs should be a defining feature of humane custody.

One extreme position is that correctional institutions
without programs are an absolute moral outrage. In this
view, a full complement of programs ought to be provided
whether or not they can be shown to facilitate institutional
management, to have a positive effect on institutional conditions (reducing violence, for example), to pay for themselves over time, or, alas, to lower recidivism rates. The
other extreme position is that correctional institutions *with*
programs are a moral outrage. In this view, giving convicted criminals educational, employment, and other opportunities that many average, law-abiding citizens cannot
obtain, and doing so at taxpayer expense, is unconscion-
able; programs ought not to be provided even if they can
be shown to improve management, to enhance conditions,
to lower costs, and/or to reduce recidivism.

Most corrections practitioners, activists, and analysts
take a position between these two extremes; so do most
Americans in general.[16] Most of us are neither so forgiving that we would rush to shower convicted criminals
with such opportunities, nor so vengeful that we would
categorically deprive them of such opportunities in sheer
spite. In deciding on the moral propriety of programs,
most of us are inclined toward a "consequentialist" approach that weighs the real or perceived effects of programs on recidivism rates, institutional management and
conditions, and our pocketbooks.

If there is one corrections professional who not only
preached but practiced this morally pragmatic view of
programs, it was the late James V. Bennett. As discussed

in chapter 1, Bennett directed the federal prison system from 1937 to 1964. He founded and institutionalized many of the agency's best programs, including the fore-runner of the aforementioned UNICOR, at a time of low financial and political support for such initiatives. Throughout his long career in corrections, he believed that programs were morally appropriate, that they might keep at least some criminals from returning to crime once supervision ceased, and, last but by no means least in his thinking, that they were an indispensable management tool for keeping inmates occupied, staff alert and engaged in their work, and corrections on the road to professional-ism. He believed deeply that every criminal should be given some opportunity for self-improvement, and that failure to provide such opportunities was tantamount to a failure to provide humane custody.

At the same time, however, Bennett acknowledged that not all offenders could or should have ready access to programs, that some programs probably were better than others, and that the primary purpose of corrections was immovably custodial: to protect the public from offenders and to protect offenders from one another in a lawful manner. He was open to systematic research into the ef-ficacy of programs as rehabilitation tools, and he encour-aged his subordinates to modify or abolish programs when they hindered rather than helped other important facets of the operation.

Bennett was also aware that the unfettered pursuit of what in his day was often termed the "rehabilitative ideal" could generate unnecessary conflicts, produce perverse and unintended consequences, and lead corrections prac-titioners and penologists astray. In his day as in ours, there stood no better monument to the limits and potential of rehabilitation as a correctional goal than Maryland's Patuxent Institution. Let me, therefore, complete this revisit to rehabilitation by conducting a brief tour of Patuxent and its checkered history.

WHITHER REHABILITATION?
NOTES FROM PATUXENT

In the fall of 1988, I spent a few days observing operations and interviewing inmates and staff at Patuxent Institution, a maximum-security prison in Jessup, Maryland, that houses several hundred inmates. My visit was in loose conjunction with a research project, sponsored by the National Institute of Justice, intended to assist Maryland corrections authorities in developing a research agenda. A week or so after my field visits to Patuxent, the prison was caught in a public controversy that made national headlines. Having spent time reviewing the prison's history and gathering archival data on it, I was not surprised by this turn of events.

Throughout much of its history, Patuxent has been at the eye of a political storm. This time the storm occurred when a newspaper reported that Robert Daly Angell, a Patuxent prisoner sentenced in 1976 to three consecutive life terms for murdering two police officers and a teenager, had been allowed by Patuxent officials to leave the prison for unsupervised visits with his family. Angell had been awarded many such unsupervised twelve-hour furloughs.

Just as the public protest over this disclosure was peaking, another Patuxent prisoner, James M. Stavarakas, escaped. Actually, *escaped* is not the right term. Stavarakas did not scale any walls but simply walked away while on work release from Patuxent. He was charged with raping a female jogger on his second day as a fugitive. The alleged rape occurred in the same Maryland park where he had raped a woman in 1978, a crime for which he was sentenced to twenty-five years.

In response, top Maryland corrections officials, legislators, and the governor's office wasted no time in expressing their shock and regret and in calling for major changes at Patuxent, including its abolition. For weeks following the incidents, stories about Patuxent dotted the lead sections and op-ed pages of the *Washington Post* and Maryland newspapers. These reports, and many of the op-ed pieces, were picked up and run by big circulation newspapers all around the country. The CBS News program "60 Minutes," which years earlier had produced and aired a segment on Patuxent, returned to the scene and broadcast an updated story on the prison.

As of mid-February 1989, the controversy was still brewing. Maryland's elected leaders and corrections chiefs remained under enormous political pressure over Patuxent. Dr. Norma Gluckstern, Patuxent's warden since 1977, had been their number-one target. She was granted a medical leave of absence. Her future, and the future of the prison, remained in grave doubt.

The Rise and Fall of the "Clockwork Orange" Prison

Patuxent's present and future should be seen against the backdrop of its rocky past. Patuxent opened in 1955 as a maximum-security institution designed to rehabilitate repeat male offenders serving indeterminate sentences. Under the prison's 1951 enabling legislation, Article 31-B, these offenders were termed "defective delinquents," defined as "individuals who, by demonstration of persistent aggravated anti-social or criminal behavior, evidence a propensity toward criminal behavior and who, on evidence of standard tests and clinical procedures, reveal either intellectual deficiency or emotional disorder, or both."

The "defective delinquent" statute was born of the notion that some criminals, though not legally insane, were so criminally asocial, antisocial, and deviant that they simply could not be housed safely in conventional prisons. In 1931, Judge Joseph N. Ulman of the Baltimore City Court sentenced the murderer Herman Webb Duker to death by hanging because, though Duker was "not fully responsible for his actions," Maryland had "no institutions specifically designed and intended for the permanent or long-time segregation of defective delinquents of this type." His opinion was punctuated by many references to the leading psychiatric texts, authorities, and jargon of the day. For example, Judge Ulman wrote:

What, then, is a "psychopathic personality"? In the first place, in Maryland, it is a legally sane person. He knows the difference between right and wrong; he is capable of appreciating the consequences of his acts. He may be a highly intelligent person. But he is emotionally unstable, abnormally self-centered, and his moral responsibility is less than that, or different from that, of a normal man. Psychiatrists, writing for scientific readers, do not find it easy to define this term. But this Court is thoroughly convinced that difficulty of statement does not, in this instance, indicate confusion of thought.[17]

Luckily for the convict Duker, Maryland Governor Albert C. Ritchie found enough "confusion" in Judge Ulman's opinion to commute the hanging sentence to life imprisonment:

What I cannot understand is how the Court could first decide—as it did—that Duker's mental disorder should be considered in mitigation of punishment, and that he should not be hanged; and then sentence him to be hanged anyhow, not for his crime, but because the Penitentiary is the only place to which he could be committed, and because of the Court's prediction that in the Penitentiary Duker would be a dangerous person. . . . I don't think he should be hanged because of anybody's prediction as to what kind of prisoner he might be.[18]

Judge Ulman's confusion, however, was resurrected on a high plane in 1947 in the form of the Maryland State Legislature's Commission to Study Medico-Legal Psychiatry. The Commission's leading members included some of the most eminent psychiatrists of the day. But after two years of study and discussion, the Commission did little more than surround Judge Ulman's "defective delinquent" notion with lots of unsubstantiated psychiatric theory and dense rhetoric, lend it false intellectual legitimacy in the eyes of a wider public, and define it in much the way it had been officially defined in Article 31-B.

The Commission was not alone in endorsing the "defective delinquent" concept. The Maryland State Board of Corrections, and the Legislative Council on Medico-Legal Procedure, advanced the concept as well; the latter body dotted the *i*'s and crossed the *t*'s on the 1951 enabling legislation for Patuxent. In essence, it appears that the logic employed by each body went as follows:

1. Some dangerous criminals are mentally deranged; others are not.
2. Those who are mentally deranged can be "treated" by psychotherapy; most of the others cannot.
3. The "incurables" might get a fixed prison term.
   a. They would cause violence and other trouble in prison.
   b. They would still be dangerous when released.
4. Thus, let us designate these "incurables" as "defective delinquents."
   a. These criminals must be held in prisons administered in ways that recognize their special criminal "deficiencies."
   b. These criminals must be assigned to these prisons and subjected to their rules and programs involuntarily.
   c. These criminals must be given indeterminate sentences and be held at the discretion of "professional" evaluators and relevant prison officials.
   d. If need be, these criminals must remain incarcerated well beyond the limits of any fixed sentence

and be released only when the responsible authorities have decided that they no longer pose a criminal danger to others.

Between 1955 and 1976, some 1,300 prisoners were
committed to Patuxent. There were four ways for a prisoner to get out of Patuxent. First, he could escape; few
did. Second, he could die; about 25 left this way. Third,
he could be released (either to another prison or to the
streets) by a court of law with the power to declare that,
contrary to the evaluation of the relevant corrections officials, he was no longer a "defective delinquent"; about
500 inmates exited on these terms. Fourth, he could be
paroled by the Patuxent Institutional Review Board; some
730 inmates were paroled by the Board, and over 300 of
them were reincarcerated for violations of parole conditions or new crimes.

From day one, Patuxent drew fire. The prison was
charged with violating inmates' civil liberties and depriv-
ing them of due process protections. In time, documented
horror stories began to circulate about sentenced criminals who, had they not be been tagged as "defective delinquents" under the impossibly vague language of Article
31-B and via the mysterious pseudoscience of the diag-
nostic methods it prescribed, would have been released
within two years but were still in Patuxent after nearly
twenty.

Though psychotherapy was not expressly mandated by
the enabling law (remember, the "defective delinquent"
was defined largely as a dangerous criminal who was beyond the reach of such treatment), it quickly became a
centerpiece of Patuxent's treatment milieu. That milieu

was institutionalized through the provisions of Article 31-B requiring that the director of the prison, one member of the board, and one associate director must be psychiatrists, and that counted among the prison staff should be at least three psychiatrists (or clinical psychologists) and four social workers.

Patuxent inmates were in a classic catch-22 situation. If they responded well to the psychotherapy and other treatment programs, then more of the same would be in order and they would continue to be incarcerated at Patuxent. But if they resisted treatment, did not admit that they had special criminal "deficiencies," and so on, then more of the same would also be in order and they would continue to be incarcerated at Patuxent.

Meanwhile, to justify their existence and their approach, the Patuxent treatment staff tried to make Patuxent a testimonial to the "defective delinquent" notion on which it was founded—and funded. Seeing a parallel between the prison's perverse medico-legal psychotherapeutic regime and the futuristic anti-utopia depicted in Anthony Burgess's popular novel, some critics dubbed Patuxent the "Clockwork Orange Prison."

Less literary-minded critics of Patuxent flourished as well. Between 1955 and 1976, in every session of the Maryland legislature at least one lawmaker proposed a bill calling for the prison's abolition. Critical newspaper reports, television spots, and other media assaults were common. Lawsuits, including several class action suits, against some or all of the "defective delinquent" provisions were filed repeatedly. Amid these controversies, high-profile commissions to study Patuxent were empaneled in 1961, 1965, and 1967.

Patuxent also had its supporters during these years, on the bench and elsewhere. In its 1964 opinion in the case of *Sas v. State of Maryland*, the U.S. Court of Appeals for the Fourth Circuit characterized Patuxent as a "new and radical approach to the problems of crime and recidivism." Many progressive and liberal supporters of prison rehabilitation programs and the medical model of corrections applauded Patuxent as a well-intentioned experiment that failed because of its involuntary procedures and its indeterminate sentencing power.

But even the most friendly critics of Patuxent in this era raised three unsettling sets of questions about it. First, they wondered how the authorities knew a "defective delinquent" when they saw one. Most Maryland criminals were not found insane ("insanity" being a legal, not a medical or a mental, status) at the time of their crimes; and most were held competent to stand trial. Just how did the responsible authorities select from this group the mentally troubled, sociopathic candidates for "defective delinquent" status who were to be Patuxent-bound? Were there meaningful differences between the convicts they selected for Patuxent and those whom they did not? And just how did they decide to lift the "defective delinquent" status? Were there any discernible and consistently applied principles of logic, any objective or objectifiable criteria, or any meaningful pattern to the decision process at the base of these decisions? Or were the responsible authorities merely exploiting the vague language of Article 31-B, following its formal procedures and doing the required paperwork, but relying on ad hoc and biased guesswork in making these determinations?

Second, critics doubted the ability of Patuxent officials

to predict accurately the dangerousness of offenders and, in conjunction, to judge their treatability. When the prison opened, the consensus among the leading researchers of the day was that such predictions were possible, reflected in the redrafting in many states of inmate classification schemes. But by the mid-1960s, serious challenges had been leveled against this heady claim. It was not clear that Patuxent officials were operating in accordance with either the discredited or the revised theories of how to predict the postinstitutional behavior of convicted criminals. Moreover, the critics doubted that the level, quality, and type of treatment being received by Patuxent inmates in the form of counseling sessions and the like were based on anything approaching a systematic inventory of each inmate's mental state, past criminal history, and related background characteristics.

Third, critics raised questions about Patuxent's success measured in terms of recidivism rates and cost-effectiveness. Other than simply keeping its charges incarcerated longer than they might otherwise have been, did the Patuxent experience really do anything to reduce their chances of returning to crime? Would their recidivism rates be any different were they made to "do time" in a conventional prison setting? Did they recidivate more or less than otherwise objectively comparable "nondefective delinquents" housed for similar crimes for similar periods in "nontreatment" prisons? And, in any case, how much was Patuxent costing Maryland taxpayers? Was its expense, particularly the part of it consumed by the activities of the professional treatment staff, justified by its performance?

These questions were never satisfactorily answered. But in 1977, amid one of the periodic bouts of hot political controversy that has defined Patuxent's history, a fatal blow to the "defective delinquent" idea was delivered. A Massachusetts consulting firm, Contract Research Corporation, issued a 190-page report (plus appendices) on Patuxent.[19] The report had been commissioned by the Department of Public Safety and Correctional Services. Based on a partial and modestly competent analysis of data (mainly statistical) related to the questions that had been raised by Patuxent's critics, the report challenged virtually every aspect of the prison's program.

The report generated some immediate responses from defenders of Patuxent. Naturally, the academic responses focused on arguable flaws and biases in the report's statistical sampling procedures, comparison techniques, theoretical premises, and on its concomitant mistakes of methodology, inference, and argument.[20] Some of the strongest responses came from those who took exception to the report's conclusion that inmate participation in psychotherapy had little or no effect on recidivism rates, though it may have helped inmates achieve positive "personal insights."[21] This statement struck a raw nerve not only among outside researchers who believed in the efficacy of such "treatment modalities," but also among the Patuxent staff who had dedicated their lives to administering them. Some of the flaws in the report were indisputably serious and bound to harm its credibility among even the most open-minded readers.[22] Three things, however, worked in its favor.

First, despite its many shortcomings, on most major points of disagreement over how to interpret the data the report was on firmer ground than were its criticisms. This is not to say that the report answered the questions it presumed to answer. But it did answer them in an academically respectable fashion that proved nothing either way, though it purported to do so.

Second, most of the readers of the report (or most of those who read the summary of the report or the abbreviated newspaper accounts of it) were not open-minded. A majority political coalition dedicated to changing Patuxent significantly or abolishing it had formed well in advance of the report's findings. The report was commissioned at their behest, and its conclusions gave them precisely the kind of intellectual ammunition they needed to attack the prison's remaining defenders. Although much of this ammunition consisted of what were, from a scientific standpoint, fake bullets, the report was credible, its findings were stated powerfully (and so lent themselves to political rhetoric about "outright failure" and "waste of money"), and the opposition was unarmed, on the defensive, and relatively weak and disorganized.

Third, though damning on every front, the report did not recommend that Patuxent be abolished. Instead, it called for major modifications that would better enable the facility to meet the goal of prisoner rehabilitation: "Nevertheless, the study team believes that the conditions that gave the initial impetus to the establishment of Patuxent Institution still exist: the need for rehabilitation programs within secure facilities, for the habitual serious offender."[23] This was no minor concession. As noted in the opening part of this chapter, in the mid-1970s the rehabilitative ideal had been taking a beating in the academic journals and in legislation in many states. Thus, to recommend in 1977 that a maximum-security prison dedicated mainly to the rehabilitation of hard-core criminals be erected on the ashes of Patuxent's discredited "defective delinquent" regime was quite a political bone to toss to the prison's defenders.

In the ensuing legislative debate over Patuxent's future (and there was not much of a debate), the institution's history was recast, even upended, to make it appear that the prison, born of the desire to rehabilitate "treatable" convicts, had been pursuing the right ends with the wrong means. Get rid of the involuntary provisions, get rid of indeterminate sentencing, rework the "treatment modalities" in accordance with the latest academic theories, revise Article 31-B accordingly, and Patuxent would fulfill its historic mission.

It did not matter that Patuxent's "historic mission" was no such thing. History could be written in the service of political compromise and to avoid further media heat and costly legal battles; besides, by 1977 most Maryland legislators thought Patuxent was kind of a crazy place. Thus, Article 31-B was revised in July 1977, and the Patuxent saga continued.

Patuxent Reinvented, 1977–1989

Since 1977, the Patuxent regime has operated under the Secretary of Public Safety and Correctional Services but without being part of the Division of Corrections. It has no formal connection with the Maryland Parole Commission or the Division of Parole and Probation. Instead, Patuxent has its own paroling authority through its Board.

Offenders at other Maryland prisons who volunteer and are accepted for treatment at Patuxent are termed "Eligible Persons" (EPs). No prisoner is sent to Patuxent against his will, and any prisoner can be transferred from Patuxent to another Maryland prison by filing a transfer request. To be an EP, a prisoner must meet certain objective requirements, but the prison's Examination/Evaluation Team—psychiatrist, psychologist, and social worker—exercises much discretion in deciding who will get in.

Until the most recent controversies, an EP at Patuxent could aim simultaneously toward three goals in his attempt to satisfy Patuxent officials. First, he could try to work his way into the prison's honor unit. Patuxent operates on a "graded-tier" system. The first tier, "receiving," imposes all sorts of conventional maximum-security restrictions on an inmate's movement, such as constant direct supervision by correctional officers and severe limits to the amount of personal property he may keep in his cell. The second and third tiers offer gradually less restrictive environments, and when a prisoner reaches the fourth tier, he is afforded the chance for "self-government." Inmates in fourth-tier units elect representatives to set living rules for their area of the prison and to serve as liaisons to the prison staff. They enjoy privileges and freedoms that are normally known only to inmates of minimum- and some medium-security prisons.

An inmate must serve minimum requisite times on each tier before being eligible for the next one. Good behavior is the key to moving from the first to the fourth tiers. New Patuxent prisoners quickly learn that "good behavior" at this maximum-security prison means more than just refraining from violence. The Patuxent *Inmate Handbook* admonishes:

Those of you who stay at Patuxent will find Patuxent different in many ways from other prisons. It is a "total treatment" Institution, which means that . . . everything you do in the Institution is important: whether or not you go to school; whether or not you try to learn a trade; the ratings you get on your Institutional job; your behavior and whether you get tickets [disciplinary reports]; and how you use the whole program will determine how fast you move through the Institution. If you get a lot of tickets, you may be considered for a return to the Division of Corrections. But just being good and staying out of trouble won't get you parole. Just doing well in psychotherapy won't get you parole. Everything has to work together.[24]

One reward of moving up the tiers, and the second goal toward which an EP could aim, is furlough. Furloughs are granted at the discretion of Patuxent officials who, in the language of the handbook, look at the total picture, including reports on whether an inmate has made progress in the various sorts of required counseling sessions.

What constitutes progress in these sessions varies depending on which Patuxent official you ask. Some, for example, stress the inmate's willingness to verbalize his feelings and to "confront his crime" and other past misdeeds. From this perspective, prisoners who maintain their innocence, minimize their responsibility for the crime, or try to "run a con" on their counselors (which may include fellow inmates) are rated poorly. Other officials place more emphasis on whether the inmate simply behaves in an orderly fashion, speaks respectfully to his peers, and does not "act out" or "get too rammy" in counseling sessions. At a session I attended, one inmate who had been described by both a "touchy-feely" and a "boot camp" counselor as having made rapid progress spoke as follows:

> I killed that girl and it didn't matter to me. I was a damn animal. I had no remorse, no guilt. But now I'm getting my head together, getting an understanding of the way I behaved and the things that I did. . . . I still can't handle stress situations the way I should, like a mature man. But I'm working on it.

Another inmate whom both counselors agreed was "doing well in here" stated:

> Shit, motherfu—ers [referring to his Patuxent peers] can lie all day and night. I can do it, I loved doing it. But who the f—k you lying to? You lying to yourself. I did the crime and I can't say I wouldn't do it again. Now, I got the motherf—k-ing sense I didn't have then, so I don't think I'd blow him away, not for nothing—maybe not for anything except he threaten my life and put a weapon to my face.

Clearly "making progress" and "doing well" at Patuxent are descriptions open to wide interpretation.

The third and biggest prize for which an EP could aim is release from custody earlier than would have been possible had he not been granted EP status and come under Patuxent's expansive paroling authority. Every official document pertaining to the prison states that inmates are selected based on their "desire to receive treatment." The truth, however, as every official knows, is that the "desire to receive treatment" is a surrogate for the desire to get out of prison and back on the streets as quickly as possible. Patuxent inmates themselves freely admit as much, especially when officials are not there to hear them. A typical comment was as follows:

> These dumb bitches [referring to the Institution officials] want you to like the way they like, do things their way, take bullshit classes and psychoshit. I play the game and I talk the talk. Smile nice, not like a f—king nut. . . . Get them to eat the bullshit and your ass is out of here.

Another, less cynical, inmate said:

> This is a prison like any other. Only here you can do certain things and get out sooner if you connect with what they expect. I don't know what this place does for you. Maybe it works. But I do know I want to get out and stay out, and that these people really want to help me do that as best as they think how.

Patuxent officials pride themselves on their ability to discriminate between "con artists" and those who genuinely seek self-improvement and want to lead a normal life upon release. At the same time, however, each of them has at least one story about getting "burned" by an inmate whom they "really went to bat for" at parole review time, which is at least once a year for every EP. Some indirect evidence indicates that they may be erring on the side of caution. For instance, an in-house study revealed an EP dropout rate of over 60 percent; over 50 percent of the dropouts had spent more than six years at Patuxent, "possibly under the assumption that they would obtain earlier release if they returned" to another Maryland prison.[25]

Many of the policymakers and administrators who have supported Patuxent over the years have failed to see that the way inmates are selected has a significant bearing on their ability to make reasonable claims on the institution's behalf. In a 1983 "Patuxent Day" keynote address, for example, Judge Alan M. Wilner stated: "Inmates are, in fact, now suing to get into Patuxent. Why? Mostly because they see Patuxent as a faster way out of incarceration and because it is a nicer place to be than the overcrowded medium- or maximum-security prisons. But, although their motives may be selfish, that gives Patuxent a terrific advantage. . . . It now can take the people it can best help."[26]

Contrary to the judge's statement, in terms of the possibility for solidly evaluating the impact, if any, of Patuxent's policies and programs, what this means is that selection bias is built in to the selection process. As one veteran Patuxent official responsible for selecting prisoners admitted: "We look for the type of prisoner who will do well. . . . It's hard to admit a mistake, and so once a man makes it here we do our best to make things work out . . . and let the little things go; but normally they don't disappoint us."

Oddly enough, however, there may be a degree of randomness built in to this selection process, and into Patuxent's inmate evaluation and paroling processes as well. In a typical response, when asked to specify the actual criteria that Patuxent officials normally use in making these decisions, and to estimate how consistently they were followed, a key Patuxent official replied:

Truthfully, there aren't any such criteria. I don't think there's any formula. We just use our judgment and size him up based on our experience at that time. Today you admit a guy; tomorrow you might reject the same guy with the same record if the name on his folder changed and he appeared before you in disguise. . . . Some of the inmates on the fourth tier would not have made it there if their cases had come up before a different group of evaluators, or even the same group on different days. The same holds for furloughs and even release decisions, though on those there's a little more of what you called "checks and balances," and more second-guessing.

Nevertheless, the way Patuxent selects its inmates makes it virtually impossible to say with confidence what impact its policies and programs have on their institutional, pre-release, and postinstitutional behavior. During the most recent controversy, for example, figures on Patuxent inmates' rates of recidivism were bandied about by the prison's critics and supporters. There are often numerous problems associated with how such statistics are calculated—for example, whether *recidivism* is taken to mean that the inmate was in violation of parole, was arrested for a new offense, was convicted for a new offense, was convicted for a new offense more serious than the prior offense of conviction, or other criteria, not to mention varying lengths of the follow-up period. But even if, as supporters claimed, it were true that on average Patuxent inmates had lower rates of recidivism than other Maryland prisoners, it would be impossible to judge the significance of this fact in relation to Patuxent's policies and programs.

Among the professional treatment staff at Patuxent, there is some resistance (though it is by no means universal) to the idea that the prison's policies and programs ought to be evaluated at all, let alone through rigorous research with random assignment (see chapter 6). The unduly beleaguered Dr. Gluckstern was open to the possibility of evaluation, and she was self-reflective and self-critical about the efficacy of Patuxent's policies and programs: "We should want to know whether what we do here, and how we do it, makes any difference not only in how inmates may feel about themselves, but in how dangerous they are to themselves and others. . . . If there are better ways of treating these types of criminals and protecting the public in a cost-effective manner, I want to discover what they are. . . . I'd change things in a minute."

Other senior Patuxent officials, however, expressed the view that such research efforts are unnecessary, destructive, or both. One official said: "Look, I'm a bleeding heart. I believe in this way of doing things. I'd do it this way even if it didn't make any difference." Another argued: "Experience on the ground is the only way to understand the effects of a place like this. I know it works, whatever the statistics and studies show."

Among the prison's uniformed correctional officers, however, just the opposite view was dominant. Officially, Patuxent officers are supposed to be involved in the treatment process. In practice, they have little involvement with it and relatively little confidence in those who do. Officers are not consulted when parole decisions are made, which galls many of them. "We know these inmates better than the psychiatrists," said one senior officer. But another quickly added: "We're not interested in making those decisions, but I'm sure we could do a better job at it than the professionals—or at least no worse."

Conclusion

The literature on Patuxent routinely ignores the custodial context in which its programs are offered. I have been to prisons and jails, federal, state, and local, in many parts of the country, and rarely encountered officers with the professional, spit-and-polish approach of those at Patuxent. Moreover, with Dr. Gluckstern's blessing and at her insistence, they have run one of the tightest maximum-security operations I have ever seen. In fact, the custodial element of the prison is so strong that it may be every bit as important as the prison's "treatment modalities" in explaining whatever impact Patuxent has on its prisoners' behavior.

As one examines Patuxent's organizational structure, it becomes clear that there are enormous differences within given treatment modalities. For example, at Patuxent, some group psychotherapy sessions are led by "boot camp" counselors, who shout and yell and stifle intimate discussion; others are led by "touchy-feely" counselors who speak little and encourage inmates to "rap" with one another on any matter that pops into their heads; some inmates move in and out of different sessions with different counselors; and so on. It may well be the case that the rehabilitative effects on inmates of participating in these programs (assuming, for the moment, that there are any such effects) come not from the substance of the treatment

but from the fact that the treatment causes them to engage others repeatedly in a more or less calm, civilized
fashion, to be at a given place at a given time, and otherwise to behave in ways that are more reflective of
straight middle-class society than of any criminal sub-
culture.

My guess is that something good is happening inside
Patuxent. I doubt that its custodial policies and correctional programs as administered during Dr. Gluckstern's
tenure made much of a difference in recidivism rates;
and, even if I were more convinced that reliable predictions in such matters were possible, I would remain
staunchly opposed in principle to furloughing murderers
and other violent criminals the way Patuxent has done.
Yet, with respect to safety, cleanliness, and cost-
effectiveness, I suspect that Patuxent's unique combination of custodial policies and correctional programs has
made a positive difference, and that it may be possible to
learn how these accomplishments were made and to ex-
port any lessons to more conventional prison settings.

There is a breath of evidence for this suspicion. An
in-house report that studied aggregate data on rates of institutional violence at Patuxent versus non-Patuxent prisoners hints that, other things being equal, Patuxent prisoners
may be less violent, more prone to participate in work
and other productive activities, and less inclined to file
costly legal suits against the prison system.[27] There is,
however, nothing even approaching a reliable data base,
or a set of in-house or extradepartmental studies, to confirm or to void this suspicion.

The future of Patuxent, and the future of the idea of

rehabilitation itself, remains in doubt. But to anyone who revisits rehabilitation in light of the latest findings of researchers and the vintage opinions of practitioners, this much should be clear: The facile notion that "nothing works" is ready for the garbage heap of correctional history.

4

Judicial Intervention: Lessons of the Past

FOR MOST OF AMERICAN HISTORY, the role of judges in corrections had been minimal. Judges heard criminal cases and issued sentences, but they did not involve themselves directly in the postsentencing process and certainly made no attempt to administer prisons and jails from the bench. Instead, they followed a hands-off doctrine, epitomized by a federal circuit court's ruling in 1954 that judges are "without power to direct prison administration or to interfere with ordinary prison rules and regulations."[1] As late as 1970, not a single prison or jail system was operating under judicial orders to change and improve.

Since 1970, however, the doctrinal wall of separation between the judge's chambers and the prison's corridors has crumbled. The courts have intervened on a wide range of prison and jail issues, including crowding, food services, sanitation, health care, due process protections for inmates, and the constitutionality of prison and jail conditions "in their totality." Federal judges in particular have abandoned the hands-off doctrine in favor of a hands-on doctrine: At the end of 1989, over three dozen corrections agencies were operating under court directives; many agencies had class action suits brought against them and were bound by population limits set by the courts; over a dozen states had court-appointed special masters, monitors, and compliance coordinators. In some prison systems, texts of court orders and consent decrees were being used as staff training manuals, and as official inmate rules and regulations handbooks.

My primary purpose in this chapter is to examine the impact of judicial intervention on the quality of life behind bars. Has judges' involvement changed prisons and jails for the better, altered correctional practices in a way designed merely to avoid unfavorable rulings in the future, or led to undesirable or simply unanticipated results? To explore this question, I will discuss three illustrative instances of judicial intervention—one case in some detail, the other two more briefly—and conclude by offering some strategic advice on how judges can work to improve (or at least not to worsen) prison and jail conditions. First, however, we need to examine briefly the reasons for judicial involvement in corrections, the chances of judges staying involved into the next century, and the conventional views on what judicial involvement has wrought behind bars.

JUDGES AS WARDENS

The rise of judicial intervention into penal systems has been part of a broader expansion of the courts' role in American government. In a few recent cases, the courts have shown some reluctance to intervene, and there is a hint of evidence that the problem of AIDS in prisons and jails may encourage judges to defer more readily to the wisdom of on-site corrections officials. But there is no reason to suppose that we are witnessing a return to the hands-off doctrine; in the 1990s and beyond, judges will continue to influence, and in many cases to dictate, how prisons and jails are organized and managed.

One might suppose that judges began to intervene in penal administration in the 1970s because, relative to previous decades, prison and jail conditions were deteriorating. In fact, however, just the opposite is true: Judges started to act as wardens at a moment when, throughout most of the country, prison and jail conditions were no worse than before—in fact, in most cases they were demonstrably better.

As early as the 1940s in many penal systems, corrections officials themselves were reforming institutions in fundamental ways that made inmates safer, better fed, better clothed, physically and mentally healthier, less subject to harsh and arbitrary discipline, and more likely to receive meaningful work and educational opportunities than they had been at any previous time in the history of American corrections.[2] Not only did the quality of cellblock life improve steadily between 1940 and 1970, but procedural reforms were made as well. To cite just one of his countless examples, Clair A. Cripe, veteran chief legal counsel of the Federal Bureau of Prisons, recalled that in 1965, ten years before the federal judiciary required such measures, the BOP adopted, and other agencies copied, elaborate due process safeguards for inmates in disciplinary hearings.[3]

If not a deterioration in objective conditions or gross

inattentiveness to due process reforms on the part of corrections practitioners, then perhaps a radical shift in judicial philosophy brought about the shotgun wedding between courts and corrections. In this vein, some have argued that the rise of judicial intervention in this area (and many others) occurred because, in the 1960s, there arrived on the federal bench a critical mass of liberal activist judges.[4] Aided and abetted by the American Civil Liberties Union (ACLU) and other organizations that instigated inmate litigation and championed the cause of inmate "writ writers," these liberal activist judges, so the argument goes, simply took it upon themselves to order and aggressively enforce sweeping changes in the country's penal systems.

There is, to be sure, a germ of truth in this explanation. In some cases, including the *Ruiz* case in Texas, to be discussed at length later in the chapter, the intervening judge was both liberal and activist. But in many if not most cases, the intervening judge was neither liberal nor activist.[5] And in no case of which I am aware did the intervening judge seem hellbent on issuing sweeping decrees and playing warden. Instead, most judges, including the legendary liberal activists, have approached institutional penal reform cases in the spirit evoked by these words from a federal circuit court decision handed down in 1988: "Judges are not wardens, but we must act as wardens to the limited extent that unconstitutional prison conditions force us to intervene when those responsible for the conditions have failed to act."[6] Almost without exception, the judges have approached intervention as a necessary evil, not as a positive good.

In any case, if the rise of liberal activist judges on the

federal bench were a sufficient explanation for the rise of judicial intervention in corrections, one might expect the Republicanization of the federal bench that occurred under President Ronald Reagan between 1980 and 1988 to have spelled a reverse trend. It has not. Political scientist Robert Bradley has studied the relationship between federal judges' propensity to intervene in prisons and jails and such factors as the political party of the president who appointed them and other related background characteristics.[7] Bradley's neat statistical analysis reinforces the experience of most corrections practitioners, including agency legal counselors such as the BOP's Cripe; namely, that contrary to the fears of some and the hopes of others, the appointment of more conservative judges to the federal bench does not presage a return to the hands-off doctrine.

Of course, Congress could in effect force a return to the hands-off doctrine by exercising its latent constitutional authority to lock the courts out of the nation's Big Houses. Section 1 of Article 3 of the Constitution specifies that "inferior courts" (all federal courts save "the one Supreme Court") exist at the pleasure of Congress, and Section 2 of the same Article specifies that the "appellate Jurisdiction" of the Supreme Court itself is bounded by "such Exceptions, and under such Regulations as the Congress shall make." In the 1980s, some conservative senators attempted to invoke this authority and to restrict the federal bench's jurisdiction in school prayer and school desegregation cases. Their efforts did not succeed in both houses, but in mid-1989 conservative senators contemplated widening this net to include prison reform cases. Under the heading "Appropriate Judicial Remedies for

Prison Overcrowding," in a section of a draft omnibus "National Crime Emergency Act," they trained their guns on limiting the scope of judicial intervention into prisons and jails. As of this writing, the fate of this initiative is undecided. But given the fate of similar court-restraining initiatives in other areas, I do not expect this section of the draft bill to become law.

THREE VIEWS OF JUDICIAL INTERVENTION

As sentencing and demographic trends conspire to make continued growth in the nation's prison and jail populations, and institutional overcrowding, virtual certainties, it is most likely that judges will continue to intervene and act as wardens. Whether one welcomes or laments this prospect may depend not only on one's beliefs about the constitutional and moral propriety of judicial involvement in this area but also on one's assessment of the consequences of that involvement measured in terms of institutional safety, civility, and cost-effectiveness. There are three basic schools of thought on the impact of judicial intervention into prisons and jails.

One school argues that judges have emboldened the inmates, upset informal order-keeping arrangements among prisoners and between inmates and staff, and gutted basic custodial controls. Members of this school blame the courts for rising tides of prison violence. For example, Kathleen Engel and Stanley Rothman have argued that court-imposed reforms have increased prison violence by undermining the "complex relationships among inmates"

153

that had "contributed to the maintenance of order and inmate solidarity."[8] The notion that such informal cellblock alliances were once a bedrock of prison order is a vivid but wholly unsubstantiated sociological myth; riots and disturbances have occurred most often precisely where prison administrators have relied upon inmates to control other inmates and have failed to run things by the book. Especially in high security prisons, those prison managers have governed best who have governed most and most formally.[9]

A second school maintains that activist judges have done no more than force prison administrators to operate in ways that secure rather than deny prisoners' rights. Advocates of this view credit the courts with improving prison and jail conditions. For example, the ACLU's National Prison Project led the litigation efforts that expanded court intervention into penal affairs; indeed, the organization spearheaded the use of special masters and monitors. One of the ACLU's primary objectives in this area has been to decrease the number of people behind bars and to force a greater use of ostensibly less harsh and restrictive alternatives to incarceration; hence, whether the actual impact on cellblock conditions is good, bad, unknown, or nonexistent, the organization counts as major victories instances of judicial involvement where population limits have been imposed and negative media attention has been focused on the prison gates.

Yet a third school believes that the courts have fostered a codification of correctional policies and procedures resulting in the bureaucratization of the institutions, which in turn has made prisons and jails more orderly and humane. This belief moves from a top-down conception of bureaucracy that focuses more on formal administrative trappings (bulky training manuals, elaborate central-office policy directives, uniform institutional training programs, and the like) than on the day-to-day work of line employees. By definition, those in a bureaucracy who perform the agency's critical tasks have little discretion; successful job performance is not highly contingent on the integrity, personality, wit, or any other special talents of the workers.

Yet, clearly, court-induced changes in the operation of prisons and jails have helped increase the complexity of the corrections officers' work by vesting them with ever greater discretionary authority and personalizing their relationships with inmates, while obliterating the guards' once simple, paramilitary routine of counting, checking, locking, monitoring, frisking, searching, and so on. To the extent that prisons and jails have undergone any sort of court-induced organizational metamorphosis, the barbed-wire bureaucracies have become less, not more, bureaucratic, and the effects of these changes on actual conditions are hard to measure.

Proponents of each view tend to agree that, whatever the effects on institutional conditions, judicial intervention has exerted upward pressure on corrections budgets. But there is argument over how much of a fiscal effect the courts have had, either in general or in specific cases.[10] And there is absolutely no consensus regarding whether court-induced spending has been worth it.

A TALE OF TWO STATES AND ONE CITY

None of the leading views of judicial intervention fares well when considered in the light of actual cases. There is a great deal of variance in the outcomes of judicial interventions into penal systems. Let us now explore three cases that illustrate the range of outcomes in relation to the intervening judge's modus operandi. As we shall see, the course and consequences of an intervention depend on many factors, but, not surprisingly, the judge's role is primary.

The *Ruiz* Intervention in Texas

Administrative and Political Context

Perhaps the single most controversial, publicized, and revealing instance of judicial intervention into a major prison system is *Ruiz v. Estelle* in Texas. The case began in 1972, dragged on into 1987, and revolutionized the way Texas ran its prisons. Nobody had a more profound sense of what the intervention had wrought than Dr. George Beto. Beto figured briefly in chapter 1; here is the denouement of this legendary practitioner's story.

In 1985, Beto, for thirteen years a professor of criminal justice at Sam Houston State University in eastern Texas, close to the prisons he had directed from 1962 to 1972, sat in stunned silence as members of his graduate seminar who worked in Texas prisons lectured the class about their experiences. Beto's head drooped as they described in graphic detail how Texas prisoners, especially new ones, were commonly raped or gang-raped; how every shake-down of cells turned up hundreds of weapons and other contraband; how certain inmate leaders ran prostitution and drug rings; how prison gangs were putting out contracts on—that is, hiring inmates to kill—staff and other prisoners; how inmate classrooms and workplaces were, like the cellblocks, sites of idleness punctuated by disorder; how demoralized officers, fearing inmate reprisals for disciplinary action and with little more than personal survival and a paycheck in view, were simply "keeping their backs to the wall" and ignoring most rule violations, major and minor.

During Beto's tenure and into the 1980s, the Texas prison system had been hailed as one of the nation's best; but in 1984 and 1985 a total of 52 inmates of Texas prisons were murdered, and over 700 were stabbed. More serious violence occurred during those two years than had occurred in the previous decade. As the disorder mounted, inmate participation in treatment and educational programs became erratic, the once immaculate inmate living quarters ceased to sparkle, and recreational privileges were curtailed.

What happened to the Texas Department of Corrections (TDC) was the product of at least two sets of related factors: a major flaw in the model of penal administration fathered by Beto and bequeathed to his successor, W. J. Estelle; and *Ruiz v. Estelle*, a landmark court case in which federal district judge William Wayne Justice brought about sweeping changes in TDC's philosophy, leadership, and day-to-day management practices while making the agency the *bête noire* of state policymakers and the press.

Beto, a tall, lean Lutheran minister with a doctorate in

education, instituted what came to be known in corrections circles as the control model of penal administration. His control model emphasized inmate obedience, work, and education, roughly in that order. Every TDC prison was run as a maximum-security operation organized along strict paramilitary lines. Official rules and regulations were enforced rigorously. In the prison corridors, for example, clean-shaven, white-uniformed inmates were required to walk between lines painted on the floors rather than moving at random down the center. Talking too loud was a punishable offense. Punishment for rule violations, major and minor, was swift and certain. Rewards for good behavior came in the form of better work assignments, sentence reductions, and "trustyships." Each inmate spent his first six months doing backbreaking stoop labor, a cog in the machine of TDC's then enormously successful agribusiness complex. All inmates were required to attend school and, if illiterate, to learn how to read and write.

As mentioned earlier, Beto earned the nickname Walking George for his practice of appearing unexpectedly at prisons and roaming through them relentlessly to see that every phase of the operation met his exacting standards. He was a charismatic leader who made both his subordinates and the inmates feel that he knew or could trace their every move; in fact, he often could. As comfortable in the aisles of the state legislature as in the cellblocks, Beto successfully courted governors, lawmakers, and other officials influential in state business, and saw to it that TDC got the legal authority and the money it needed to run its custodial and treatment programs in accordance with his correctional precepts.

Beto was perhaps the most well read man ever to run

a prison system; the influences on his thinking about how to govern prisons ranged from the Bible (which he read each morning in ancient Greek) and classic works of moral and political philosophy, to writings in public administration and texts by leading sociologists of the prison. It was in deference to the last of these that Beto fashioned as part of his control model the building tender system in which inmates were used to control other inmates.

In return for watching the officers' backs, providing information, turning cell doors, tending to the physical upkeep of the institution, and other duties, Beto's building tenders were officially rewarded with better food, job assignments, and other amenities. The building tender system was a calculated gamble aimed at turning the "natural" leaders of the society of captives into the official allies of the government of keepers.

Beto did everything imaginable to keep the tender system honest. For one thing, he handpicked his "supertrusties,"choosing inmates who were tough but not predatory. He permitted neither the building tenders nor the staff to "get too big for their britches." Any officer who violated his trust was fired, usually on the spot. Any building tender who exercised or demanded illicit privileges in return for his services was sent back into the fields to do stoop labor flanked by "fish" (new inmates).

When in 1972 Beto resigned amid pleas from all over the state that he remain as director of TDC, most of his control model had been well institutionalized: the paramilitary procedures, the liberal awarding of good time, the stress on inmate discipline, work, and education. The building tender system, however, was never a well-integrated part of the model. Beto and his top aides were

159

aware that, without unremitting efforts to keep it honest, the building tender system could easily degenerate into the very system of inmate dominance and corrupt inmate-staff relations it was meant to forestall. As one high-ranking veteran of TDC noted perceptively:

> The tenders were always like a sort of sore thumb of the control model. . . . I mean here you had the bosses [officers] and the "Yes, sirs," and the steady discipline, all of it done formal-like and run by the authorities. . . . But then there were the tenders, inmates who were "first among equals" so long as they did our bidding. . . . But you know Dr. Beto, he'd never let it get out of control!

Under Beto's handpicked heir, W. J. "Jim" Estelle, the number of TDC inmates increased by the thousands and the agency's prisons more than doubled to over two dozen institutions. Though in many respects a brilliant prisons man, Estelle was no "Walking Jim." Under Beto, the building tender system had been a sharpened knife wielded by a master chef in a calm kitchen. This knife was handed to Estelle who, by comparison, was a good short-order cook behind a busy counter. Estelle was a younger man with a mostly officebound style of executive leadership; word of abuses did not always trickle up to his head-quarters in Huntsville, and there were no independent channels of information such as had enabled Beto and his aides to check on the veracity of reports from the field and caused them to notice when no such reports were forthcoming.

Predictably, while most other parts of the control model survived and were strengthened under Estelle, the building tender system ran amok and became nothing more than a con-boss system in which selected inmates were allowed to carry weapons and were given illicit privileges for "keeping things quiet." In some instances, this meant administering beatings to fellow inmates who had defied an officer or refused to work. At a few TCD institutions, the administration became a virtual hostage to the building tenders, relying on them to perform many or most custodial functions. In at least one prison, the weekend staff consisted of only a dozen officers supervising some forty building tenders who made counts, searched cells, frisked other inmates, and administered harsh and arbitrary discipline.

In 1978, the state's first Republican administration in 105 years took the reins in Austin and wasted little time in shaking things up. With new appointees, the Texas Board of Corrections, a body once dominated by leading Texas businessmen who had never been anything but supportive of TDC, started to cast unprecedented split votes and to voice public criticism of the agency. Political pillars of TDC such as Texas State House Appropriations Chairman Bill "The Duke of Paducah" Heatly and H. H. "Pete" Coffield were passing from the scene. Meanwhile, the state's oil revenues were drying up, forcing Texas policymakers to scratch for ways to be even stingier than customary with financial support for public agencies. Estelle lacked the political instincts that had made Beto so successful with the state's political establishment; TDC lost its "sacred cow" status and was targeted for budget cuts.

Judge Justice Intervenes

In this context the case of *Ruiz v. Estelle* was litigated, beginning in 1972 shortly before Estelle's appointment. Inmate David Ruiz, a chronic offender who had been incarcerated many times, sent a handwritten petition to Judge William Wayne Justice of the Eastern District Court. While in prison, Ruiz had stabbed several of his fellow inmates and had often been placed in solitary confinement. In his petition, Ruiz charged that conditions in "the hole" were inhumane. He claimed that he slit his wrists so that prison officials would release him from isolation. Ruiz challenged conditions of confinement in TDC under section 1983 of the U.S. Civil Rights Act. In 1974, Judge Justice combined Ruiz's petition with those of seven other TDC inmates, thereby framing a class action suit.

Unaffectionately called "Willie Wayne" by TDC officials, Judge Justice came to the *Ruiz* case with a record of strong judicial activism in education and other areas. He separated the damage claims at stake in the case from the injunctive issues, thereby making his control over the litigation absolute. In addition, he instituted a procedure whereby issues not raised by the inmate plaintiffs—crowding, recreational facilities, prison land use, and many others—also came under his review. He appointed a few of the country's leading prison litigation attorneys to represent the inmates and brought in the U. S. Department of Justice as an adversary to the state of Texas.

The trial began in 1978. In the preceding four years, Judge Justice had imposed a number of orders on TDC. In 1975, for instance, he prohibited prison authorities from censoring inmates' mail. In 1980 his 248-page memorandum opinion required scores of changes in the Texas prison system, among them: an end to the use of building tenders; a requirement that the agency double its officer force and retrain veteran officers; a revision in the procedures for handling inmate grievances; a complete overhaul of the prisoner classification system that would reduce the number of maximum-security designations; a division of the prison population into management units of not more than 500 each; a radical improvement in health delivery systems that would give inmates easy access to state-of-the-art medical treatment; and the provision of a single cell for each inmate. All the major issues in the case were decided wholly in favor of the plaintiffs. The judge dismissed without formal comment TDC's contention that certain of his requirements were likely to spawn inmate violence; and he rejected summarily the agency's plea that the timetables he had established for implementing these changes were unrealistic.

In 1982, a decade after the litigation had begun, the U. S. Circuit Court of Appeals for the Fifth District upheld Justice's central findings about the unconstitutionality of conditions inside Texas prisons, but overturned several provisions of the original order. "Taken as a whole," the three-judge panel wrote, "the district court's decree administers a massive dose when it is not yet demonstrable that a lesser therapeutic measure would not suffice." At the same time, however, the panel chided TDC officials for failing to run better prisons and warned that the "implementation of the district court's decree can become a ceaseless guerrilla war, with endless hearings, opinions and appeals, and incalculable costs." The panel also warned Judge Justice and his team of monitors to "respect the right of the state to administer its own affairs so long as it does not violate the Constitution."

Unfortunately, neither the judge and his monitors nor the TDC officials fully heeded the panel's warnings. The litigation continued at full boil for three more years amid bitter charges and countercharges. Estelle was the proud director of a proud agency. He challenged TDC's critics on the bench and elsewhere to measure its performance in terms of safety, cleanliness, programs, and costs. Compared to prisons in California, Michigan, and many other major jurisdictions, TDC prisons had measured up favorably: For example, between 1973 and 1980 there was a total of 19 homicides in Texas prisons, while there were 139 in California; rates of prison assaults in Texas ran well below the national average while costs per inmate were the lowest in the country; and TDC boasted the only fully accredited prison educational system in the nation.

These and other elements of TDC's management regime were worth preserving. In 1982, with Estelle still in the director's chair and with a live possibility of measured, effective organizational changes that could provide most of the remedies mandated by the court, a blue-ribbon panel noted that TDC had been described as both "the best example of slavery remaining in the country" and "probably the best prison system in the world"; as the panel's report concluded, the reality "lay somewhere in between."

The judge, however, painted an unrelievedly bleak image of TDC while his staff acted in ways that were almost calculated to breed ill will, confusion, and low morale among the very persons—from the director to the junior officers in the cellblocks—who would ultimately have to translate the court's decree into administrative action. No matter how Estelle and his staff moved to bring the agency into compliance with the court's sweeping orders, public criticism and a barrage of new orders followed. Echoing the complaints of cellblock workers, a central office administrator observed:

> Compliance of staff to our orders or of inmates to staff orders was never really a major problem here. . . . But now, with the court action and the rest, every day has become a goal line defense. . . . Officers must look at the bulletin board each day to see if the essence of the job they had the other day has changed. . . . How would you like to be given a new syllabus every day to teach from? One day you emphasize one theme, the next day another. Pretty soon everyone is confused; people get disgusted, some quit, and things just break down.

Estelle's defense of the agency, like the judge's attack, was undiscriminating, even desperate. He fought fiercely to protect Beto's control model and to shore up staff morale. By 1983, however, Beto himself recognized that the building tender system was a cancer ripe for the cutting, a rotten administrative crutch that TDC could and should drop at the judge's invitation in order to preserve and strengthen the rest of the system. These decisions, however, were not up to Beto. Under fire from the Board of Corrections, and having had the agency's budgetary requests rebuffed by a state legislature that was about to launch critical investigations into TDC's financial management, Estelle resigned in late 1983.

The principled intransigence of the fallen director was

mirrored, albeit crudely, by his staff. The thrust of the court's decree was caricatured by many of the uniformed officers. In a typical remark, one veteran officer stated: "The judge says an inmate can spit in your face. I won't have it. That's no good for the inmate! What does that teach him but to misbehave the way he's always done?" A warden asserted: "We don't need people coming in here—judges, monitors, politicians, professors—telling us what to do. We have our lives invested in these prisons. Our inmates are kept well. They're not getting raped right and left. . . . But I guess that's what the judge and them others want."

Estelle's replacement, Raymond Procunier, was a salty-mouthed man with a brash leadership style. Known in corrections circles as "the pro," Procunier had directed several major corrections agencies, usually leaving them in turmoil. But state leaders got from Procunier what they wanted: a promise to rush TDC into the latter stages of compliance with the judge's orders. After a brief honeymoon with his staff, Procunier fired employees who did not jump to cooperate, subjected officers to lie detector tests, and took other actions that undercut his popularity within the department. Within months of his arrival, political support for his administration crumbled as murders multiplied, inmate-on-officer assaults skyrocketed, programs were disrupted, costs escalated, prison gangs organized along racial and ethnic lines blossomed, and outside contractors were brought in to do the agricultural and other work once solely the province of TDC inmates.

As more TDC inmates were being buried, turnover of staff reached an all-time high, and officers took the unprecedented step of unionizing. Judge Justice, who had not once set foot inside a TDC prison since the *Ruiz* case began, continued to pressure the agency. The court's actions came as repeated stabs against the officers' sense of mission and encouraged TDC workers at all levels to abdicate responsibility for the inmates, enervating any desire they might have had to go above and beyond the call of duty at a time when enormous demands were being made on them. Judge Justice and his staff made it clear that they were out to revolutionize TDC, not to reform it, acting, as one of the court's aides later confided, on the assumption that TDC was "rotten from top to bottom, that everything had to change."

What Beto and Estelle had taken twenty years to build, Judge Justice, aided and abetted by Estelle's successor and by grandstanding state policymakers eager to make fresh political hay and headlines out of the system's legal troubles, helped to put asunder, by making the task of formal prison governance inside Texas prisons much harder and personally more unrewarding. TDC employees were sensitive to how the agency's detractors on the bench and elsewhere had portrayed them, in the words of one officer, as nothing but a "bunch of redneck guards and contraband carriers." In a typical remark, one veteran TDC employee recalled: "Nobody felt like keeping it up. All you heard was that we beat the inmates, we didn't care for the inmates, that we let them rip up each other. . . . Then the outsiders are giving us orders. . . . So we let go, let everything go."

The *Newman* and *Pugh* Intervention in Alabama

Administrative and Political Context

In a strange but telling twist of courts and corrections history, Dr. George Beto of Texas also figured directly in the sweeping judicial intervention into Alabama's prison system that began in 1972 as *Newman v. Alabama* and ended in 1988 in combination with *Pugh v. Locke*.[11]

In 1971, an Alabama inmate filed a lawsuit charging that six fellow inmates had died in the state prison hospital because of inadequate medical treatment. If anything, "inadequate medical treatment" is a euphemism here. Sick and dying Alabama inmates simply went unattended. Such medical facilities as existed were decrepit, understaffed, and without basic equipment. Maggots crawled through patients' festering wounds. In short, Alabama's prison health care complex was a cesspool.

But horrible health care was only one of the many horrible things about Alabama's prisons. Unlike in the case of Texas, over the years the Alabama prison system won few plaudits from disinterested outside observers, and rightfully so: The system had little to brag about. Even the most severe critics of Texas prisons as they existed under Beto had to admit that the institutions were clean and that they provided educational services, protected most inmates from violence, and offered inmates work not only out in the fields but in prison industries and other areas.

Alabama prisons had no such advantages. Instead, the institutions were filthy, programs were nonexistent, cellblocks were violence-ridden and overcrowded, and most inmates were left idle. Disciplinary practices in Alabama remained pretty much what they had been in the antebellum era. Unruly inmates were tossed into the "doghouse," a dank isolation chamber without light, where they were beaten and all but starved to death.

Moreover, Alabama corrections officers were extremely ill trained and undertrained. Within their ranks, there was no TDC-style esprit de corps or sense of mission, no well-practiced paramilitary security routine, and no tradition of openness to outsiders, including legislators, journalists, and extradepartmental researchers. Whereas Texas prisons in the decades leading up to the *Ruiz* litigation had always enjoyed sufficient political and budgetary support, in the decades leading up to the *Newman* and *Pugh* intervention, Alabama prisons had been political and fiscal orphans.

Judges Johnson and Varner Intervene

In October 1972, Federal District Judge Frank M. Johnson found the Alabama prison system's medical facilities so poor as to be in violation of the Eighth Amendment's prohibition against "cruel and unusual punishments." He ordered major changes in medical facility staffing and other areas.

Initially, Johnson thought that these changes could and would be made within about six months. But his orders encountered fierce resistance from the Department of Corrections and from many of the state's political leaders. As Judge Justice did in Texas, Johnson might have responded to this initial political and bureaucratic resistance by immediately bringing other parts of the prison system under his review, piling unmet order upon unmet order until the appeals court had its say. He did not.

Instead, Johnson remained focused on the medical issues, expressed his determination to see needed improvements made in the prison health care facilities, rolled with the verbal punches thrown at him by disgruntled agency and political officials, and simply let it be known that he would resort to contempt citations and other measures if some significant degree of compliance was not forthcoming. As a result, the department followed many of his orders, and by 1974 the state's prison medical facilities had improved somewhat.

But the institutions remained violent, overcrowded, and plagued by other serious problems. Thus, in 1976 Judge Johnson assumed control of the entire Alabama prison system. He appointed a committee of thirty-nine Alabamans to offer "advice and consent" as he attempted to remedy the system's defects. But the state's political leadership simply would not budge on budgeting for the needed reforms.

By 1979, a showdown between the judge and the department and its political allies appeared imminent, but two things happened to avert it. First, Johnson moved to the appellate court, and Federal District Judge Robert E. Varner took the reins. Second, Governor George C. Wallace, who was among those who rallied the department and the legislature against the judge and fought the intervention tooth and nail, left the office and was succeeded by Fob James.

Governor James saw the prison system's troubles as the product of poor management. Judge Varner, like Judge Johnson before him, was determined to make the necessary changes, with the department's consent and cooperation if at all possible but without it if absolutely necessary. Varner appointed James temporary receiver for the Alabama prison system. James appointed a new, reform-minded director of corrections, Robert Britton.

Britton had worked in TDC under none other than Dr. George Beto and considered Beto a great administrator. Britton's reputation as a no-nonsense Texas-style executive preceded him to Alabama and put him in favor with the prison rank-and-file. He immediately set about the task of building alliances with the state's political establishment, instituting officer training programs, improving food services and sanitation, and addressing other problems identified by the court.

In the course of Britton's Beto-like reform efforts, Judge Varner appointed Beto himself to serve on a four-member expert committee charged with overseeing implementation of the remaining court orders. Beto and his peers steered the Alabama prison system toward institutional reforms that would have been inconceivable only a decade earlier, including an aggressive prison construction and renovation program to relieve overcrowding and the introduction of early release and good time policies.

In December 1988, Beto's committee recommended that Judge Varner dismiss the seventeen-year-old suit, which he did. Most observers, including state officials who had initially opposed the judge's "interference," agreed that though the intervention had by no means perfected Alabama's prison system, it had helped to catalyze remarkable improvements at a reasonable human and financial cost—or at least without the tragic explosion of murders and assaults, the utter demoralization of staff, and the other severe problems that had accompanied the *Ruiz* intervention in Texas.

There was thus a sad irony in Beto's involvement in the Alabama intervention. In Texas, an intervening judge had clumsily revolutionized that state's prisons rather than attempt to preserve and build upon the good things that Beto had built there; but at the same moment in Alabama, the second of two more judicious judges called upon a Beto-tutored director and Beto himself to bring an equally massive and disruptive intervention to a safe landing.

The *Rhem* Intervention in New York City

Judge Lasker Intervenes

Our third and final exploration of an illustrative instance of judicial intervention takes us from prisons south of the Mason-Dixon Line to jails in New York City. In chapter 1, we peeked at the role of Federal District Judge Morris E. Lasker in helping to reform the city's jails. Let us now return to the Tombs and Rikers Island for a closer look.[12]

When the case of *Rhem* began in January 1972, everyone who mattered—the mayor, key corrections officials, and jail-beat journalists—knew that the Tombs was filthy, dilapidated, and unfit for human habitation, and that pretrial detainees there were repressively and routinely handled as dangerous maximum-security felons. Led by Mayor Abraham Beame, however, city officials stonewalled Lasker's decree to upgrade the jail.

In response, Lasker gradually turned up the heat. After

granting the department numerous delays and threatening officials with contempt citations, in July 1974 he gave the city thirty days to deliver to his chambers a detailed plan to remedy the unconstitutional conditions at the jail. The "or else" in this ultimatum was hard for anyone to ignore: Plan and budget the needed reforms or the jail will close at once. The city appealed this improve-it-or-close-it decision, but the Second Circuit Court backed Lasker.

The judge thought he had succeeded, but Mayor Beame's response surprised him. The city opted to close the jail rather than comply with the court's orders to reform it. At that point, Lasker performed what can only be described as an artful act of judicial jujitsu. He held that inmates transferred from the Tombs to other institutions were entitled to the living conditions specified in *Rhem*. Again, the city appealed, and again the Second Circuit Court backed Lasker. But the city made no effort to comply.

Thereafter, inmates at the city's House of Detention for Men (HDM) filed a lawsuit claiming on behalf of all HDM detainees the protections specified in *Rhem*. In 1975, HDM was the scene of a summer riot in which hostages were taken. The rioters requested that Lasker come to the jail; he did so. But it would not have taken a crisis to bring Lasker into the jails: He made a habit of visiting the institutions he was trying to help reform.

Eventually, Lasker brought the entire city jail system under his review. Under his direction, a new Tombs jail was built in Manhattan, and the corrections department improved its management practices there and on Rikers Island (see chapter 1). After 1978, a complicated set of plaintiffs' attorneys and others became involved in the process of negotiating and implementing court-ordered reforms. But Lasker managed to keep nearly everyone focused on what he treated as their common objective: to bring the city's jails up to minimum constitutional muster by making them safe and civilized.

At the end of 1989, the jails remained under Lasker's supervision. In the previous years, he had fought many political and bureaucratic battles—including one to keep unpopular jail reforms on the agenda when the city was falling into bankruptcy—but in each case he prevailed and the jails in question improved markedly.

In contrast to Judge Justice in Texas, at no point in the intervention did Lasker bully or belittle corrections officials. Even when there was clear evidence of bureaucratic footdragging and worse, the judge's response was measured and restrained. This made converts among many who had strongly opposed Lasker's efforts. For example, city corrections chief Benjamin Malcolm recognized that he had earned a contempt citation but was grateful to Lasker for not slapping him with one. As a result, Malcolm's attitude toward the court changed over the course of the intervention, causing him to revise his "early view of Lasker as a judge overstepping his boundary to that of a judge who had the guts and courage to stand up and keep the system in line."[13]

Lasker, however, did not dispense grace to corrections officials to the point of noncompliance with his orders. Coming from the other side of the intervention, Joel Berger, a project director for the Prisoners' Rights Project of the Legal Aid Society, characterized Lasker's modus operandi as follows: "Lasker was going slow in the way he was implementing things, but he wasn't cutting back on substance."[14]

As I myself learned in 1986 when I served as a consultant to the New York City Board of Corrections, Lasker's slow but steady, tough but temperate approach extended to the granting of variances with his orders, including those pertaining to jail population limits. Whereas Judge Justice in Texas reflexively threatened to punish the prison system with huge fines for going over his magic population number, Lasker listened to reason. As one Board of Corrections official told me: "Lasker set the tone back in 1974. The tone was, 'You play fair with me, and I'll respect your legitimate limits and needs.' He would take two steps forward and one step back to give the department and the city administration time to get the job done, and to prepare the staff psychologically; but everyone understood that his patience could be exhausted. He was cautious and liked to operate by consensus, but he never sent mixed signals."

TOWARD EFFECTIVE JUDICIAL INTERVENTION

The Texas, Alabama, and New York City cases, together with what I know about dozens of other instances of judicial intervention into prisons and jails, lead me to certain opinions about how judges can intervene most effectively. Before stating these "lessons of the past," however, let me hasten to make one qualification.

My advice about how judges can best proceed is based

175

on an analysis of exploratory studies that do not lend themselves to systematic comparisons. Unfortunately, the available empirical data on judicial intervention do not offer much in the way of natural experiments. And except as a mental experiment, we cannot hold everything else constant and see what would have happened if, say, Judge Lasker (or a more Lasker-like judge) had presided in the Texas as well as the New York City cases.

Just the same, there are four general lessons to be drawn from an analysis of the record of judicial intervention into prisons and jails from 1970 to 1989.

By now, the first and foremost of these lessons should be obvious: Intervening judges must proceed in a judicious manner, move in incremental steps, and avoid antagonizing the people who must translate their orders into administrative action in the cellblocks. They must seek to reform, not to revolutionize, the institutions, taking pains to preserve those organizational elements that are worth preserving. Judge Justice's mistake in Texas was in attempting to punish corrections officials for their real or perceived slights against his authority; Judges Johnson, Varner, and Lasker managed both the symbols and the substance of their respective interventions more deftly. The political and bureaucratic resistance to judicial intervention was every bit as intense in Alabama and New York City as it was in Texas. But only Judge Justice reacted to the opposition in a way that even his most inveterate academic apologists admit created an atmosphere of distrust, in addition to deepening efforts to resist court-approved reforms.[15]

The second lesson is that as judges attempt to make changes in the way prisons and jails are run, they should visit the institutions, make firsthand observations, and talk to inmates and staff. The ethic of a bench that confines itself to interpreting the laws is hardly appropriate for judges who make and oversee the implementation of laws; responsible activist judges must leave the serenity of their chambers. Judges will learn more from such field trips than they will from reading all the books, essays, and neatly typed depositions in the world. They will be in a far better position to predict and weigh the real costs and benefits of any court-induced changes and to appreciate the constraints under which prison administrators at all levels operate. They will be able to see for themselves whether institutional practices are in need of repair, and to judge whether cells are cramped, food is decent, health care is available, and so on. In the bargain, they will become less captive to aides and attorneys who by inexperience, self-interest, or ideological predisposition are less than fit to be the eyes, ears, and arms of the court. Finally, they will come to know the prison staff and be in a position to guide them should major reforms prove necessary. Again, our cases illustrate the point, for only Judge Justice scrupulously avoided ever seeing the inside of the institutions he sought to reform.

The third lesson is that judges need to approach intervention with one eye on the dynamics of complex organizations. They need not trade their legal texts for monographs on organization theory (heaven forbid!), but they must understand the agencies they are seeking to reform as delicate human organisms. Infusing the members of any large, complex organization with a genuine sense of mission and identification with their agency is no easy task. Corrections is a dangerous, dirty, difficult, and thankless profession. It is crucial, therefore, that judges respect what in chapter 1 we defined as "organizational culture." "Respect" does not mean surrender. But it does mean a sympathetic recogniton of the agency's past achievements.

More concretely, it means recognizing that administrative stability at the top of a corrections department is hard-won and precious. Between 1973 and mid-1987, in less than one-third of all corrections agencies did corrections commissioners enjoy an average tenure of five years or more; in over one-third they held office for an average of three years or less. Judges should try not to exacerbate this problem of fluctuating executive leadership, for it is largely responsible for the fact that prisons and jails have been ill managed, undermanaged, or not managed at all. And they should recognize how truly difficult is the task of the line corrections officer even when performed under the most stable and supportive conditions; we would all be better off if most judges (and all professionals) had the practical wisdom, public-spiritedness, and professional integrity of the average prison or jail worker.

Trailing back to our cases, whereas Judge Justice was, in the words of one veteran officer, "all over us like stink on a skunk," Judge Lasker made converts of combatants within the bureaucracy; again the results in each case were what one would predict. And whereas Judge Varner imported the talents and symbolic authority of a Dr. George Beto, Judge Justice warred with Beto's successor and gave Beto no role in steering the intervention.

The fourth, final, and most general lesson is that intervening judges should make a broader application of the idea that prisons and jails must be governed in ways that make them constitutional. In the Madisonian formulation of *The Federalist* 51, constitutional government springs from the recognition that "men are not angels"; those who rule must be strong enough to control the governed, but obliged to control themselves. Prison and jail managers are the government of the institution. They must be given enough formal authority to govern inmates who are most decidedly not angels. At the same time, however, they must be subjected to internal and external checks and balances: professional standards, peer review, legislative inquiries, media scrutiny, openness to extradepartmental researchers, and, last but not least, responsible judicial intervention and oversight.

5

Privatization or Nationalization?

EVERY GENERATION, IT SEEMS, has its magic cure for the ills of American corrections. In the 1960s and early 1970s, one popular cure was to stop building secure institutions and to deinstitutionalize offenders—"to tear down the walls." In the 1980s, amid the ongoing search for meaningful alternatives to incarceration, proposals have been made to give the private sector a significant role in the administration, finance, and construction of correctional facilities and programs—"to sell the walls." The former solution proved bankrupt; what should we expect from the latter?

THE RISE OF PRIVATIZATION

Several states have enacted laws authorizing privately operated state correctional facilities, while more than a dozen others are actively considering the option. In 1985, Corrections Corporation of America (CCA), a leader among the twenty-odd firms that have entered the "prison market," made a bid to take over the entire Tennessee prison system. Though this bid was unsuccessful, CCA now operates several correctional facilities, among them a Federal Bureau of Prisons halfway house, two Immigration and Naturalization Service facilities for the detention of illegal aliens, and a 370-bed maximum-security jail in Bay County, Florida. On January 6, 1986, U.S. Corrections Corporation opened the nation's first private state prison, a 300-bed minimum-security facility in Marion, Kentucky, for inmates who are within three years of qualifying for parole. In addition, over three dozen states now contract with private firms for one or more correctional services or programs—in most cases, medical and mental health services, community treatment centers, construction, remedial education, drug treatment, college courses, staff training, vocational training, and counseling.

The paramount question in the debate over the privatization of corrections is not whether private firms can succeed where public agencies have ostensibly faltered, but whether the privatization movement can last. Some observers believe that the movement, though barely a decade old, is already running out of steam. They point to the failure of CCA to win control of the Tennessee system, Pennsylvania's statutory moratorium on private prison initiatives, the rushed campaign by CCA and other firms to establish themselves in foreign markets (mainly Great Britain and France), and the fact that private prison operations have not advanced much beyond the proposal stage in most jurisdictions (and are not even on the draw-

ing board where public-employee relations are strong—
that is, outside the South).

Other observers, myself included, see privatization as a
response to three main conditions: soaring inmate populations and caseloads; escalating costs; and the widespread
perception that public corrections bureaucracies have
failed to handle convicted criminals in ways that achieve
public protection, deterrence, just punishment, and the
rehabilitation of criminals in a humane and cost-effective
manner. As each of these conditions intensifies, so too will
private corrections initiatives.

Three sets of issues are raised by the privatization of
corrections. First, can private corrections firms outperform public corrections agencies? Can they produce and
deliver more and better for less? Second, should the authority to administer criminal justice programs and facilities, to deprive citizens of their liberty, and to coerce
(even kill) them, be delegated to contractually deputized
private individuals and groups, or ought it to remain
wholly within the hands of duly constituted public officials? Third, does privatization present a single either/or
bundle of policy alternatives, or does it pose multiple
choices?

THE COST OF PRIVATE PRISONS

At this stage, it is impossible to answer most of the empirical questions about the comparative cost-effectiveness
and the efficiency of private correctional operations.
Though publications on the subject now number in the
hundreds, the necessary research has simply not been done

and relevant empirical data remain scarce. Theoretical speculations, anecdotes, and raw statistics abound, but there is as yet little dependable information to tell us whether or how privatization can work, and at what human and financial cost.[1]

Of course, this lack of policy-relevant knowledge has not prevented a shower of assertions on both sides of the debate. Proponents of privatization claim that it can shave anywhere from 10 to 25 percent off the nation's correctional budget. In support of this contention, they invoke several stock arguments in favor of privatization. Unlike government bureaucracies, advocates argue, private firms are freed, to a degree, from politics, bureaucracy, and costly union contracts. Private companies must answer to their investors and satisfy the terms of their contract with the government or risk losing it. As in any open market, the firms must compete with one another to maximize services while minimizing costs, or else they go out of business. While government agencies enjoy a virtual monopoly and need not strive to improve the quality and quantity of services, it is argued, private firms will have every incentive to economize and will be held accountable at every turn.

Some proponents add that privatization engenders a legislative climate receptive to the production and sale of prison-made goods. Operators of private facilities, it is claimed, have incentives to produce and sell inmate-made goods, and might help to persuade lawmakers to authorize prison industry as an effective cost-saving measure and thus to join in efforts to transform prisons and jails into "factories with fences."

Opponents of privatization claim that major cost cut-

ting can be achieved only at the expense of humane treatment. Private firms, it is reasoned, have no incentive to
reduce crowding (since they may be paid on a per-prisoner
basis) or to foster less expensive (and, to the private firm,
less lucrative) alternatives to incarceration. Indeed, critics
charge, since prisons have traditionally been financed
through tax-exempt general-obligation bonds, privatization encourages costly prison construction. Elected officials can pay for construction through lease agreements
that fall within government's regular appropriation process, thereby avoiding the political headaches involved in
raising debt ceilings or gaining voters' approval of bond
issues. The firms' staffs, it is predicted, will be correctional versions of "rent-a-cops": ill trained, underedu-
cated, poorly paid, and unprofessional.

In theory, concerns about staffing, compliance with
professional standards, use of force (lethal and nonlethal),
strikes, fiscal accountability, and the like can be addressed
through tightly drawn contracts. But opponents assert
that, in practice, either government regulation will prove
inadequate or the costs of effective regulation will more
than consume any savings from privatization. Critics also
argue that privatization can neither minimize the liability
of governmental units under federal civil-rights laws (under which most "conditions of confinement" litigation has
been brought) nor relieve the government of its constitutional duty to administer the criminal justice system.

In this crossfire of empirically ungrounded claims about
private corrections, only one argument has been mortally
wounded by the existing evidence; namely, that government can construct prisons and jails as quickly and as
cheaply as private firms can. Over the last few years, the

advantages of private construction arrangements have become so clear in so many cases that not even the most inveterate opponents of private involvement in corrections can deny them. In California, for instance, one of the most ambitious prison-building projects in history was stalled until complete responsibility was transferred to a private, Arizona-based construction-management firm.

THE MORALITY OF PRIVATE PRISONS

In discussing and writing about the morality of private corrections, critics have rarely been able to avoid two pitfalls. First, they have tended to substitute empirical for normative criteria, giving rise to the notion that if it could be shown beyond a reasonable doubt that private involvement improves (or worsens) correctional services, lowers (or increases) correctional costs, and exceeds (or falls below) constitutional requirements, then the normative questions would thereby be resolved. While some academics commit this mistake, it is made more often by correctional policymakers and practitioners. For example, in *A Handbook for Decisionmakers*, distributed by the American Correctional Association, the nation's leading association for corrections professionals, it is tacitly assumed that while "government has the ultimate authority for corrections," the moral standing of private management is wholly unproblematical as long as it conforms to "professional standards" and contributes in tangible ways to the "effectiveness and efficiency" of correctional operations.

The second pitfall in discussions of the morality of private corrections is made less often by policymakers and

185

practitioners than by academics who focus on the profit motive of the privatizers. They suppose that the central moral problem of private corrections is not whether the authority to administer justice ought to be delegated by contract to private, nongovernmental parties, but whether the private contractors ought to be paid or to profit financially for their services. In effect, they worry less about whether the government's responsibility to govern ends at the prison gates than whether (and how much) the gatekeepers get paid.

The question of whether it is ever right to profit from the misfortunes of criminals and their victims is a serious one. But it must be understood that there have been, and continue to be, several nonprofit, nonpublic corrections enterprises (for example, Florida's Okeechobee School for Boys, run by the Eckerd Foundation). A properly constructed moral case for (or against) private involvement cannot turn simply, or even mainly, on whether the private contractor reaps huge or moderate profits—or none at all. By analogy, if one reasons that it is morally wrong (or right) for a married man to have sex with a woman other than his wife, then it matters little (if at all) whether the act is done with a high-priced call girl, a cheap prostitute, or the girl next door.

Conceptually, if not morally, the privatization of corrections is often construed as a simple either/or issue. In fact, however, the issue of corrections relates to prisons and jails, probation and parole, and various nontraditional community-based programs ranging from compulsory drug-abuse treatment to fines and restriction. Most correctional programs have administrative, financial, and construction components, any of which may be public or private. Thus there are numerous possible permutations of private involvement in corrections, only some of which are bound to provoke substantial controversy.

Far and away the most heated part of the privatization debate concerns the private management of prisons and jails. It is here that most of the money is at stake, and here that the moral and constitutional issues seem most thorny. Should the care and custody of citizens detained or incarcerated for the commission (or suspected commission) of crimes be entrusted to nonpublic, profit-making organizations? What benefits, if any, might be expected from private penal administration? Who should manage our prisons, how, and by what authority? The best available answers to these questions can be discovered by examining the historical, administrative, and moral dimensions of the issue.

The Historical View

Yesterday's Private Prisons

In 1833, Alexis de Tocqueville and Gustave de Beaumont expressed their grave reservations about the role of private contractors in the administration of penal facilities. They chronicled the horrors of the contracting system in France, and noted that even in the United States, a country whose general penal practices they greatly admired, "the presence of the contractor or his agents in the prisons has been found to be not without its inconvenience."[2]

For much of the nineteenth century and as late as the 1960s, prisons and jails in many parts of the United States were privately owned and operated. In the current debate over private sector involvement in corrections, these precedents have not been duly acknowledged. In Texas, California, Michigan, Louisiana, Oklahoma, and many other states, all or part of the penal system has at one time or another been administered privately. As a few examples should suffice to show, the premonitions of Tocqueville and Beaumont were, if anything, too mild. The pre-1980s record of private sector involvement in corrections is unrelievedly bleak.

In the nineteenth century Texas leased its penitentiary (which survives today as the Huntsville "Walls" unit) to private contractors. For a few dollars per month per convict, the contractors were allowed to sublease their charges to farmers, tanners, and other businessmen. It was not long before the inmates began to appear in poor clothing and without shoes. Worked mercilessly, most convicts died within seven years of their incarceration. Not surprisingly, escapes and escape attempts were frequent, and some inmates were driven to suicide. Others maimed themselves to get out of work or as a pathetic form of protest.

The Civil War decimated several penal systems in the South. Louisiana, Arkansas, Florida, Virginia, and Georgia were among the states that responded by leasing out their entire convict populations to private contractors, or by granting contracts for work to be performed behind the walls. Even in the antebellum South, however, contracting was not unknown. The state of Louisiana, for example, began contracting in the 1840s. By the Reconstruction era, the state's prisoners were living under one of the most corrupt and brutal regimes in penal history.

Well into the 1940s, the Louisiana penal system was a business administered by leaseholders out to make profits from the labor of unskilled and semiskilled convicts. Public officials used the system as a patronage mill, awarding contracts to friends, relatives, and political loyalists. The same basic story can be told about other jurisdictions.

The era of for-profit corrections, stretching roughly from 1840 to 1960, came to an end in most places largely as a result of three factors. First, public scandals and journalistic exposés revealed the contract system's weaknesses. Second, there was a decline in the demand for the kinds of products that unskilled, uneducated convicts could produce and a concomitant increase in the mobilization of political (mainly labor-union) pressures against the production and sale of prison-made goods. Third, politicians and prison officials, often at great risk to their careers, spoke out against the system and argued in favor of the public administration of prisons and jails.

Clearly, the record of private sector involvement in corrections is not heartening. But what, if anything, does this history teach us? Are these lessons proper guides for the present and the future? Could such gross abuses occur today, beneath the eye of a watchful court and a scrutinizing media? Probably not, but we should nonetheless be careful.

Today's Private Prisons

Over the last few decades, enormous, substantive progress has been made in the professionalization of the corrections field. Many of the twenty-odd firms in private operation that have sprung up since 1980 are no doubt

189

fly-by-night enterprises; several, however, such as CCA, are led by some of the most seasoned and respected corrections professionals in the country. No private institutions or programs have yet been plagued by serious, systemic cases of inmate abuse or political corruption. Indeed, CCA and its competitors have kept an enviably clean slate.

History, however, teaches us to be wary of the oft-made claim that this slate will remain clean as long as contracts are detailed in accordance with the highest contemporary correctional standards. Writing and enforcing highly detailed contracts may help to guarantee accountability, but it does so at the expense of administrative flexibility. A major selling point of the privatizers is that they can be more innovative (and ultimately more efficient) than public providers of correctional services. A contract that "counts nails," however, makes it difficult for the contractor to allocate resources freely, to make staffing changes, and so forth. As a public corrections official with years of experience in these matters stated: "Either the contractors will be allowed to run wild as they did in the old days, or we'll make the specifications, regulations, and monitoring so rigid that the firms will become as bureaucratized and inefficient as we are—killing the goose before he lays any eggs."

CCA officials claim that all of their facilities are accredited by the American Correctional Association. While their claim is accurate, it is also true that the accreditation process leaves much to be desired; some accredited facilities number among the worst in the nation. And because CCA and its competitors covet accreditation (if only as a rough-and-ready shield against litigation), they are prone to engage in what critics call "correctional creaming":

assuming control of modern, lower-custody facilities where populations are small and offenders are not hard-core (for example, juvenile centers), and staying away from institutions and programs that are more costly and difficult to manage (for example, most existing maximum-security prisons).

One unchanged historical reality about prisons in the United States is that those who are incarcerated come overwhelmingly from the lowest rungs of the socioeconomic ladder. Criminologists and others may debate both the empirical and the moral issues related to this fact, but none deny the simple truth that U.S. prisons house disproportionate numbers of poor, dark-skinned persons. Historically, race and class prejudices have combined with the low visibility of penal facilities to make the average American unconcerned about what happens inside prisons and jails. It seems likely that societal pressures against inmate abuse and political corruption will be at a low ebb when these largely underclass and minority offenders are placed in nonpublic hands. Opponents of privatization worry that the sigh of relief that public officials may breathe after turning over all or part of their penal complex to private firms may presage a death rattle for inmates' legal and constitutional rights.

But such possibilities become less frightening in light of the single most important post-1970 change in the operating environment of prisons and jails; namely, the rise of judicial intervention into penal affairs. Since 1970, dozens of correctional systems have fallen under court orders. And while there continues to be disagreement about the causes and consequences of judicial intervention in this area, most analysts agree that activist state and federal

191

judges have become a permanent part of the correctional landscape. While I harbor some serious reservations about the judges' involvement (see chapter 4), I cannot deny that the courts can and do provide a salutary barrier against any repeat of the kinds of unmitigated horrors that characterized the previous era of for-profit corrections. If anything, the courts may prove especially eager to keep the corrections corporations on a short leash.

With regard to deciding whether the authority to administer prisons and jails ought to be delegated to private contractors, history is an ambivalent tutor, counseling both openness and vigilance. Our last experience with private corrections was hellish, but in the intervening decades much has changed. We can neither dismiss the possibility that the problems may recur, nor assert that history is bound to repeat itself. We can, however, gain an additional perspective on the wisdom of privatization by considering its administrative dimensions.

The Administrative View

Most claims that private corrections firms can outperform public corrections agencies rest on two assumptions. The first is that there are significant differences between public and private management, that business firms are necessarily more "efficient," "effective," and "innovative" than government agencies, and that these advantages of private management are universal; they obtain whether the task is picking up garbage or locking up prisoners. The second assumption is that the public sector's admin-

istrative experience in corrections has been an unmitigated disaster: Prisons and jails have been, and continue
to be, horrible places horribly run.

In my judgment, both assumptions are false. The former is the product of faulty logic, poor conceptualization,
and lazy moralizing; the latter results from an inadequate
appreciation of the fact that the performance of public
corrections agencies has varied enormously and in ways
that are clearly traceable to differences in public management practices.

There is more than human caprice behind the fact that
some tasks are in public rather than private hands; there
are real reasons why we have both government and business, both politics and markets, both public agencies and
private corporations, both MPAs and MBAs. In the public sector, the relationship between valued inputs (people,
money) and desired outputs (less crime, better public
health) is often unclear and may even be impossible to
specify with any degree of precision; hence, "efficiency"—
being able to maximize output for a given set of inputs
or minimize the inputs needed to achieve a given level of
output—is hard to measure. The political and legal constraints on what work gets done, how, and by whom tend
to be far greater in the public arena. "Sophisticated"
management theories and techniques may or may not help
in the private sector, but they are almost always more
likely to come away limping when applied to public tasks.
Such verities about public versus private management
have been discovered by successive generations of top-
flight business people who have entered government service only to find that the lessons of Wall Street have
limited application in government.

Nevertheless, suppose we wanted to make hard-and-fast evaluations of public versus private correctional management. What performance measures could we use? Most students of corrections would agree that there is little, if any, clear relationship between institutional penal practices, on the one hand, and rates of recidivism, on the other (see chapter 3). Prisons and jails yield an imprecise mix of incapacitation, deterrence, retribution, and rehabilitation—or so we tend to believe. It is difficult, however, to specify the relationship between any of these ends and the way penal facilities are managed. There are, however, at least three performance indices that may be less ambiguously related to managerial practices: order, amenity, and service.

By *order*, I mean the absence of individual or group misconduct that threatens the safety of others behind bars—simply stated, no assaults, rapes, riots, suicides, or murders. By *amenity*, I mean anything that is intended to increase the inmates' comfort: clean living quarters, good food, color television sets. By *service*, I mean anything that is intended to enhance the inmates' life prospects: programs in remedial reading, vocational training, work opportunities, and so on.[3]

Measured accordingly, are America's prisons and jails simply wretched, or are some relatively safe, humane, treatment-oriented, and productive? There are extremist views on both sides of this question, but the available data suggest that public penal institutions have been, and continue to be, a terribly mixed bag: some are clean, others filthy; some are orderly, others riotous; some offer many programs, others none at all; some cost over $30,000 a year per inmate, others under $10,000. Certain public corrections agencies have improved over time; others have gotten worse; and still others have changed little, if at all. One thing, however, seems clear: The quality of life inside prisons and jails depends mainly on the quality of penal management. As discussed in chapter 1, through more humane and intelligent institutional management, prisons and jails can be improved, even when budgets are tight, facilities dilapidated, and inmate populations large and dangerous.

The crucial point is that the administrative performance of public prisons and jails has not been uniformly bad, and there is no reason to suppose that the performance of private facilities would be uniformly good. To believe otherwise would be to believe that there is something magical about the private sector. In the world of the economics textbooks, a world of perfect competition and *ceteris paribus* assumptions, the market *is* magical. In this world, it is certain that efficient market-driven organizations can give us whatever bundle of goods and services we demand, from "widgets" to more complex commodities. But in the real world, organizations—public or private—tend to succeed when they combine good workers with sufficient resources under the right conditions, and to fail when they do not.

The core administrative issue here is not public versus private correctional management, but the possibility of *competent* correctional management. The performance of public sector corrections agencies has varied. By probing the political, budgetary, and other conditions associated with the better institutions and programs, public managers can learn from one another's mistakes and successes. Rather than considering abandoning governmental stewardship of prisons and jails in favor of private management, we ought to give public administration a chance.

The Moral View

For the sake of argument, let us suppose that, contrary to the foregoing discussion, corrections corporations can operate successfully on a wide scale, constructing, financing, and managing everything from tiny new community centers to massive old maximum-security prisons. And for the sake of argument, let us concede, without any qualifications, that private firms can indeed maximize services while minimizing costs in an abuse- and corruption-free environment, satisfying all political, legal, and other such constraints. In other words, let us grant for the sake of argument that private prisons and jails are eminently feasible. Must it then follow that they are desirable? Is the private operation of prisons and jails, however instrumental it may prove to be in reducing costs and bettering services, justifiable morally? Does the government's responsibility to govern end at the prison gates? Who ought to administer justice behind bars?

Behind each of these questions lies a string of related issues. For example, where (or how) does one draw the line between "contractually deputized" private individuals and "duly authorized" public authorities? Since the authority wielded by public administrators is delegated to them by "the people," by what strange metaphysic does the delegation of that authority to private firms constitute any sort of a moral (or constitutional) problem? The fact that "many different officials contribute in many different ways to decisions and policies in the modern state" gives rise to what has been aptly labeled "the problem of many hands": deciding who in government is responsible for political or policy outcomes.[4] The private management of prisons and jails, however, brings into focus what may be termed the problem of *whose* hands: deciding whether the moral responsibility for given communal functions ought to be lodged mainly or solely in the hands of government authorities.

In my judgment, to remain legitimate and morally significant, the authority to govern behind bars, to deprive citizens of their liberty, to coerce (and even kill) them, must remain in the hands of government authorities. Regardless of which penological theory is in vogue, the message that those who abuse liberty shall live without it is the philosophical brick and mortar of every correctional facility—a message that ought to be conveyed by the offended community of law-abiding citizens, through its public agents, to the incarcerated individual. The administration of prisons and jails involves the legally sanctioned exercise of coercion by some citizens over others. This coercion is exercised in the name of the offended public. The badge of the arresting police officer, the robes of the judge, and the state patch of the corrections officer are symbols of the inherently public nature of crime and punishment.*

---

*Charles H. Logan makes light of this notion in *Private Prisons*, countering that, if it is "symbols" we want, the contract between the state and the firm is "a powerful symbol of legally enforceable obligations and responsibilities in both directions." To me, the notion of a signed, sealed, and delivered for-profit contract as the symbolic moral equivalent of traditional public law trappings is unpersuasive; it would certainly have raised a chuckle for Sir William Blackstone, Professor Kingsfield, nineteenth-century slave traders,

197

The moral implications of privatizing the administration of this central communal function—administering justice for acts against the public welfare—can be felt by entertaining morally analogous situations. Suppose, for example, that the question were not, Who ought to administer justice to the community's offenders? but Who ought to administer rewards to the community's heroes? Consider the following hypothetical scenario. You have worked tirelessly on behalf of your fellow citizens. You have discovered a cure for cancer, or negotiated successfully with our foes abroad, or made a major contribution to the performing arts. For your good deeds, you are to receive a National Medal of Honor. The big day arrives. The crowd is assembled on the White House lawn. The Marine Band begins to play. You gaze into the crowd and notice that the distinguished-looking guests (and the "Marine" musicians) have little pins on their lapels that read "MCA" (for Medals Corporation of America). The ceremony is grand. The crowd roars as your name is called and the "president" (better-looking than the real commander-in-chief) shakes your hand and embraces you. You know for a fact that by every tangible measure—the physical quality of your medal, the warmth of the presenter, the duration and intensity of the crowd's ovations, the sound of the music—MCA gave you a ceremony that was far superior to what you would have received had the government and its officials presided. Moreover, MCA spent only one-third of what the government would have spent. Are you satisfied?

---

used-car dealers, and others familiar with the place of contract in the theory and practice of Anglo-American law. Just the same, however, Logan's book is outstanding.[5]

Or, imagine that a private consulting firm consisting of the nation's wisest, most seasoned, and most widely respected statesmen could do a superb job of selecting our next president, at a tiny fraction of what it now costs to stage primaries and a general election. The very thought sends a chill up my spine because I believe, as most Americans no doubt do, that the public, democratic nature of the process of presidential selection has a value independent of the outcome. Thus, in a situation where it was certain that Candidate X was going to be selected regardless of whether the choice was delegated to the presidential headhunting firm or left in the hands of the voters, I would not hesitate to choose the public process even though it was far more expensive. Indeed, I would probably do the same even if the "private presidents" corporation would select my favorite candidate while the voters would not.

Or, suppose that CCA has made it really big. They have proved that they can do everything the privatizers have promised and more. The corporation decides to branch out. The company changes its name to CJCA: the Criminal Justice Corporation of America. It provides a full range of criminal justice services: cops, courts, and corrections. In an unguarded moment, a CJCA official boasts that "our firm can arrest 'em, try 'em, lock 'em up, and, if need be, fry 'em for less." Is there anything wrong with CJCA?

In each case, the relevant human collectivity can be said to have abdicated its duty to reward, to choose among, or to punish its members: the nation at large, its heroes; the electorate, its leaders; the community of law-abiding citizens, its criminals. Implicit in the "farming out" of such responsibility is a denial of the group's moral integrity. Ought not the nation to express its gratitude directly through the agency of its elected and duly appointed public representatives? Is it not the voters alone who may bestow authority and legitimacy on occupants of the Oval Office? Is it not the community of law-abiding citizens that is offended by criminals and should dole out their punishment?

The Moral Writ of the Community

If every tangible advantage belongs clearly to private management, does it matter whether the corrections officer's patch reads "Corrections Corporation of America" or "State of Tennessee"? Where the governing of prisons is concerned, is management by private hands morally distinguishable from management by public hands? At a minimum, it can be said (both in theory and in practice) that the formulation and administration of criminal laws by recognized public authorities is one of the liberal state's most central and historic functions; indeed, in some formulations it is the liberal state's *raison d'être*. In the opening chapter of his *Second Treatise of Government*, Locke defines political power itself as "a right of making laws with penalties of death, and consequently all less penalties, for the regulating and preserving of property, and of employing the force of the community, in the execution of such laws . . . , and all this only for the public good."[6] Criminal law is the one area in which Americans have conceded to the state an almost unqualified right to act in the name of the polity, and hence one of the few places in which one can discern an American conception of political community that is not a mere collage of individual preferences. It is not unreasonable to suggest that "employing the force of the community" via private penal management undermines the moral writ of the community itself.

But what about the argument that the community's moral writ remains intact so long as the pre-sentencing process remains in public hands? Returning to our earlier illustration, one might assert that CJCA would be wrong, but not CCA. There are two main problems with this position. First, it rests on the wholly untenable presumption that the administration of penal facilities involves little or no exercise of discretion on the part of the administrators, or at least none that would affect the duration of an inmate's stay or the basic conditions of his confinement. There is a mountain of empirical studies that show how much discretion at every level—from the commissioner's office to the cellblock—is of necessity vested in those who run prisons and jails. Any normative case for private penal management that hinges upon a resurrection and acceptance of the discredited notion of a politics/administration dichotomy is prima facie too weak to require a rebuttal.

Second, it is simply unclear how one can distinguish morally between private and public courts, and between private and public policing, and yet see no moral difference between private and public corrections. The moral logic required to embrace a CCA while rejecting a CJCA stems from a species of moral confusion of the same sort that underlies discussions of the death penalty in which supporters of privatization declare that while corporations may "play jailer" (even for life), only the government should "play executioner." Those who claim that a CCA is morally legitimate have little basis for rejecting not only private police but also private judges, juries, and executioners.

PRIVATIZATION: FALSE PROMISES

Privatization efforts have been fueled by the belief that public correctional institutions are too crowded; but the crowding problem is less acute than is commonly supposed. Privatization initiatives have been offered as ways of tightening the reins on galloping correctional budgets; but the public sector has made innovations that promise to reduce the corrections tax bill. Privatization ventures are driven by the perception that public corrections managers have failed; but the public record is by no means unremittingly bleak, and in some respects it is quite impressive. The problems of crowding, rising costs, and failed management are most evident in the area of high-security prisons and jails, but at present the privatizers offer no help for these institutions.

When privatization proponents assert that the firms will do better because they, unlike their public-sector counterparts, will be immune from the political, administrative, and financial woes of governmental red tape, they should be reminded that "one person's 'red tape' may be another's treasured safeguard."[7] Even a cursory review of the historical, political, and administrative issues surrounding private prison and jail management raises grave doubts, and not a few fears, about the prospects of privatization in this area.

The central moral issues surrounding private prison and jail management have little to do with the profit motive of the privatizers and much to do with the propriety, in a liberal constitutional regime, of delegating the authority to administer criminal justice to nonpublic individuals and groups. For much of American history, government has allowed too many of the community's prisons and jails to be ill managed, undermanaged, or not managed at all. Especially in light of the progress that has been made over the last two decades, no self-respecting constitutional government should again abdicate its responsibility to protect and guide criminals in state custody.

The most promising corrections alternative is to get down to the nitty-gritty business of governing prisons well with the human and financial resources available in the public sector. Where public corrections agencies have managed their discretion and coercive powers with common sense and compassion, prisons and jails have been relatively safe, clean, and cost-effective. But far too many institutions remain unsatisfactory, and more progress in public corrections management can and must be made. Arguably, the surest way to make such progress is not to privatize the country's prisons but to nationalize them.

NATIONALIZATION: FALSE HOPES?

Nationalization of corrections can mean many things short of direct federal government responsibility for all facets of prison operations throughout the country. As is true of all governmental activities, prison operations have three basic dimensions: (1) policy-making, (2) financing, and

(3) administration. In the extreme case, nationalization would mean that the Federal Bureau of Prisons would operate every prison in the nation—setting its policies, paying for it out of the federal budget, and staffing it with federal employees.

At least on academic grounds, such an extreme nationalization scheme is not a completely crazy idea. The BOP already houses over 7 percent of the nation's prisoners. By the mid-1990s, its share of that total will probably increase to around 10 percent. Between 1970 and 1990, the BOP developed a regional administrative structure that, if expanded accordingly, could probably carry ten or more times its present operational weight without buckling or breaking. In the past, the BOP has grown by leaps and bounds without losing its capacity to run safe, clean, programmatic, and cost-effective institutions. There might well be economies of scale from centralizing the administration of the nation's prisons under the BOP's direction.

Some observers of corrections have argued that the existence of the BOP in its present form, let alone any expansion in the agency's jurisdiction, is an affront to the principles of federalism.* But as a student of American politics who has taught introductory and advanced courses on American government, I find such arguments bogus. There is nothing in the U.S. Constitution and the Amendments, nothing in *The Federalist Papers*, and nothing in

---

*For example, William G. Nagel, one of the nation's most prominent and well respected penal reform activists, has taken this position. Nagel has credited the BOP with running safe and humane facilities, but he takes issue with the constitutional propriety of a prison system run by national government authorities.

Anglo-American traditions of criminal justice administration to bar the nationalization of prisons. And to the extent that one wishes to invoke national public opinion on the subject, there is no evidence to suggest that most citizens would in principle be opposed to such a move; if anything, there is evidence to indicate that a majority might support a greater federal role in this and several other areas once the sole preserve of the states.*

To take the idea a few steps further, consider the fact that since 1970 the nation's prisons have been undergoing an ad hoc process of "nationalization" via the federal courts. As we saw in chapter 4, in 1970 not a single state prison system was operating under federal court orders; at the start of 1990, over three dozen jurisdictions were subject to such orders. Moving from the hands-off doctrine to the hands-on doctrine, federal judges in Alabama, Texas, and many other states have had an enormous impact on prison operations.

In most cases, judges have foisted upon the states some version of the American Correctional Association's recommended policies, procedures, and accreditation standards. As I argued in the preceding chapter, while the results of federal court intervention have been mixed,

---

*Perhaps the best (albeit still weak) evidence is in the area of education. In a 1989 Gallup poll, 69 percent of the respondents said they would favor requiring local public schools to conform to national achievement standards and goals; 77 percent said they would favor national testing programs to measure the academic achievement of students. In the same poll, however, 53 percent also said they would like to reduce federal involvement in determining the educational program of local schools. In criminal justice, a 1987 Gallup poll found 80 percent of all respondents in favor of a national law that would raise the legal drinking age in all states to twenty-one years; similar majorities have supported an expanded federal role in local law enforcement efforts directed against drug dealers.

there is no reason to suppose that judges will intervene less in the future. This gives one leave to ask whether a systematic and well-planned executive-led process of nationalizing prison operations could produce better consequences at a lower human and financial cost than the current ad hoc, catch-as-catch-can judicial-led process; I think it might.

In addition, there are arguably compelling moral reasons to contemplate seriously some variant of the nationalization option. Why should a U.S. citizen convicted of felony X and imprisoned in state A live under radically different rules and experience radically different conditions of confinement than a U.S. citizen convicted of the same felony X and confined in state B? One traditional answer takes the form of unbridled federalism: The citizens of each state, through their duly elected officials, are entitled to enact penal codes that embody their respective views about crime and punishment. If the communal consensus in state A is that persons convicted for felony X ought to be imprisoned for Y years under what are known to be miserable, spartan conditions, then, barring flagrant violations of prisoners' constitutional protections and statutory rights, that is the state's prerogative; the same, however, goes for citizens of state B who agree that the same felony X deserves .5Y years under decent, eminently livable conditions.

A general concern for equity, and considerations of intracriminal equity, militates against the position of unbridled federalism and argues in favor of "punishing like cases alike." Here, however, my immediate purpose is not to perform the moral-reasoning gymnastics that might constitute a meaningful justification for this view. Rather, it is to briefly raise the possibility of a compromise form of nationalization, one that preserves the role of the states in sentencing and in financing prison operations, but that vests administrative control in the federal government via the BOP.

In simplest terms, under this plan state A could still issue a sentence of Y years for felony X; state B could still issue half as long a sentence for the same offense. It would be a "pay-as-you-lock" system, so that, were state A consistently twice as punitive as state B, it would effectively pay twice as much per offender into the federal treasury through an appropriate intergovernmental financing scheme. But the direct, day-to-day administration of the facilities would be in federal hands. Administrative policies, procedures, and practices would be uniform. A maximum-security felon in state A would live under the same basic administrative regime, and enjoy much the same basic level of services and amenities, as a maximum-security felon in state B (or a maximum-security felon in a federal prison).

Obviously, this variant of nationalization routes the expression of relevant state differences in penal codes through length of confinement, not *both* length and conditions of confinement. To the unbridled believer in states' rights, that limitation would be enough to trash the idea. But even to one willing to speculate along these lines, enormous problems and muscular counterarguments appear quickly on the horizon.

Even in the blissful ignorance of abstractions, a slew of potential logistical, political, and other complications conspire to make any strong variant on full-scale nationalization seem impractical. The mere thought of trying to

207

come up with an inmate classification system that would rationalize over four dozen penal codes is enough to make one flee from the imaginary republic of a nationalized prison system—if the nightmare of devising uniform recruitment, training, and personnel policies does not cause one to flee from it sooner. Possible latent dangers of centralizing prison administration in one federal superagency, such as having it turn into a kind of "American Gulag," cannot be taken lightly. Nor can one dismiss the very real chance that, even if some such plan were debated, adopted enthusiastically, and implemented on a phased, incremental basis, and even with so successful an agency as the BOP in the administrative cockpit, a national prison system could well prove to be an organizational Mission Impossible. And to the extent that it could be achieved, nationalization might well give rise to perverse and unintended consequences, and new and unprecedented cellblock horrors.

Though I believe that the idea of nationalization deserves at least as much of a hearing in the 1990s as the idea of privatization received in the 1980s, I recognize that there are all manner of problems with the option, and I am ever mindful of the maxim, "Be careful of what you wish, for you may get it." Moreover, I recognize that other criminal justice and corrections scholars at other times have researched and speculated along these lines, all for naught. For example, in a 1936 book entitled *Local Democracy and Crime Control*, Arthur C. Millspaugh examined the intergovernmental (mainly state and local) mechanics of the administration of criminal justice and how they might be improved. "Co-ordination purely on the local level has been difficult to bring about," he observed, "and no state has yet seriously attempted to integrate its numerous crime control agencies into a single, centrally commanded, technically equipped, mobile, and effective force."[8]

Millspaugh's fascinating little book was written as the thirty-second in a series of "Studies in Administration" sponsored and published by the Brookings Institution in Washington, D.C. From what I can tell, the book had a fairly wide audience of influential readers. Its "centralizing" drift and litany of problems with "co-ordination" were echoed in virtually every subsequent major report on federal, state, and local criminal justice agencies; indeed, today, to observe that the American criminal justice system is actually a loose confederation of thousands of agencies in hundreds of jurisdictions—a "nonsystem"— is to utter a commonplace. Nobody really expects any part of that "nonsystem" to change fundamentally, least of all in the direction of a nationalized prison system.

Finally, the opinions of corrections practitioners I have interviewed and observed over the years convince me that, for now at least, talk of any full-blown nationalization scheme is idle intellectual prattle. In a typical remark, one veteran official said, "Nationalize? Do you have any idea of what that would mean? . . . It could never work. I thought you had common sense." Another veteran official, this one with the BOP, stated: "Don't do us any favors! You think we're doing a fine job, but that would kill us." Yet another veteran official, this one with a state agency, remarked: "That's got to be the nuttiest idea yet, nuttier than privatization even. Bring in the feds, deputize us, what's next? Run prisons on Mars? Let the Martians run them, maybe. C'mon, you know better than that." As

209

usual, I defer to the superior wisdom of the practitioners, but leave the door open to the possibility that their wisdom on the subject might change.

CONCLUSION: FOR PUBLIC ADMINISTRATION

In the meantime, there is one quite modest nationalization proposal that most corrections practitioners, federal, state, and local, do endorse; namely, an enhanced federal funding commitment to, and a broadened mandate for, the National Academy of Corrections. The academy is a creature of the National Institute of Corrections, itself a research arm of the BOP with a tiny budget. The academy should be expanded to serve as a national anchor of corrections research and training that regularly brings together federal, state, and local policymakers and practitioners to share information, to promote promising strategies, and to educate the wider public. For an estimated $10 million a year—which would not even qualify as static in the federal budget machine—the academy could run a first-rate operation involving thousands of corrections workers from all around the country.

This proposal is not terribly sexy or immediately far-reaching. But it is a valuable incremental move that can be made well within the budgetary and political constraints of current national policy-making. In politics and policy-making, symbols matter. And, if nothing else, the proposed academy would symbolize the nation's long overdue recognition of corrections as a vital area of public concern and give those who work in this most demanding and thankless area of public service a greater sense of public support.

In conclusion, while corrections firms like CCA have run admirable juvenile centers and other facilities, we are most likely to improve our country's prisons and jails if we approach them not as a private enterprise to be administered in the pursuit of profit but as a public trust to be administered on behalf of the community and in the name of civility and justice. The choice is between the uncertain promises of privatization and the unfulfilled duty to govern. In fulfilling this duty, the federal government, which spends far less on "domestic defense" (law enforcement and corrections) than it does on social welfare, education, health, and other vital public functions, can and should play a leading role.

6

Social Science and Corrections

THE RELATIONSHIP BETWEEN SOCIAL SCIENCE RESEARCH, on the one hand, and correctional policy-making and administrative practice, on the other, can be described in three main points. First, there is no meaningful body of social science research on corrections; second, even if there were such a body of research, it would probably not affect the way most correctional policies are made or implemented; and third, except to academics, policy analysts, consultants, and others who have a direct intellectual, occupational, or financial interest in believing (and having the rest of us believe) otherwise, it is by no means clear that correctional supervisees, correctional staff, or average taxpayers would be better off were a social science of corrections to exist.

To appreciate these three points, and to enable me to append a few hopeful qualifications to them later in this chapter, we need to understand some fundamental concepts: (1) the basic differences between social science and other ways of understanding and explaining human behavior; (2) the main alternative conceptualizations of the relationship between social science research and "real-world" activities; and (3) a strategy for social science research on corrections that may result in small positive changes in correctional policy-making and administration.

THE SOCIAL SCIENCE ENTERPRISE

Social scientists, when they are "on duty," and policy analysts, consultants, and others whose expertise consists essentially in their ability to explain seemingly complex things after doing (or appearing to do) their social science homework, generally aim to produce statements about human affairs that are (1) empirically true, (2) intellectually interesting, and (3) practically useful. In part because these aims often prove mutually contradictory, and in part for other reasons, social scientists rarely succeed in producing such statements, though they often claim to have done so and often succeed in convincing others that they have done so. Let me begin by explaining their basic aims.

By *empirically true*, I mean statements based on observation or experimentation that are subject to falsification by methods open to and accepted by most rational investigators. Empirical statements have three main qualities that distinguish them from nonempirical statements. First, they are public: that is, they refer to places, persons, and relationships that can be seen or described in much the same way by most observers. Second, they are communicable: that is, observers can communicate fully what they have observed, and how they have observed it, to most nonobservers. And third, they are potentially falsifiable: that is, new observations, or a reordering of existing ob-

213

servations, can be used to test the findings and conclusions derived from previous observations and the analyses based upon them.

To the full-blooded empiricist, a charismatic preacher who claims from the pulpit to be inspired by Divine Will, to have had a religious revelation, or to have touched the face of God, is neither right nor wrong; the preacher's claims are merely insensible (meaning not based on normal sense experience) and hence beyond the pale of empirical discourse. The preacher's statements are based on a type of human experience that is private, impossible to express fully, and incapable of being tested by others (except, perhaps, by "the faithful"). The empiricist *qua* empiricist has nothing to say about the preacher's statements, except that they are nonempirical. By the same token, the empiricist has nothing to say to ideologues who make nonempirical claims, regardless of whether they are political radicals, liberals, conservatives, or reactionaries; whether their inspiration is drawn from overtly political tracts or literary theories about the nature of "meaning"; or whether they use facts, statistics, words in books, and other empirical referents in making their claims. If their statements express articles of faith, and if they are offered accordingly in ways that do not enable others who may or may not share these beliefs to know whether their statements are objectively valid, then the empiricist has nothing to say in response.

On the other hand, the empiricist may be on perfectly good speaking terms with average citizens and other non–social scientists who do think empirically; and, of course, he is completely at home in communicating with others who are themselves self-consciously and systematically empirical in their statements about human affairs.

A preacher might say, for example, that rising violent crime rates are the work of wicked souls whom God has visited upon us for our sins. A political radical might say that the rise is the "inevitable result" of the "racist, oppressive nature of the bourgeois society in the United States." An avant-garde literary theorist might say that it is "meaningless" to interpret the world in terms of "rates." For his part, however, the empiricist may look upon rising violent crime rates (once he has defined and documented this phenomenon) as a "dependent variable" that may or may not be related systematically and in objectively measurable ways to any number of specifiable factors, such as a decline in imprisonment rates or an increase in the availability of guns. The preacher may denounce his secular approach; the radical may laugh at his political naïveté; the literary luminary may balk at his simplemindedness, call his thoughts "bloodless," and joke about his plodding "barefoot empiricism." But most average citizens will understand him pretty well; and his is the only approach to such questions that does not lend itself to as many stylized answers as there are questioners.

By *intellectually interesting*, I mean statements that stimulate the intellect or excite the active mind. To most social scientists, to be intellectually interesting, a statement must be counterintuitive, theoretical, or both.

Counterintuitive statements rebut common sense and reveal what "everybody knows" to be a false or partial understanding of the reality in question. Thus, a respected introductory sociology text begins with the following all-purpose statement of disciplinary purpose:

> The aim of any discipline ought to be two things: to be clear and to be nonobvious. . . . Sociology does know some important principles [that] . . . go beneath the surface of ordinary belief. The principles had to be discovered by professional scholars, including some of the major thinkers of the past; they are by no means obvious.[1]

Similary, Claude Lévi-Strauss has argued that "true reality is never the most obvious; and the nature of truth is already manifest in the care it takes to remain hidden."[2]

Theoretical statements posit a relationship between two or more variables that is supposed to hold under specified conditions. In essence, empirical theories are generalizations about the way the world works. As Alexis de Tocqueville stated elegantly, "God stands in no need of general ideas."[3] But we mere mortals are forced to employ general ideas or theories lest we be paralyzed by the endless stream of particular realities that bombard us, or lost in the endless quest for those that elude us. If we could grasp every particular reality in its infinite details, and if we could set these particulars in some nonrandom relation to one another, then theory building would be a moot enterprise. But we cannot, and so we must rely on theories as intellectual economizing devices.

Unlike the rest of us, however, when it comes to statements about human affairs, the card-carrying social scientist attempts to theorize self-consciously and with precision. Also unlike the rest of us, he strives on these terms to concoct theories that "capture" as much of reality as possible based on as few simplifying assumptions as possible. He finds such theories especially interesting because they are powerful yet parsimonious. In deciding between two theories about the same phenomenon, he naturally chooses the one that explains the most with the least (unless, of course, the weaker theory is his own).

By definition, no theory explains "everything." What is not explained by the theory the social scientist calls "unassimilated data" or (where theories are predicated on statistical analyses) "residuals," "outliers," or "noise." Of course, to him the most intellectually interesting theory would explain "everything" with reference to just two variables—the causal (or "independent") variable, and the thing caused by it (or "dependent") variable: "If X, then Y." But he does not normally strive for such grand theories, knowing them to be rare in the natural or hard sciences (physics, chemistry), and virtually unheard of in the scientific study of human affairs. In fact, in most cases, he feels no need to account for the existence of things that are not explained by the theory. Rather than pining for "If X, then Y," a statement such as, "If X, under condition A, then in 72.2 percent of all cases, Y" would more than tickle most social scientists.

Certainly, however, this would not tickle most of the rest of us. To pluck the beam from my own social scientist's eye, it may be true that, *ceteris paribus*, and in most cases, certain types of management approaches are better than others at making certain types of prisons and jails safe, civilized, and cost-effective (see chapter 1). But in the real world, *ceteris* are hardly ever *paribus*. Moreover, the "management variable" does not account for all the observable variance in the quality of institutional life; and, as I shall hint later in this chapter, the practical value of such "findings" is unclear to say the least.

Because they are out to generalize to the extent possible, social scientists have little interest in theories that involve rare, arguably random, or unique causal agents. Indeed, except with a knowing wink or in a disparaging tone, they are reluctant to characterize such statements as "theories." Thus, for example, to them the "great man" theories that explain important historical events largely or solely with reference to the thoughts and deeds of one individual (for example, Hitler and the rise and fall of Nazi Germany) are to be avoided (and caricatured) at all costs.

Instead, social scientists reflexively opt for what may be dubbed "great causes beget great effects" theories. Such theories relate broad social, political, economic, and other "forces" to one another and are normally expressed by words ending in *-tion*: for example, how industrialization in conjunction with urbanization have increased rates of criminal victimization and led eventually to ghettoization in conjunction with deindustrialization. Such supraindividual forces are called "structural" factors (or other catch-all terms that the social scientist usually leaves undefined).

Finally, theories that center on complex and remote "structural" factors (often translated by journalists and pop social scientists as "underlying factors") are more interesting to social scientists than theories that center on simple and proximate variables (those that Aunt Tessie would cite when explaining the same phenomenon), in part because the former stand a higher probability of generating counterintuitive conclusions about the way the world works.

A few examples are in order. The economic theory of supply and demand is an example of a powerful social science theory that is not counterintuitive. Four-year-olds of average intelligence can be made to understand it; college students in introductory economics courses can learn it, plus learn all sorts of neat ways to express it mathematically and graphically. But they must normally enroll in the intermediate-level courses before they can learn much about things that do not fit the theory of supply and demand (such as backward-bending supply curves). And it is only those lucky few who go on to graduate study in the field who learn how to make economics "intellectually interesting" by using advanced math to produce complex statements about economic "equilibria" (or the lack thereof) that have little or no basis in commonsense reality, and that only their fellow Ph.D.s can understand.

On the other hand, the sociological theory of prison riots is an example of a powerful social science theory that is counterintuitive to boot. For years, leading sociologists have argued that the more prison officials do to crack down on inmate predators, to maintain tight security procedures, and to run things strictly by the book, the more likely it is that prison riots will occur.[4] This theory has been based on selective interpretations of a few prison riots, and, as both common sense and existing evidence make clear, it is demonstrably false.[5] But its radically counterintuitive appeal has enshrined it for the last three decades as a piece of conventional sociological wisdom.

Aunt Tessie would guess that a maximum-security prison where inmates are frisked, cells are searched, crowds are dispersed, and contraband is controlled is far less likely to have a riot than one where security-conscious procedures are not followed on a routine basis; and, empirically, she would be right. And Aunt Tessie has lived long enough to reckon that a prison run by a warden who is "wet behind the ears" is more likely to be troubled than one with an experienced, no-nonsense administrator; and, again, the empirical record, so far as anyone can reconstruct it, would bear her out.

But her "obvious," "banal," "trite," and "pedestrian" theory of prison violence spoils the social scientist's fun; and, if forced to choose between making statements that are interesting and making statements that are true, the social scientist has every professional and occupational incentive to choose the former at least as often as the latter. After all, there is no *Journal of Obvious Realities*, and no self-respecting, "theory-minded" social scientist or "expert" would publish in it if there were.

By *practically useful*, I mean statements that tell one how to achieve an operational goal. An operational goal is an image of a desired future state of affairs that can be compared unambiguously to an actual or existing state of affairs.[6] "Good will on earth" is a nonoperational goal; the cessation of armed combat between two enemy nations is an operational goal.

Closer to our topic, the "spiritual reformation" of prisoners is a nonoperational goal. We can give the incarcerated convict a Bible, preach to him, and exhort him to be good day and night (or at least the Pennsylvania Quakers of the eighteenth century could). And we can observe that whereas once he hit, spit on, and cursed at everyone who came within ten feet of his cell, he now shakes hands, smiles, and says "Have a nice day." But whether he has "torn the evil from his heart" or "repented" is beyond our power to observe.

On the other hand, the "rehabilitation" of prisoners is an operational goal if by *rehabilitation* we mean simply getting persons who behaved illegally in the past to behave legally in the future. Tocqueville breathed the distinction between reformation and rehabilitation when he wrote that the "change of a wicked person into an honest man" may be beyond our power to effect, and implied that, in any event, we would not be able to tell whether anything we had done was responsible, in whole or in part, for the change. But we could, he reasoned, make the offender "more obedient to the laws" and observe the change by observing "the convict's behavior in prison" and his newly "honest habits."[7]

The rehabilitated criminal may still be a cruel, violent person "inside." But so long as he does not observably translate these impulses into illegal behaviors as he once did, he has been rehabilitated, and our operational goal (if not necessarily our "higher" nonoperational aspiration of spiritual or moral rebirth) has been achieved.

Inherent Limitations of Social Science

For the sake of what is intellectually interesting, social scientists purposefully tend to work at a level of generality that most citizens find remote from "real life"; hence the image of the Ivory Tower intellectual and related characterizations.[8] While these characterizations sometimes run into caricature, the truth remains that even public policy-minded social scientists rarely do work that has meaningful practical implications. In practical human affairs, the theoretical is the enemy of the particular, and the real-world problems confronted by policymakers and administrators involve particular people, particular places, and particular situations; and they require highly particularized responses.

For example, if the operational goal is to reduce prison line staff turnover rates, it does little good to know that, in general, staff turnover rates tend to be lowest where inmate overcrowding and related job stresses are lowest, informal worker associations are frequent and positive, and the history of union-management relations is smooth. It may, however, help to know whether particular shift supervisors or officers are "pains in the ass" (prison staff have more earthy but unprintable expressions) who can be transferred or fired. But that is precisely the kind of knowledge that, while readily available to agency insiders, will be found nowhere in the reports of social scientists (or other "experts").

Even if done with the utmost care and respect for scientific methodology, any generalizations based on an analysis of, for example, inmate counseling sessions, would be suspect; moreover, they would be of doubtful practical value. For example, suppose it was "found" that, other things being equal, of every 100 inmates who participated in counseling sessions for ten hours a week for at least two years, 25 recidivated, while among otherwise comparable inmates who did not participate in these sessions (or did not participate in them for the requisite time), 40 of every 100 recidivated. And suppose that the recidivism rates for participants who had different styles of counselors varied as well, and that only 20 percent of the inmates who participated mainly in sessions with "touchy-feely" counselors recidivated, while 30 percent of those who participated in sessions with "boot-camp" counselors recidivated.

What, precisely, would, should, or could corrections policymakers and administrators actually do with these findings? Should the veteran "boot-camp" counselors be made to undergo sensitivity training or be forced to retire? Do the findings justify an expansion in the number of hours inmates are required to spend in counseling? Given funds and time for research, social scientists would be able to provide general answers to many such follow-up questions. But policymakers and administrators do not operate in a political, administrative, legal, or (one hopes) moral vacuum. Nor can even a handful of the situations that pop up, or the decisions that they must make and enforce each day, be put on hold until the next social science project has issued its "findings" several months or years from now.

Moreover, the political, administrative, legal, and moral context in which research is produced may severely limit both the possibility of doing meaningful social science research on corrections, and the practical value (if any) of such research. Politicians and political appointees have stakes in what research gets done and how its findings are broadcast and interpreted; correctional administrators may see their work (for example, psychotherapy counseling sessions) as an end in itself that ought not to be evaluated according to whether it has much, some, or no statistically discernible impact on inmates' institutional or postinstitutional behavior; judges may intervene in ways that make the policy or administrative implications of the research moot because they are at odds with prisoners' rights or other legal requirements; and so on.

The practical inutility of most social science research on crime and other subjects has been discussed artfully by Thomas Sowell.[9] As Sowell observed, you can give a farm boy a big empty pail and tell him to go back to the barn and fill it with milk—and fully expect to see a pail filled with milk when he returns. And you can give a criminologist a big open-ended grant and tell him to go back to the university for surefire advice on how to reduce crime rates—but you would be foolish to expect to see anything other than (at best) a bunch of factual, fascinating, and practically useless monographs when he returns (months or years later). By the same token, social scientists have established ad nauseam that a disproportionate number of predatory street crimes are committed by poor young males living in inner cities. So what? Can we cure poverty? Are we to outlaw teenage and young adult malehood? Do we ship them out to the country?

Policy-oriented social scientists aim to produce general but precise statements about human affairs that are at once empirically true, intellectually interesting, and practically useful. Social scientists of corrections have not fared terribly well on any of these counts, especially the last. The same, of course, might be said about social scientists of schools, police departments, armies, mental institutions, public hospitals, and other institutions. But, perhaps because I have been closest to the research record in this field, it appears to me that social scientists of corrections have had the most complete failures.

In examining three distinct conceptualizations of the relationship between social science research and "real-world" activities—those of Edward Banfield, Charles Lindblom, and Richard Nathan—we can begin to see a way of reversing these failures. These three views differ mainly in how unbridgeable a gap they discern between researchers and practitioners (both policymakers and administrators).

SOCIAL SCIENCE AS "METAPHYSICAL MADNESS"

In the first conceptualization, represented well in many of the writings of Harvard University's Edward C. Banfield, the gap between researchers and practitioners seems almost wholly unbridgeable.

In his essay "Policy Science as Metaphysical Madness," Banfield draws inspiration from the following words of the eighteenth-century British philosopher-statesman Edmund Burke:

A statesman differs from a professor in a university; the latter has only a general view of society; the former, the statesman, has a number of circumstances to combine with those general ideas, and to take into his consideration. Circumstances are infinite, are infinitely combined, are variable, and transient; he who does not take them into consideration is not erroneous, but stark mad—*dat operam ut cum ratione insaniat*—he is metaphysically mad.

225

Broadening "professors" to include social scientists and policy analysts, and broadening "statesmen" to include policymakers and bureaucrats, the crux of Banfield's Burkean argument runs as follows:

> It is a dangerous delusion to think that the policy scientist can supplant successfully the politician or the statesman. Social problems are at bottom political; they arise from differences of opinion and interest and, except in trivial instances, are differences to be coped with (ignored, got around, put up with, exorcised by the arts of rhetoric, etc.) rather than puzzles to be solved.[10]

Banfield's message is that social scientific ideas about human affairs may or may not be intellectually interesting and empirically true, but they are almost never practically useful. Policymakers and administrators worth their salt will stay immersed in the particulars of what they do, be wary of "sophisticated" general ideas, and avoid professional researchers like the plague. The researchers must have a passion for the general, the nonobvious, and the intrinsically interesting; the practitioners must have a passion for the particular, the obvious, and the practically useful. Each enterprise is legitimate and worthwhile in its own right, but it is foolish to think that they can be merged, and dangerous to try.

The American Founding Fathers, adduces Banfield, were able to build a new national government that worked because they were civic-spirited men of practical affairs who consulted not abstract notions but their own experiences, and the hard facts of history, in their political deliberations. And, indeed, *The Federalist* does contain several disparaging references to men of affairs who proceed as "theoretic politicians."

Banfield argues that educating the leaders and managers of organizations (public and private) in theories of administration and the like is a waste of time; if anything, it makes those who receive the training less capable of functioning effectively than they would have been in the absence of any such schooling. To paraphrase one of his memorable quips, one no more needs a theory of organizational leadership to be a successful executive than one needs a theory of kinship to be a good cousin.[11] Thus, he observes:

> The science of organization, and science in general, has nothing to contribute. . . . Science cannot tell [the executive] how to make a value judgment or a moral judgment. . . . In matters that are subject to statistical treatment—i.e., that involve many instances of the same thing—science has a great deal to say about probability. But, alas, the matters the executive is called upon to decide are almost never of this kind. He must make probability judgments about unique events, and in this science has no help to offer. . . . [F]ormal training, especially when it is in subject matter alien to the concrete manner of behaving (as social science, even at its best, is alien to concrete behavior "in" organization), may only succeed in instilling a "trained incapacity" for suitable behavior. . . . So far as [the executive] needs knowledge about organization at all, he needs knowledge about his particular organization [which] . . . can be most economically provided by word of mouth instructions from fellow employees.[12]

In short, Banfield's advice to policymakers and administrators (though, given the cast of his argument, he would

227

not offer it as such) is to forget social science generalizations and to rely upon common sense and knowledge of particulars. The implication is that persons with good natural intelligence and judgment skills will do well, while persons without these talents will fare badly. Resorting to social science analytics, he implies, will only make both the naturally skilled and the unskilled less able to do a good job.

Political-Choice Versus Technical-Choice Problems

This sort of sentiment about the irrelevance, or detriment, of social scientific training makes people who teach in schools of public policy (like me) nervous; they are reluctant to respond to these "obviously ridiculous" assertions about the efficacy of their craft. But in all honesty, nobody knows whether, other things being equal, and at any level of government service, people with MPAs are more effective or efficient public servants than people who have not had such formal training. And nobody can cite many credible examples of social science studies or consulting reports (1) being taken seriously by policymakers and administrators (that is, not commissioned and used merely to support positions they had already held), (2) containing recommendations that were acted upon without vast modifications, or (3) having unambiguously positive results once implemented. But there are many examples of advice being given by social scientists and acted upon with unintended consequences, many of them negative.

At the core of Banfield's conceptualization of the relationship between social science and "real-world" activities is an important distinction between what may be termed "political-choice" and "technical-choice" problems.[13] Social science (mainly economics), he argues, may be useful in addressing, and in helping non–social scientists to address, the latter problems, but it has nothing but trouble, confusion, and false hopes to contribute in addressing the former problems.

To understand the distinction between these two types of choice, think of choosing between two diamonds versus choosing between two candidates for a Rhodes Scholarship. The value of a diamond is established in accordance with four criteria: color, cut, clarity, and carat. There are established rates of exchange between each of these criteria, so that diamonds that differ on one or more value will be priced differently by any competent and disinterested professional jeweler (or "gemologist"). If Diamond A and Diamond B have the same color, cut, and clarity, but Diamond B has more carats, then it is worth more. If you were offered these two gems and told that you could keep either one, you could go to any experienced jeweler and learn that Diamond B is the more valuable gem (say, by $500). Of course, other considerations might affect your decision. If, for instance, Diamond A had belonged to your grandmother and thus held a special sentimental value for you, you might choose it instead. Or if you had a passion for smaller stones, you might do the same. By the same token, if the diamonds differ in cut but in no other way, and you do not consider a diamond a diamond unless it is pear-shaped, you might choose a less monetarily valuable pear-shaped stone over a more valuable oval one.

In most cases, however, you would gladly and reflexively take the more valuable diamond. In this "technical-choice" situation, the *data* (two glistening stones), the *criteria* (color, cut, clarity, and carat), and the *decision rule* (choose the one that is worth more in dollars and cents) are unambiguous and uncontroversial; any trained jeweler (or experienced diamond maven) could make the "right choice" without consulting others, and nobody would much care.

But now consider an either/or choice between two candidates for a Rhodes Scholarship. Again, there are four established criteria: scholastic ability, athletic prowess, civic character, and leadership ability.[14] But in making this choice, the data, criteria, and decision rule are not quite so clear-cut.

The "data" are two living, breathing, aspiring young persons, not two lifeless stones. The two candidates may differ in ways that, though not directly relevant to the choice, are objectively noticeable, and possibly significant (such as race or gender), to those who make the choice. The criteria are relatively unclear; reasonable people could be uncertain in their own minds, and could disagree fundamentally with reasonable others, about how to define and measure one or more of them. And the "rates of exchange" among the criteria are controversial; reasonable people could disagree fundamentally over how, if at all, to count one quality against another or others. Thus, it is difficult, some might say impossible, to discern anything but a vague decision rule ("choose the worthier candidate") in this case.

It is no accident, therefore, that we do not normally entrust such decisions to a single individual, however wise or experienced in such matters he or she may be. Instead, we normally make such decisions via some kind of committee process. The essential feature of such a process is that, by design, it involves more than one person; indeed, one or more wise heads may structure the decision-making body so that it reflects and registers all or most of the range of reasonable views about how to define, measure, and trade off the multiple and competing values that are at stake in the decision (for example, in the Rhodes decision, no ardent anti-intellectuals or uncompromising anti-footballers).

But as anyone who has ever served on such a committee will tell you, even with a stellar assemblage of reasonable-minded committee members, and even in the academic cloister where professional norms and collegial protocols preclude shouting at co-workers or engaging in fisticuffs, the disagreements over which candidate is, in absolute or relative terms, more "worthy" than the next can be intense. The decision process may well involve everything from give-and-take discussion, subtle attempts at persuasion, and head-on debate, to semi-friendly bargaining ("I'll vote for your superjock, you vote for my pencil-neck genius") and unfriendly "arm twisting." Often, the process ends when some aggregative measure of consensus (for example, one-person, one-vote voting in which a majority rules) is taken and the decision is "made."

Political-choice situations (like the either/or choice between two Rhodes candidates) differ from technical-choice situations (like the either/or choice between two free diamonds) in that the data, criteria, and decision rules involved in making the former choices are more complex, ambiguous, and controversial than those involved in making the latter choices. In essence, political-choice situations involve conflict over ends, while technical-choice situations involve a search for the best available (perhaps the most foolproof or cost-effective) means to achieve agreed-upon ends. For the most part, technical problems can be solved, while political problems can only be resolved (often over and over again, and not always in the same ways).

Conceptually, "pure" political-choice situations are at one end of a continuum, and "pure" technical-choice situations are at the other. Today, for example, the abortion issue is at the far political end of the continuum. The data (Is a fetus a life? When? At conception? At ninety days?), the criteria (Do medically specifiable health risks to the mother matter? Do the mother's non–health-related preferences matter? Do the circumstances surrounding the birth—such as rape or incest—matter?), and the decision rule (Are the mother's preferences primary? Is the child's life primary?) are so unclear and controversial that we often cannot even agree about how to structure the legal power to make and enforce the choice (whether federal courts, state legislatures, constitutional amendments, or some other way). And those who are unhappy with how a given process has resolved the issue may work to have it re-resolved by the same process or by a different one (such as a new ruling by the Supreme Court, a constitutional amendment, or "tossing the decision back" to the state legislatures).

Of course, if tomorrow morning nearly everyone decided to be pro-choice (or pro-life), and to resolve each question related to the issue in the same way, then this choice situation would slide rapidly to the technical end of the continuum, having become "depoliticized." And, indeed, a favorite trick of astute political actors is to get their opponents to focus on means instead of ends. (For example, savvy pro-choicers may be covertly happy to debate how, whether, or to what extent the federal government funds abortions, so long as abortions remain legal and widely available to most women who want them.) But where such ploys fail, or where compromises cannot be reached among contending single-issue activists or extremists unwilling to take "half a loaf," then conflict continues, sometimes to the point of a physical confrontation that decides the issue by a sheer test of might (as with slavery and the Civil War).

By the same token, long-resolved technical-choice problems may become "politicized" by those who attack the value premises on which they rest. (For example, some proponents of school prayer argue that the Founding Fathers did not erect a "wall of separation" between church and state, and challenge the Supreme Court's 1963 ruling that enshrined "secular humanism"). And bubbling beneath what looks like a technical-choice situation may be a host of political-choice problems. For instance, those who wonder why the national budget deficit cannot be "solved" in obedience to the simplest canons of arithmetic by raising taxes, cutting spending, or both, ignore the fact that different people want and value different things and will be affected differently by any given choice on the matter: Some citizens will win financially, some will lose; some will feel that their values have been reified by the choice, others will feel that their values have been "trashed" by it; and some (normally the majority) will just quietly pay the bills.[15]

In such political-choice situations, technical rationality (that is, general statements about how to make and implement choices consistent with given ends) will get mugged repeatedly by political rationality (that is, general statements about what ends ought to b achieved, how, and for whom). Mr. Dooley was right that "politics ain't beanbag"; but neither is it simply a messy, irrational, roundabout way of doing academic benefit-cost analysis.[16]

Federal, state, and local elected officials tend to be sensitive to political realities and, in consequence, are reluctant to make "hard"—that is, highly political—choices. Politicians long for "win/win" solutions; but much of the time they must adopt "win/lose" resolutions or do nothing. Much the same can be said of experienced bureaucrats and administrators, especially those who work for agencies that handle "hot" issues. And, indeed, much the same can be said of most people who live and work in the real world.

At least when they are "on duty," however, social science researchers are not terribly sensitive to the political realities that surround the sorts of real-world choice situations that policymakers and administrators must face (or duck) each day. At their worst, social scientists *qua* policy analysts think that any political problem is merely a technical problem disguised by the ignorance, prejudice, and unfounded fears of the contending individuals or groups. Their faith is that once they have shed the light of rational analysis on the situation, the "optimal solution" will become apparent, the silly "political rhetoric" on all sides will stop, and, with their "expert" guidance, our elected and appointed officials will go on to "solve" other problems without delay.

Whenever the real or perceived costs and benefits of a decision fall upon different persons or groups, whenever ends conflict and goals are multiple, vague, and contradictory, the operative word in a free society is (and, one could argue, ought to be) *politics*, not *analysis*. The skill of the politician and the public administrator consists largely in finding practical ways of working in and around political-choice situations while taking into account a host of hard-to-navigate constraints, among them legal prohibitions, public opinion, and the capacity of disaffected citizens to make waves and bring pressures (including violence) to bear.[17] The skill of the social scientist *qua* policy analyst is, in effect, to ignore such real-world realities, freeing himself to conceptualize the problem in a more general, systematic, tractable, and intellectually satisfying fashion.

Implications of Banfield's View

If Banfield (via Burke) is to be heeded, then we would want to do everything in our power to keep the "statesmen" and the "professors" as far apart as the natural exercise of their respective skills permits. Just as journalists often use them for "expert" quotes, and attorneys use them as "expert" witnesses, so policymakers and administrators may from time to time use social science researchers as "facilitators" at agency workshops; as staffers,

235

consultants, or "hired guns" who marry research to political aims; or as reliable "reference tools" who know how to locate reliable factual (especially statistical) information, sift through it quickly, and summarize the results as needed. Such a relationship between social scientists and responsible officials, Banfield implies, is harmless.

But for government officials at any level to take social scientists seriously enough to give them any real hand in making and implementating public policies, domestic or foreign, to govern in accordance with social scientists' latest ideas and "findings," would be, or so Banfield teaches, at once the dumbest and most dangerous form of "metaphysical madness."

To the chagrin of most persons who work in the research units of corrections bureaucracies, policymakers and upper-level administrators tend to behave in precisely the way that Banfield would have them behave. The "researchers" in these positions often complain about doing nothing more than summarizing prison admission and release statistics in annual reports, responding to "ASAP" requests for factual information about given inmates from legislators, and other mundane tasks. "I wish they would let us do some *real* research," said one veteran corrections department research chief, "but they don't understand the value of it—they don't understand it, period."

Of course, corrections agencies have commissioned studies from consulting firms and the like. Usually, however, they have done so to buy time with which to work out the politics of the situation; as a public relations gesture intended to demonstrate "openness," "innovativeness," or "good will" toward political adversaries; and for other reasons having little or nothing to do with a longing for social science generalizations about their work. Most often, the final consulting reports commissioned by corrections agencies have been testimonies to bad social science, inept theorizing, and poor writing; often, the main conclusions of the "research" could have been spoken by any honest agency worker with more than a few years on the job. In many cases, the price to the taxpayers for this pseudo-academic drivel has been hundreds of thousands, even millions, of dollars.[18]

Few policymakers or top corrections officials, however, go so far in Banfield's direction as Dr. George Beto. As discussed in chapter 1, Beto directed the Texas Department of Corrections from 1962 to 1972. He has spent most of the last two decades as a professor of criminal justice at a Texas university. In his view, "any organization that needs a management study needs new management." Stated a bit differently, if the officials are competent to request and meaningfully evaluate the consultants' work, then they do not really need it; and if they are not so competent, then it matters not what advice they are given.

On the other hand, there are present and former corrections policymakers and administrators who, unlike Beto, would find themselves somewhat at odds with Banfield's views. Norman A. Carlson directed the Federal Bureau of Prisons from 1970 to 1987 and now teaches in the University of Minnesota's Department of Sociology. Carlson has always been a true believer in the possibility that social scientists and other professional analysts might have something of practical value to teach corrections policymakers and administrators. In the spirit of that belief, he supported the development of an experimental federal

237

prison in Butner, North Carolina, administered to test ideas about prison management advanced by the University of Chicago's Norval Morris; and he commissioned several studies, including one by the National Academy of Public Administration.

Like Beto, however, Carlson did not base his management decisions on systematic research of any kind. Outside researchers had relatively little influence; in-house researchers had even less. So far as one can tell, Carlson, like Beto, drew mainly on his vast personal experience, general education, personal moral precepts, considered judgment, and intuitive "prison sense" in making decisions.[19]

In their official written instructions to applicants, criminal justice funding agencies like the National Institute of Corrections (NIC) and the National Institute of Justice (NIJ) stress that research proposals that may reasonably be expected to yield ideas of practical utility to practitioners are more likely to be chosen for funding than those that do not hold such promise.[20] I have held NIC grants and served as a referee on proposals to NIJ, and I know that both agencies are serious and well intentioned on this score. But with few exceptions, it is clear that this shotgun wedding between research and practice has rarely if ever come off as desired.

This would neither surprise nor displease one who views the relationship between social science research and real-world activities the way Banfield does. The same could be said of the fact that in the concluding section of a leading corrections textbook, under the heading "Scientific Guidance for Correctional Policies," there appear four essays that offer plenty of high-toned opinions, management proverbs, anti-incarceration rhetoric, and ideological rallying cries, but nothing that even vaguely resembles practically useful empirical generalizations generated through scientific methods.[21]

SOCIAL SCIENCE AND "MUDDLING THROUGH"

In a second major conceptualization, the gap between social science on the one hand, and policy and practice on the other, is viewed as necessarily wide and invariably strewn with mighty obstacles, but not unbridgeable. This view is captured nicely in several writings by Yale University's Charles E. Lindblom.

In his justly famous 1959 essay "The Science of 'Muddling Through'," Lindblom describes two ways of making public policy and related administrative decisions.[22] The first is decision making by "root," or the "rational-comprehensive" method. The social scientist strongly favors this method, in which the decision maker posits an objective (for example, reduction of inmate-on-officer assaults); ranks the direct and indirect benefits that would result if the objective were achieved (fewer injuries, better officer morale, less use of disability leave, and so on); specifies alternative ways, or combinations of ways, to achieve the objective (tighter restrictions on contraband, increasing the penalties for assaults, and so on); and chooses the best or "optimal" alternative, the one that most nearly maximizes the objective (in this example, the one that brings the assault rate as close to zero as possible) while minimizing the human and financial resources needed to achieve it.

Decision making by root is "rational" because it systematically relates means to ends, desired outputs to valued inputs, process to performance, resource allocation to goals. It is "comprehensive" because it involves logically "scanning" all relevant ends, all relevant means, and all relevant relationships among ends and means, in accordance with one's ranked preferences.

The second decision-making process discussed by Lindblom is by "branch" or "successive limited comparisons." To the disappointment of the policy analyst, the real-world decision maker naturally follows this method. In the branch method, the decision maker pursues an objective that is not selected rationally but instead is foisted upon him by others (such as legislators, unions, public opinion). The objective is fixed (for example, a legal requirement) and is constrained by other objectives (for example, reduce assaults without reducing face-to-face inmate-officer interactions). Because deciding to pursue new objectives may please some internal and external constituencies and upset others by "rocking the boat," and because the decision maker faces too many immediate problems to permit a consideration of all possible objectives, all possible benefits of achieving them, and all possible ways of achieving them, he avoids bold steps. Instead, if he is wise, he consults his own personal experiences and considers a few limited options, each of which can be pursued with the resources (including legal, administrative, and political authority) already on hand. When necessary, he proposes "sensible" incremental measures that have immediate practical relevance, and do not ruffle many feathers.

Lindblom argues that there are six reasons why decision making by root is inescapably distant from and, given the practical demands of the world beyond the academic cloister, superior to decision making by branch.

First, actual decision makers do not have the unlimited resources (including time) necessary to make comprehensive decisions; an option that is "good enough" must suffice. They cannot wait to discover the "best" alternative while "Rome burns" or calls for action go unheeded.

Second, in a free, democratic society such as ours, people are entitled to disagree over policy objectives, and to have most of these disagreements reflected in both policy choices and administrative actions. Besides, nobody can objectively rank multiple, vague, and contradictory values; and, as Lindblom says, even "when an administrator resolves to follow his own values as a criterion for success, he will often not know how to rank them when they conflict with one another as they usually do."[23]

Third, means and ends (process and performance, inputs and outputs) are often indistinct. For one thing, they are often hopelessly intertwined; if the end is, for example, slum clearance, the means is to clear the slum. For another, people often value not merely what is achieved but how it is achieved; for example, one might think that a "better" president could be selected by an elite group of bipartisan wisemen, yet resist surrendering the right to vote because one values the public, democratic nature of the electoral process independent of (or merely in addition to) its outcomes.

Fourth, at least in the arena of public policy decisions, every decision must meet the test of minimum acceptability to all parties affected by it. Aside from the intrinsic joys of democratic consensus, if the decision is one that the "losers" (those who perceive that their interests are harmed, their beliefs ignored, or both, by the decision) cannot at least grudgingly accept or "live with" without resorting to extreme, even violent, measures against the organizations, groups, or individuals who made it, then the decision may be purchased with the currency necessary to make decisions ("optimal" or not) in the future.[24]

Fifth, at least in the public arena, most decisions are never final. Issues can rise to the top of the public agenda, fall off, and then rise again in response to events over which neither policymakers nor administrators have much or any direct control.

Sixth and finally, given the necessarily pluralistic and incremental nature of the decision-making process, policymakers and administrators must rely mainly on the political art of compromise, rather than on the fledgling science of policy analysis, to get the job done. Indeed, as Lindblom conceives it, their job is to seek and find compromise decisions that represent an agreement among contending parties.

Lindblom handily chose an example from criminal justice to illustrate a key part of his argument:

> For example, without a more comprehensive theory about juvenile delinquency than scholars have yet produced, one cannot possibly understand the ways in which a variety of public policies—say on education, housing, recreation, em-

ployment, race relations, and policing—might encourage or discourage delinquency. And one needs such an understanding if he undertakes the comprehensive overview of the problem prescribed in the models of the root method. If, however, one merely wants to mobilize knowledge sufficient to assist in a choice among a small group of similar policies—alternative policies on juvenile court procedures, for example—he can do so by comparative analysis of the results of similar past policy moves.

In the penultimate section of his essay, under the pregnant heading "Theorists and Practitioners," Lindblom added:

> This difference explains—in some cases at least—why the administrator often feels that the outside expert or academic problem-solver is sometimes not helpful and why they in turn often urge theory on him. And it explains why an administrator often feels more confident when "flying by the seat of his pants" than when following the advice of theorists. *Theorists often ask the administrator to go the long way round to the solution of his problems, when the administrator knows the best available method will work less well than more modest incremental comparisons.*[25] [Emphasis added.]

In several crucial respects, Lindblom's "muddling through" makes the relationship between social science and real-world activities seem every bit as unbridgeable as it appears to be in Banfield's "metaphysical madness." But Lindblom's conceptual organizing metaphor—decision making by "root" versus by "branch"—is a sure clue that his view is significantly more moderate than

Banfield's: a root and a branch can be different, mutually supportive parts of the same healthy tree.

Thus, near the end of his essay, Lindblom noted that while those who approach decisions by root (like most social scientists and policy analysts) and those who approach them by branch (like most actual policymakers and administrators) confront a deep "barrier to communication, an understanding of it promises an enrichment of intellectual interaction in policy formulation. Once the source of the difference is understood," Lindblom reasoned, "it will sometimes be stimulating for an administrator to seek out a policy analyst whose recent experience is with a policy chain different from his own."[26] And though he has never been at a loss to stress the severe limits of social science as a worthwhile guide to making and implementing policy decisions, in some of his subsequent writings, Lindblom suggested that at least some types of policy analysis under some conditions may constitute "usable knowledge."[27]

Beyond "Muddling Through"

It has been left to other researchers to explore Lindblom's thinking about the nexus between social science theory and real-world practice, often under banners highly evocative of his "muddling through." Recently, for instance, Robert Behn wrote positively about public management by "groping along," and Thomas Miller followed shortly thereafter with "gut-level decisionmaking."[28] While recognizing the many limits to the relationship, Behn,

Miller, and others have sought creative ways to overcome them.

In this regard, Miller's work is a natural follow-up to Lindblom's. He distinguishes three types of decision making: rational (which parallels Lindblom's "root"), political (which parallels Lindblom's "branch"), and intuitional (which is the most radically contra-analytical of the three). Table 6.1 summarizes Miller's neat decision-making "trichotomy." He stresses that policy analysis "does not now give what even gut-level policy makers might be inclined to notice—proof rather than probability," adding that

> gut-level decisionmakers exist precisely because they see nothing better in practice or in the fruits of the scientific community that is more credible or reliable than their own gut feelings. Forecasts, impact studies, citizen surveys, cost-benefit analyses, and other stock in trade of the policy analyst frequently identify as many questions as answers. Analysis thus makes decisions more difficult, not easier for the decisionmaker.[29]

Miller offers four strategies for bridging the gap. First, there is "whistle blowing," a strategy in which the analyst informs the public that information relevant to government policy is being ignored by policymakers. Second, there is "job shuffling," a strategy in which the analyst (especially the in-house departmental researcher) passes his analysis (or his services) on to individuals and groups who are more receptive to it than those for whom he is currently working. Third, there is "becoming your own client," a strategy in which the analyst gets himself elected or appointed to a relevant position of actual decision-

TABLE 6.1

Three Modes of Decision Making

Presumptions behind the decision	Rational	Political	Intuitional
Nature of truth	One truth discoverable by analysis	Competing truths resulting from conflict	No truth susceptible to intersubjective verification
Relationship of evidence to politics	Insulated	Immersed	Irrelevant
Effect of analysis on decision maker	Influence	Pressure	Confusion
Source of knowledge	Credible, objective data	Testimony from constituents, pressure groups, and analysts	Feelings
Value of knowledge from systematic evidence	It's good	It can be good or bad	It's bad
Role of scientific information	As means to social good	As end "proving" decision makers are objective	As obstacle to what I want
Use of policy study	As tools for betterment	As weapon or ammunition	As something for scientists
Essential decision criterion	What is the net social benefit?	How many votes or contributions will result?	Do I like it?
Most common method	Logical-empiricism	Quasi-legal advocacy	Blind faith, intuition, or ideology

Source: Thomas I. Miller, "Gut-Level Decisionmaking: Implications for Public Policy Analysis," *Journal of Policy Analysis and Management*, 8, no. 1 (Winter 1989): 122.

making authority. And fourth, there is "improving our product," a strategy in which the analyst strives to make first-rate applied social science serve the real needs of real decision makers.[30] As a fifth strategy, I would add to Miller's list (or submit as a variant on his "job shuffling") "mixing it up," meaning efforts to immerse the analyst in the world of the practitioner and (though such efforts are more rare) vice versa. This strategy is the implicit justification for the scores of university-sponsored government internship programs that have flowered since the end of World War II.

In the light of this Lindblomian conceptualization of the relationship between policy analysis and real-world activities, the bleak record of social science research on corrections would appear not to be the inevitable product of insurmountable differences between analysts and practitioners à la Banfield, but to be the improvable product of a lack of concerted effort on both sides to understand that there are different types of knowledge that can be brought to bear on policymaking and administration, each of which has its strengths and limitations and is appropriate in its own sphere; and that the two can sometimes (but only sometimes) be married successfully if both sides are willing to give and take, to listen and learn.

Because, however, policymakers and administrators are normally more constrained than analysts in what they can say and do, the burden for establishing this sort of positive relationship falls more heavily on the analysts. As former Congressional Fellow Carol Weiss has observed, it is a burden that at least some social scientists are beginning to understand and to shoulder:

> Most policy researchers, particularly those in the universities, are more comfortable trying to produce analysis that eschews political allegiances and strives for "truth." But truth is not the name of the game on the Hill, and people in Congress doubt that analysts are after truth, either. . . . [But when] analysis makes values explicit, rigorously analyzes good data, and makes clear the implications for coherent action, the results tend to fit the staff's needs for coherent policy packaging. . . . Scholars are trying to adapt the methods of analysis to fit the realities of political decision making.[31]

Another statement along these lines was made in a 1987 essay by the criminal justice analyst Mark H. Moore of Harvard University. After offering numerous examples of how policy analysts have produced significant and positive effects on policy, Moore counseled that analysts must become more willing to interact productively with actual policymakers and administrators, deemphasizing the norms of "objectivity and distance" and producing work that does not "crumble into academic irrelevance."[32] And in an earlier essay which he wrote partially in response to Banfield's "Policy Science as Metaphysical Madness," Moore concluded:

> Social science is neither a substitute for nor a major threat to public officials' ability to think intelligently and responsibly about the decisions they face. To the extent that formal applications of social science come to dominate policy debates, there is some risk that debate will be substantively and procedurally impoverished. But it is not clear that any sensible policy maker would allow this to happen. . . . The possibilities for statesmanlike decisions might be enhanced by the development of structures and processes that mediate

between the institution of social science and the policy process. I do no want to exaggerate the importance of establishing such links. . . . But in a world of particular substantive choices and a growing social science establishment, this relationship is becoming relatively important. As a result, managing this relationship is becoming a priority matter.[33]

Implications of Lindblom's View

From this perspective, the sterile relationship between social science and corrections may be attributed largely to a failure on the part of the analysts to establish the necessary links. Behn, Miller, Weiss, Moore, and others who have moved away from an essentially Lindblomian conceptualization of the relationship between social science and real-world activities, have offered constructive (if easier-said-than-acted-upon) suggestions about how to strengthen the connections between "root" and "branch." They share the view that social scientists must take the initiative and tailor their analytic skills to the needs of policymakers and practitioners. Indeed, especially in Moore's writings, policy-oriented social scientists are made aware that they have at least as much to learn from the practitioners as the practitioners have to learn from them.

There are, of course, other views on how to structure the relationship. One is that analysts ought to interact directly with practitioners only infrequently and at a respectable distance. The analysts remain outside the processes by which policies are made and implemented, except insofar as their ideas trickle down to practitioners through books, essays, speeches, and so forth. This, quite

249

frankly, is the view of many professors who reside in schools of public policy.

Another view is that analysts should interact directly and frequently with practitioners, but only on a one-way street where social scientists are assumed to have the intellectual right-of-way. This view was expressed rather fully by the political scientist Aaron Wildavsky in his 1979 book *Speaking Truth to Power*. As Wildavsky sees it, the two necessary ingredients of good policy-making and implementation are truth (or systematic knowledge) and power (or the authority and influence to make and enforce policy decisions). In his understanding, analysts have the "truth"; policymakers and administrators have the "power." Wildavsky's book is a sort of extended memo to the former about how to maintain their intellectual and personal integrity while serving as "truth" missionaries to the latter. Thus, writes Wildavsky: "How to help ourselves [policy analysts] gain access to public life without becoming politicians is the challenge."[34]

Most corrections "experts" have taken either the "trickle-down" or the "speaking-truth-to-power" approach. To build real links with practitioners, however, researchers must have enough intellectual flexibility and sympathetic capacity to care about the problems that corrections policymakers and administrators face *in the ways that these officials care about them*; and to do so, the analysts must identify in a nontrivial way with the tasks that corrections officials must perform.

Most corrections researchers simply have not identified themselves with corrections practitioners in this way. Either they have been lost in interesting but practically irrelevant (and often poorly executed) statistical gymnastics (or theoretical speculations) about one or another aspect of the subject, or they have been relentlessly critical rather than constructive in studying what practitioners do, how they do it, and how (if at all) they can do it better and in a more cost-effective fashion. The academic literature on corrections officers is just the most obvious example of many.[35]

It is no secret that many of the field's leading analysts, mostly sociologists, have historically been far to the left politically, and more interested in fawning over "criminal cultures" than in finding ways to keep lawbreakers from victimizing citizens (including each other) on the streets and behind bars. Most corrections officials, especially those with years in the administrative trenches, know this all too well. As one veteran corrections officer remarked: "Most academics . . . don't really want to know about what we do. They like to write about the criminals, not the 'keepers.' They write about how we're a bunch of stupid ogres lording over a bunch of fallen angels . . . and wasting money, getting fat pensions, taking too much overtime. . . ." Not surprisingly, the "truth" these analysts have spoken to "power" has normally fallen on deaf ears. The exceptions are too few to be encouraging. To extend Lindblom's metaphor, in corrections the roots have turned rotten and the branches have been snapped.

SOCIAL SCIENCE AS DEMONSTRATION RESEARCH

A third conceptualization of the relationship between social science and "real-world" activities holds that the gap between the two is significant but bridgeable, and offers a single potent strategy for building that bridge. This view was advanced strongly by Princeton University's Richard P. Nathan in his 1988 book *Social Science in Government: Uses and Abuses.*[36]

Unlike Banfield, Lindblom, and other important commentators on the subject, Nathan draws on substantial "real-world" experience of his own. Before becoming a professor, he worked as a top-level official in the United States Office of Management and Budget, and in the Department of Health, Education, and Welfare. He spent years as a senior analyst at the Brookings Institution, a leading public policy "think tank" in Washington, D.C., and has also been Chairman of the Board of Directors of the Manpower Development Research Corporation in New York.

The author of numerous books and articles, Nathan's work on social science in government begins by acknowledging that faith in the practical value of social science research has waxed and waned. In the 1960s and 1970s, many believed that social scientists, mainly economists, could do no wrong. "Social scientists," observes Nathan, "were feeling their oats. . . . There was a feeling of ebullience about the potential for applied social science in national domestic policy. That optimism has faded."[37]

The essential reason it has faded, as Nathan sees it, is that social scientists simply failed to deliver on their promise of applied policy-relevant knowledge. They failed because they did not recognize that "the relationship between social science and social policy should be a two-way street. *The conduct of applied social science research is not only a matter of what social science can do for the real world. It is also and very much a matter of what the real world can do for social science*" (emphasis in original).[38]

Nathan highlights three "bad habits" of modern social science that are at the core of this failure. First, it has tended to emulate the natural sciences and to strive impossibly toward the elegance and predictive power of many natural scientific theories; no science of human behavior can achieve what sciences of inanimate matter have achieved, nor would we necessarily want that degree of understanding and control if it were within our grasp. Second, there has been a tendency toward overspecialization such that the modern social scientist is someone who knows a lot about a little and often cannot see the forest for the trees. Third, modern social science heralds quantitative research designs and techniques while disparaging qualitative research methods and data (participant observation, interviewing, and so on) as "soft," "unrigorous," and "unscientific." Here Nathan cites Abraham Kaplan's "law of the instrument": "Give a small boy a hammer, and he will find that everything he encounters needs pounding." The contemporary social scientist's hammer is the computer, which enables him to "work with large data sets to demonstrate mastery of the latest bells and whistles of mathematical practice that have mesmerized the social science industry (and other industries, too)."[39]

In Nathan's view, the one proven way of overcoming

253

this failure, and of effectively negotiating a mutually satisfactory relationship between the world of social science theory and the world of public policy and practice, is "demonstration research." Demonstration research is "a type of applied social science research systematically conducted under conditions in which independent, trained researchers apply their expertise to provide knowledge that can be used by policymakers in deciding whether to adopt a particular course of action or type of program."[40] Demonstration research has certain key features.[41]

First, researchers in a demonstration study seek to determine the impact of a new policy or program by measuring selected characteristics of the members of the affected group before, during, and after the new policy or program has taken effect. These characteristics are compared to the characteristics of a group that was not affected by the new policy or program. Based on this comparison, the researchers determine whether the new policy or program made a difference and, if so, the kind and the degree of difference it made.

At core, researchers in a demonstration study seek to determine what would have happened had there been no new policy or program. Strictly speaking, it is impossible to make this determination since, for obvious reasons, the same group cannot be both affected and unaffected by any given policy or program any more than a person can be in two places at one time. But demonstration researchers have several clever ways of getting around this problem, each one designed to make the comparison as meaningful as possible by making the affected and the unaffected groups as similar as possible. For if the "only" meaningful objective difference between the affected and the unaffected groups is that the former was affected by (that is participated in or was subjected to) the new policy or program while the latter was not, then any differences between them can be logically attributed to the new policy or program.

By far the best way to do this is to choose the members of the affected and unaffected groups on a random basis, as in a lottery. This way prevents the conscious or unconscious biases of those involved in setting up and administering the study from "loading the deck" in a way that might influence the results of the comparison. For example, if a diehard proponent of new inmate rehabilitation programs were free to choose which 50 of 100 maximum-security felons were to participate in psychotherapy and counseling sessions, he might well assign inmates who, based on his prior knowledge of their criminal and institutional histories, seemed most likely to "stay clean" upon release. But if the participants in the program were selected on a random basis, say, by tossing their names into a hat and selecting fifty, then the chance that such biases could determine the results of the comparison would be minimized.

Random assignment is a basic experimental technique that has been used by medical researchers and other scientists. In the social sciences, however, ethical, legal, and other considerations have often prevented researchers from using this technique of choice; and policy analysts have not made concerted efforts to find acceptable ways around these problems, or to get the relevant government officials (such as program administrators) to do the same.[42] Thus, much of applied social science has been based on "quasi-experimental" studies—demonstration studies that do *not* use random assignment. In a quasi-experimental study, for example, a new policy or program may affect inmates in a maximum-security prison in Michigan. The impact of the policy or program on these Michigan inmates may be determined by comparing their behavior "against itself" before and after the initiative took effect (for example, rates of inmate-on-inmate assaults at that prison before and after the policy or program took effect); by comparing their behavior to the behavior of otherwise comparable but unaffected inmates (inmates not subjected to such a policy or program) at another maximum-security prison in Michigan or elsewhere; or both. Often, quasi-experimental researchers use "data sets"—objective information about the relevant characteristics of the groups being compared—to determine the impact (if any) of a new policy or program. The statistical methods they employ in analyzing the data are often referred to as the "simulation" or "econometric" techniques.

As even the reader who has no more knowledge of demonstration research than what has been sketched in the foregoing paragraphs can probably sense, every step away from applied social science research with random assignment toward quasi-experimental research without it is a step away from the possibility of research findings that are (1) grounded fully in the logic of scientific inquiry, (2) subject to only one or a few logical interpretations, and (3) likely to be taken seriously by most policymakers and administrators whether or not the findings jibe with their existing interests and prior beliefs about the policies or programs in question.

In demonstration research with random assignment, the findings come close to "speaking for themselves" and are

256

less easy to ignore, to distort, or to enlist in any way (or in any grand or petty cause) one wishes. Even the uninitiated reader of the research report can normally tell (without peeking at the report's "Summary and Conclusion" section) whether the new policy or program worked, did not work, or had no discernible impact.

In demonstration research *without* random assignment, however, the wizardry of high-powered statisticians is often the only reliable road to interpreting the findings and gauging their significance. Indeed, in reviewing a demonstration research report, a rough clue to whether the study being reported involved random assignment can be gleaned by flipping through its pages to estimate the ratio of "mathematical bells and whistles" (including funny-looking graphs, calculus equations, and passages punctuated by words such as *heteroscedastity*) to easily understandable charts, tables, verbs, and nouns. The higher the ratio, the less likely it is that the study involved random assignment. And the higher the ratio, the more likely it is that each policymaker and administrator concerned with the report will employ his favorite statistical wizard to interpret the findings as he wants them interpreted, and to do intellectual combat over legitimate (versus "trumped-up" or red-herring) points of interpretation with the wizards employed by his real or perceived political and administrative adversaries.

Corrections has been the scene of very little meaningful demonstration research, virtually none of it done with random assignment. That is why social science research on corrections has normally done more to fuel ideological and political controversy than to forge intellectual and academic consensus. And it is in part why there are as

257

many "leading schools of thought" on tight custodial controls in relation to prison violence, the efficacy of given rehabilitation efforts, the cost-effectiveness of given alternatives to incarceration, and so on, as there are professional researchers and "sage" practitioner-penologists.

Lest the reader think that I exempt myself from any role in this comedy, let me hasten to note that my own ("quasi-quasi-experimental") work in this field is certainly no shining exception. But in this regard, if not in most others, I am like most of my social science brethren and other "experts" in this excessively politicized field. Rather than engaging in research that may truly bridge the gap between social science and real-world activities, we have normally engaged in research that begins or intensifies fights on both sides of the bridge and across it—researcher against researcher, official against official, and researcher against official.

Social Science and Welfare Reform: A Hopeful Example

There is, however, some evidence that those of us in all walks of corrections can do better. What *can* be achieved by practitioners and researchers via demonstration research with random assignment in even the most highly politicized policy areas is illustrated by Nathan's career and documented magnificently by him in *Social Science in Government*. His best example concerns "supported work and welfare reform."[43]

As noted earlier, Nathan has been Chairman of the Manpower Development Research Corporation (MDRC), a nonprofit corporation based in New York City that manages demonstration research projects. The studies done by MDRC between 1974 and 1987 focused on the value of various job-training, employment, and social service programs in helping members of the most economically disadvantaged groups in society.

When MDRC began its work, there was nothing approaching a consensus about how, if at all, to help these groups through such programs. Leading conservative officials and social welfare researchers often caricatured the problems of the disadvantaged and derided the possibility that they could be helped by such measures. Leading liberal officials and social welfare researchers often dramatized the problems of the disadvantaged and heralded the possibility that they could be rescued by any well-intentioned, well-funded measure. The former group circulated stories about "welfare queens"; the latter group responded with stories about starving babies. The academic debates on the subject were no less rancorous than the political ones; and they threw as much ideological heat as objective light on the problem.

MDRC helped to change all that. Among other projects, it undertook large-scale work/welfare reform demonstration studies in eight states. In six of them, the demonstration programs differed from conventional public welfare programs in that they obliged heads of families on welfare to *do something* in order to receive their benefits. The "something" could be searching for a job, working in the community, accepting an available job, or some combination of these and related activities.

These work/welfare programs did not constitute a new idea, but only carried out an old one. Previous efforts had

been made at the national and state levels to require welfare family heads to do these sorts of things in exchange
for welfare benefits. But these programs amounted to a
loosely administered bluff that welfare family heads knew
they could call without losing their benefits. The demonstration programs, on the other hand, sanctioned welfare
family heads who did not cooperate. Under such "workfare" programs, Aid to Families with Dependent Children
(AFDC) was converted from an "entitlement" program to
a "conditional" program.

Some of the states stressed the mandatory nature of the
demonstration program more than others, but all of them
imposed some meaningful employment-related requirements designed to get recipients off welfare and into the
labor force, thereby breaking the link between welfare dependency and any social ills it caused.

What, if any, impact did these new-style workfare programs have? Compared to otherwise comparable welfare
recipients not affected by the program, how did those
affected by it fare? Did the program have its desired effect, the opposite effect, or no discernible effect whatso-
ever on the groups affected by it? In most cases, the work/
welfare projects had small but positive impacts. Participants in the new programs were more likely than comparable nonparticipants to secure employment and to
reduce their welfare dependency. Moreover, these people
tended to believe that the mandatory approach was fair;
indeed, in one state the welfare recipients assigned to the
unaffected ("control") group complained that they were
not eligible for the mandatory services.

Based in part on the findings of the MDRC studies,
California and other states have adopted such programs.

The work of the MDRC has influenced the design of state-level workfare programs that, in turn, influenced the design of the new federal welfare policy signed into law by President Reagan shortly before he left office.

More broadly, it has given rise to a "new consensus" on welfare reform that would have been inconceivable just a decade ago.[44] This is not to say that ideological and political wrangling over the making and implementation of welfare policies is a thing of the past; nor is it to suggest that the MDRC demonstration studies were perfect, or that there is no research left to be done on welfare reform.

For our purposes, the important point is that the MDRC studies validated neither the fondest hopes nor the worst fears of those who had argued for and against such welfare reform measures. People on both sides were made to stop, look, and reconsider. The major lesson of this work for the future of social science and corrections is clear: Good applied social science is normally a spur to political compromise, because the empirical (if not the moral) "truth" about such matters often *demonstrably* (through demonstration research with random assignment) lies somewhere between the opinions of the main contending parties.

Implications of Nathan's View

Nathan's "can-do" conceptualization of the relationship between social science and real-world activities is better evidenced, more revealing of the hidden links between rigorous analysis and consensual politics, and (given his own background and research experiences) more authoritative than Banfield's musings about "metaphysical madness" and Lindblom's ideas about "muddling through." Of course, Nathan is a rare bird—an accomplished scholar, a former first-rate practitioner, and a man capable of moving gracefully between the worlds of social science and governmental practice, all rolled into one. This fact alone is reason enough to take seriously both Banfield's cautions and Lindblom's "root" and "branch."

Nevertheless, having weighed their conceptualizations against his, I am not convinced by Banfield that the gap is unbridgeable and that efforts to bridge it belong in the annals of human follies; nor do Lindblom and others convince me that the gap can be bridged only rarely and via a great exercise of strategic skill on the part of the most energetic and public-spirited of analysts.

Rather, I see in Nathan's work reason to believe that the gap can be bridged more regularly, and more easily, than is commonly supposed, and than the existing record in corrections and most other fields permits one to hope. It is not merely a question of getting especially gifted, strategic-minded, and tireless scholars into the business of bridging the gap as some sort of special academic favor to the officials and the public they serve. It is also very much a question of getting the right kinds of scholars to work with practitioners under the right conditions for their mutual benefit. This exchange need not be predicated on the intellectual equivalent of noblesse oblige by social scientists, for through demonstration studies, policy-oriented scholars have at least as much to gain intellectually (in the way of discovering things that are general, interesting, and true) as they have to contribute practically (in the way of arriving at ideas that can be used to achieve good public ends). Nathan hints at this when he writes:

> We [social scientists] need to know what is in the "black box," how the treatment works, what agencies and organizations are involved, and how they operate. The analysis also emphasizes the missing links between social science disciplines and variables, and between quantitative and qualitative research methods in the design and conduct of these studies.[45]

For both social scientists and practitioners, the charms of demonstration research with random assignment are twofold: It enhances scientific understanding, and it generates sound practical advice. Of course, such studies are expensive and hard to carry out. Thus, in the chapter of his book that eloquently describes "the hurdles of demonstration research," Nathan tempers his own clearly stated preference for random assignment as follows:

> All . . . alternatives to random assignment raise substantial issues for the conduct of demonstration research. The main point is that some of these less-good approaches . . . are better than others. The selection of a research design depends on a variety of factors. The research hurdle of selection bias is high and crucial. Nevertheless, I do not believe that its importance justifies the position, which unfortunately is widely held among researchers, that there are no acceptable alternatives to random assignment for demonstration research.[46]

On this point, I must qualify my near-total agreement with Nathan as follows: Demonstration research without random assignment may be acceptable, but *only* in fields where there is already a significant body of demonstration research with random assignment. In lodging this qualification, I hold corrections uppermost in my mind. At this stage, to add anything less than the most scientifically credible types of demonstration studies to the sickly piles of existing social science "research" on corrections will do little good. The field is currently too politicized, too mired in shoddy research, and too important to opt for anything short of demonstration research with random assignment.

In this regard, far and away the most important report issued by the National Institute of Justice in recent years was the 1988 pamphlet "Experiments Help Shape New Policies," which documented a small number of criminal justice demonstration studies with random assignment and presented summaries of their results. It also offered advice to criminal justice policymakers, administrators, and analysts about how to work together on such research. One of the nine "critical issues in designing experiments" stressed in the report was the need to "rigorously maintain the random assignment of persons, cases, or other units into treatment and control groups throughout the experiment." In his preface to the report, NIJ Director James K. Stewart wrote: "Increasingly, criminal justice professionals and researchers are forging stronger bonds, recognizing the important role that each plays in efforts to learn what works in criminal justice. They realize that cooperative relationships between researcher and practitioner are the key to progress."[47]

Stewart, a former police officer, is a good, wise, and public-spirited man. The past of social science and corrections has been abysmal because it has not brought practitioners and researchers together in the ways he suggests. The future of social science and corrections, the future relationship between "those who study" and "those who do," can be brighter than its past. It will be brightest if all concerned—analysts, policymakers, administrators, funders—make a concerted effort to conduct only demonstration research with random assignment.

With this possibility, there is some reason to hope that the future of social science and corrections will be slightly better than its past. But I would not bet the house—the Big House, that is—on it.

7

Conclusion:
The American Penal Credo

IN EACH OF THE PRECEDING CHAPTERS, I have drawn extensively on the ideas and experiences of the hundreds of federal, state, and local corrections practitioners whom I have interviewed and observed over the last decade. In discussing the future of American corrections as it relates to prison and jail management, alternatives to incarceration, rehabilitation programs, judicial intervention, privatization, and applied social science, I have made recourse to relevant research monographs and reports by academic analysts and other "experts." But my main source of information and insight has been the commissioners, wardens, prison and jail officers, probation and parole agents, and others who know corrections from the inside out and from the ground up.

I have no doubt that some of my academic colleagues will hear a note of intellectual heresy in my willingness to defer as such to the opinions and anecdotes of practitioners. If so, they hear right. And I have no doubt that most elite penal reformers will excuse me for taking into account the views of top-ranking agency officials, but will

266

accuse me of giving equal or greater weight to the views of less "sophisticated," lower-level staff, especially uniformed guards. If so, I plead guilty.

The library is filled with books and articles about crime and corrections. Many of these studies feature the most advanced sorts of statistical gymnastics. A few aisles over from these works are countless government-sponsored reports by blue-ribbon commissions, management consulting firms, or "research institutes." And in the same general area of the library are the embittered memoirs of violent ex-convicts and the sociological treatises on the colorful world of inmates and their leaders.

I have read through more of these pages than I care to recall. Much of it is intrinsically interesting (at least to me), and some tiny fraction of it is relevant to understanding and improving correctional policies and practices. But I would gladly trade this material—scientific, pseudoscientific, and silly—for a day spent talking to and watching almost any veteran corrections worker. My only comparative advantage as a scholar is that I have had the time and the resources to witness and learn from a variety of practitioners in diverse settings.

Let me complete my heresy, therefore, by deferring to corrections practitioners once again, this time on the question of how convicted criminals ought in general to be treated. Few people who work in the field have been exposed to the great works of political and moral philosophy; they would not know Kant from "clearing the count." But, on this subject, veteran corrections practitioners have a more profound source of wisdom; namely, they are decent, law-abiding citizens who spend most of their working hours handling and getting to know persons

267

who have criminally violated the life, liberty, and property of others. This gives them a unique moral perch from which to pronounce on the question of what our public philosophy of punishment—our penal credo—ought to be. On the one hand, corrections practitioners know better than anyone else just how utterly depraved, wicked, and calculating some of their charges have been and continue to be. On the other hand, corrections practitioners also know better than anyone else that many of their charges, including the worst "heavies" and "hard-asses," come disproportionately from miserable homes and hopeless neighborhoods, and suffer disproportionately from untreated mental and physical debilities.

"What I do here," remarked one maximum-security prison worker, "is protect, feed, and try to educate scum who raped and brutalized women and children; who robbed a convenience store and then, just for kicks, shot the old man and old lady who ran it; who didn't get paid for the drugs they sold and so killed to enforce the deal; who, if I turn my back, will go into their cell, wrap a blanket around their cellmate's legs, and threaten to beat or rape him if he doesn't give sex, carry contraband, or fork over radios, money, or other goods willingly. And they'll stick a shank [knife-like weapon] in me tomorrow if they think they can get away with it."

A parole official characterized his job as follows: "It's about helping punks, perverts, and predators, most of whom have no remorse for the harm they've inflicted on others, the innocent lives they've upset or ruined, or the hardship they work on the whole society. You can work your ass off for them—get them a job, help with their personal problems. Most will still do crime." A veteran city probation officer confided: "After decades working with criminals, God forgive me, sometimes I think we'd all be better off if they were just dead."

But that is only half of the practitioners' moral picture of their charges. The anger and frustration most of them experience as they gain an intimate knowledge of offenders is mitigated by their equally intimate knowledge of the typical offender's life circumstances.

Thus the probation officer just quoted was quick to acknowledge that persons who become offenders have, in most cases, "been treated like dirt for most of their lives. You take almost any one of them, you read their jackets [folders containing criminal record and personal background information], and you say, 'There but by the grace of God go I.' Beaten and abused as kids. Many had no folks, or a father or somebody else in jail, a mother and every other adult they know except drug dealers on welfare, and always in poverty. Some are mentally retarded or borderline retarded, but the schools didn't take care of them."

Similarly, after his diatribe against the "scum," the maximum-security officer added: "Of course, you have to feel a little sorry for these bastards. Nobody ever gave them a break. Nobody ever taught them right from wrong. . . . I work with them every day, and, except when I'm forced to think about it or there's a stabbing or something, I see them as no different from you and me. They can be friendly, considerate, caring. They can laugh at jokes. They can be good people. . . . Don't go away with the wrong idea. There's bad boys and bad homes, too. But I just don't think it's all their fault, what they are, or were. Some of them, yes. But not all of them, not all."

Finally, the parole officer qualified his remark about the "punks, perverts, and predators" as follows: "It's ten percent . . . that's the number of rotten-to-the-core mother-f—kers. One in ten I've known could change for the better but chose not to. One in ten chose crime because it paid better than other ways of life, because they got off on hurting and terrorizing and felt they could get away with it. The rest are half and half. Half want help, but never get it, or don't get enough. The other half you can't read, you can't figure. Are they rotten or are they struggling? Almost all of them, though, have had pretty lousy lives before getting in my hands."

These practitioners speak for most of their profession. Whatever criminologists find or claim about sociology, biogenetics, or opportunity in association with criminal activity, practitioners are inclined to hold individuals responsible for their actions and to see them punished. At the same time, however, they recognize that behind "bad souls" may be some mix of bad homes, bad genes, and bad incentives. Their penal credo is thus neither logically consistent nor terribly elegant, and it begs fundamental questions regarding free will, determinism, and the like.

But so be it. Toward most criminals, the practitioners' approach to punishment calls forth both care and custody, both revenge and forgiveness. As such, it has deep roots in the Judeo-Christian tradition of punishment in the form of justice tempered by mercy. The Judaic side of the tradition is often caricatured as purely punitive, vengeful, and justice-seeking, while the Christian side is often caricatured as purely forgiving and merciful. But the Mosaic injunction calling for "eye for eye, tooth for tooth, hand for hand, foot for foot" means only that injuries must be compensated, while the New Testament injunction to "turn the other cheek" by no means prohibits retribution against wrongdoers.[1]

For their part, most corrections practitioners take it as axiomatic that their charges deserve to be treated firmly but fairly, to suffer no unnecessary pains beyond the loss of liberty, and, in virtually all cases, to have a chance to return to the bosom of the free, law-abiding community once supervision ceases. Most of them would agree entirely with the following words from Francis Lieber's introduction to the English edition of Alexis de Tocqueville's and Gustave de Beaumont's monumental study *On the Penitentiary System in the United States and France*— the first study of its kind, and still one of the few studies to take seriously the penological views and moral wisdom of practitioners.

The penitentiary has not escaped the common fate of all questions of vital interest to society; many of its opponents as well as its advocates run to extremes; the former, judging by vague impressions derived from superficial knowledge, both of the character of convicts and the penitentiary system, assert not infrequently, with a kind of levity, that criminals ought to suffer severely for their crimes, and should not be treated with tenderness; the latter, carried away by pious zeal, often believe that an individual who from early childhood received bad impressions, imbibed vicious principles, and has allowed himself to be governed during his whole life by unchecked desires and unbridled appetites . . . [may] become a contrite sinner, and, soon after, change into a saint. It is always to be borne in mind, that a convict is neither a brute nor a saint, and to treat him as either, is equally injurious to himself and to society.[2]

271

The history of American corrections can be read as an imperfect effort to fashion policies and practices that embody this sort of balanced moral vision about crime and punishment. Whatever else is decided, let us hope that the future of American corrections permits no escape from this delicate moral balancing act.

Notes

CHAPTER 1. BETTER MANAGEMENT EQUALS BETTER PRISONS AND JAILS

1. For a more thorough discussion of Bennett's leadership, see John J. DiIulio, Jr., *Barbed Wire Bureaucracy: Leadership and Administration in the Federal Bureau of Prisons, 1930–1990* (New York: Oxford University Press, forthcoming).
2. James V. Bennett, *I Chose Prison* (New York: Knopf, 1970).
3. For a more thorough discussion of Carlson's leadership, see DiIulio, *Barbed Wire Bureaucracy*.
4. For a fuller discussion of the penitentiary in Marion, see John J. DiIulio, Jr., *Prisons That Work: An Overview of Management in the Federal Bureau of Prisons* (Washington, D.C.: National Institute of Corrections, June 1989), pp. 17–22.
5. For example, see the following: John J. DiIulio, Jr., *Governing Prisons: A Comparative Study of Correctional Management* (New York: Free Press, 1987), esp. chap. 4; Steve J.

Martin and Sheldon Ekland-Olson, *Texas Prisons: The Walls Came Tumbling Down* (Austin: Texas Monthly Press, 1987); and Ben M. Crouch and James W. Marquart, *An Appeal to Justice: Litigated Reform of Texas Prisons* (Austin: University of Texas Press, 1989).

6. See "The Three Faces of Ruiz," chaps. 2, 3, and 4, in *Courts, Corrections, and the Constitution: The Impact of Judicial Intervention on Prisons and Jails*, ed. John J. DiIulio, Jr. (New York: Oxford University Press, 1990).

7. See DiIulio, *Governing Prisons*.

8. Bert Useem and Peter Kimball, *States of Siege: U.S. Prison Riots, 1971–1986* (New York: Oxford University Press, 1989). For an essay linking the findings of this book to my work, see Bert Useem, "Correctional Management: How Do We Govern Our 'Cities'?" *Corrections Today* (February 1990): 88, 90, 94.

9. Christopher A. Innes, *Population Density in State Prisons* (Washington, D.C.: Bureau of Justice Statistics, December 1986).

10. For a good summary of these studies, see Jeff Bleich, "The Politics of Prison Crowding," *California Law Review* 77 (1989): 1125–80.

11. John Irwin, "Donald Cressey and the Sociology of the Prison," *Crime and Delinquency* (July 1988): 335.

12. James Q. Wilson, *Bureaucracy: What Government Agencies Do and Why They Do It* (New York: Basic Books, 1989), p. 91.

13. Alexis de Tocqueville, *Democracy in America*, vol. 2 ed. Phillips Bradley (New York: Vintage Books, 1945), p. 26.

14. Wilson, *Bureaucracy*.

15. This alliterative phrase is from Richard A. McGee, *Prisons and Politics* (Lexington, MA: Lexington Books, 1981). McGee directed the California penal system for several decades.

16. For example, see Lucien Lombardo, *Guards Imprisoned: Correctional Officers at Work* (Cincinnati: Anderson, 1976; 2nd ed., 1989), and Kelsey Kauffman, *Prison Officers and Their World* (Cambridge: Harvard University Press, 1989).

17. DiIulio, *Governing Prisons.* See chap. 4, which discusses the "keeper philosophy."

18. On schools, see James S. Coleman, Thomas Hoffer, and Sally Kilgore, *High School Achievement* (New York: Basic Books, 1982), and John Chubb and Terry Moe, *What Price Democracy?* (Washington, D.C.: Brookings Institution, 1990). On armies, see William Daryl Henderson, *Cohesion: The Human Element in Combat* (Washington, D.C.: National Defense University, 1985). On police departments, see Robert Trajanowicz and Bonnie Bucqueroux, *Community Policing* (Cincinnati: Anderson, 1990). For a complementary discussion of schools, armies, and prisons, see Wilson, *Bureaucracy,* esp. chap. 1.

19. For a fuller statement of that "faith," see John J. DiIulio, Jr., "Recovering the Public Management Variable: Lessons from Schools, Prisons, and Armies," *Public Administration Review* (March/April 1990): 127–33.

CHAPTER 2. PROMISING ALTERNATIVES TO INCARCERATION

1. For example, see Edward E. Rhine et al., "Parole: Issues and Prospects for the 1990s," *Corrections Today* (December 1989): 78–83, 146–47.

2. This insight comes from Richard McCleary, *Dangerous Men: The Sociology of Parole* (Beverly Hills, CA: Sage, 1978). This is one of the few good scholarly studies of what field agents do and why they do it. In the annotated bibliog-

raphy of my *Governing Prisons: A Comparative Study of Correctional Management* (New York: Free Press, 1987), an overeager production assistant mistakenly changed my reference to *Dangerous Men* and assigned its authorship to Richard H. McCleery, a political scientist turned corrections official who has written several excellent studies about prisons. I take this opportunity to set the record straight, and to endorse McCleary's underappreciated book.

3. See John J. DiIulio, Jr., "Underclass: The Impact of Inner-City Crime," *The Public Interest* (Summer 1989): 28–46.

4. Katherine M. Jamieson and Timothy J. Flanagan, eds., *Sourcebook of Criminal Justice Statistics—1988* (Washington, D.C.: U.S. Government Printing Office, 1989), p. 219.

5. John Doble et al., *Prison Overcrowding and Alternative Sentences: The Views of the People of Alabama* (New York: Public Agenda Foundation Report, November 14, 1988).

6. William G. Nagel, address delivered at the Brookings Institution in Washington, D.C., 1979. Nagel's most influential written work is *The New Red Barn: A Critical Look at the Modern Prison* (New York: Walker, 1973), which concludes with a call for a moratorium on prison construction.

7. Perry M. Johnson, speech delivered at the ACA's conference in New Orleans, Louisiana, 1987.

8. For an overview of Johnson's achievements as director of the Michigan Department of Corrections, see DiIulio, *Governing Prisons*, esp. chap. 4.

9. For examples, see the following: "Revolving Door Prisons," *Detroit Free Press* (September 22–28, 1985); "Michigan Prisons: From Bad to Worse," *Detroit Free Press* (November 1987).

10. Johnson, speech at ACA conference, 1987.

11. National Conference of State Legislatures (NCSL), *Legis-*

lative Finance Papers (Denver, CO: NCSL, August 1987), p. 42.

12. Edwin W. Zedlewski, "Making Confinement Decisions," *Research in Brief* (Washington, D.C.: National Institute of Justice, July 1987).

13. Franklin E. Zimring and Gordon Hawkins, "The New Mathematics of Imprisonment," *Crime and Delinquency* (October 1988): 425–36.

14. Richard B. Abell, "Beyond Willie Horton: The Battle of the Prison Bulge," *Policy Review* (Winter 1989): 32.

15. As of this writing, I am working with Ann Piehl, a Princeton Ph.D. candidate in Economics, on a project that may result in a more valid approach to calculating incarceration benefit-cost ratios.

16. For example, see the references to articles published in such places as *Reader's Digest* in Robert James Bidinotto, "Crime and Consequences," *The Freeman* (July, August, and September 1989).

17. Michel Foucault, *Discipline and Punish: The Birth of the Prison*, trans. Alan Sheridan (New York: Pantheon, 1978).

18. For example, see Richard A. Berk and Peter Rossi, *Prison Reform and State Elites* (Cambridge, MA: Ballinger, 1977); George W. Downs, *Bureaucracy, Policy, and Innovation* (Lexington, MA: Lexington Books, 1977); Stuart Nagel et al., eds., *The Political Science of Criminal Justice* (Springfield, IL: Charles C Thomas, 1983); Barbara Lavin, "Political Theory and Correctional Politics: Policies and Rhetoric," paper presented at the September 1983 meeting of the American Political Science Association, Chicago, Illinois; Julia Gordon, "Under Lock and Key: Correctional Policymaking in Massachusetts" (unpublished thesis, Harvard University, Cambridge, MA, March 1985).

19. Blake McKelvey, *American Prisons: A History of Good Intentions* (Montclair, NJ: Patterson-Smith, 1977).

20. David J. Rothman, *The Discovery of the Asylum: Social Order in the New Republic* (Boston: Little, Brown, 1971); idem, *Conscience and Convenience: The Asylum and Its Alternatives in Progressive America* (Boston: Little, Brown, 1980).

21. Nagel, *The New Red Barn.*

22. Douglas C. McDonald, *Punishment Without Walls: Community Service Sentences in New York City* (Rutgers, NJ: Rutgers University Press, 1986).

23. For an overview, see Billie S. Erwin and Lawrence Bennett, "New Dimensions in Probation: Georgia's Experience with Intensive Probation Supervision," *Research in Brief* (National Institute of Justice, Washington, D.C., January 1987).

24. For an overview, see Frank J. Pearson, *Research on New Jersey's Intensive Supervision Program* (National Institute of Justice, Washington, DC, November 1987), and his "Evaluation of New Jersey's Intensive Supervisions Program," *Crime and Delinquency* 34 (October 19, 1988): 437–48.

25. Walter J. Dickey, *From the Bottom Up: Probation Supervision in a Wisconsin Community* (Madison: Occasional Paper, University of Wisconsin Law School, August 1988), pp. 21–23.

26. Neal R. Pierce, "No Bars, No Guns: Punishing Without Prison," *National Journal* (November 21, 1987): 2987.

27. Neal R. Pierce, "On Letting the Punishment Fit the Criminal," *National Journal* (December 5, 1987): 3107.

28. Quoted in Pierce, "No Bars."

29. DiIulio, "Underclass: The Impact of Inner-City Crime."

30. For example, see Todd Clear, *Research in Corrections: Statistical Prediction in Corrections* (Washington, D.C.: National

Institute of Corrections, March 1988), including the reviews by two practitioners offered in pp. 41–52.

CHAPTER 3. REHABILITATION REVISITED

1. Douglas Lipton et al., *The Effectiveness of Correctional Treatment: A Survey of Treatment Evaluation Studies* (New York: Praeger, 1975).
2. Robert Martinson, "What Works?: Questions and Answers About Prison Reform," *The Public Interest* (Spring 1974): 25.
3. Lee Sechrest et al., eds., *Rehabilitation of Criminal Offenders: Problems and Prospects* (Washington, D.C.: National Academy of Science, 1979).
4. For example, see Robert Martinson, "New Findings, New Views: A Note of Caution Regarding Sentencing Reform," *Hofstra Law Review* 7 (1979): 243–58.
5. Ibid.
6. For a sample of this work, see: Paul Gendreau and Robert P. Ross, "Revivification of Rehabilitation: Evidence from the 1980s," *Justice Quarterly* (September 1987): 349–407; Paul Gendreau and D. A. Andrews, "What the Meta-Analyses of the Offender Treatment Literature Tells Us About 'What Works,' " unpublished paper (September 1989; forthcoming in *Canadian Journal of Criminology*); Francis T. Cullen and Paul Gendreau, "The Effectiveness of Correctional Rehabilitation: Reconsidering the 'Nothing Works' Debate," in *American Prisons: Issues in Research and Policy*, ed. Lynne Goodstein and Doris MacKenzie (New York: Plenum, forthcoming).
7. Cullen and Gendreau, "Effectiveness of Correctional Rehabilitation," p. 39.
8. See reference to Conference on Issues in Corrections, footnote p. 104.

9. Marcia R. Chaiken, *Prison Programs for Drug-Involved Offenders* (Washington, D.C.: National Institute of Justice, October 1989); quotation from p. 1.

10. Cullen and Gendreau, "Effectiveness of Correctional Rehabilitation," pp. 1, 32.

11. Gendreau and Andrews, "Meta-Analyses," p. 12.

12. For example, see Gendreau and Ross, "Revivification of Rehabilitation," esp. pp. 349–53, 394–96.

13. For an overview, see John J. DiIulio, Jr., *Barbed Wire Bureaucracy: Leadership and Administration in the Federal Bureau of Prisons, 1930–1990* (New York: Oxford University Press, forthcoming).

14. Ronald J. Waldron and Peter L. Nacci, eds., *Research Review, Butner Study: The Final Analysis* (Washington, D.C.: Federal Bureau of Prisons, June 1987), p. 5.

15. For an overview, see John J. DiIulio, Jr., *Governing Prisons: A Comparative Study of Correctional Management* (New York: Free Press, 1987), pp. 40–43.

16. For example, see Katherine M. Jamieson and Timothy J. Flanagan, eds., *Sourcebook of Criminal Justice Statistics—1988* (Washington D.C.: U.S. Government Printing Office, 1989), p. 221. In the survey reported here, rehabilitation was one of six discrete "purposes of punishment" that over 58 percent of all respondents deemed "very important." In fact, while 79.2 percent rated deterrence as "very important," 71.5 percent rated rehabilitation as "very important." Only 25 percent deemed sheer retribution "very important" as a purpose of punishment. These results are echoed in scores of other credible surveys conducted between 1975 and 1989.

17. Mimeo of "Case of Herman Webb Duker . . . October 3, 1931," pp. 5–6, 8.

18. Ibid, pp. 10–11.

19. Contract Research Corporation, *The Evaluation of Patuxent*

Institution: Final Report (Hunt Valley, MD: Contract Research Corp., February 25, 1977).

20. For example, see Robert A. Gordon, "A Critique of the Evaluation of Patuxent Institution, with Particular Attention to the Issues of Dangerousness and Recidivism," *The Bulletin of the American Academy of Psychiatry and Law* 5, no. 2 (1979): 210–55.

21. Contract Research, *Evaluation of Patuxent*, pp. 83–86.

22. For example, see Gordon, "Critique of the Evaluation of Patuxent," p. 243, on the report's erratic use of statistical controls.

23. Contract Research, *Evaluation of Patuxent*, p. vi.

24. Patuxent Institution, *Inmate Handbook*, February 1988, pp. 3–4.

25. Report prepared by Patuxent Institution Research Office for Judge Byrnes of the Baltimore City Circuit Court, "Report on Lifers and Non-Lifers Evaluated for Admission to Patuxent Institution, FY 1978 to FY 1988," September 30, 1988.

26. Judge Alan M. Wilner, "Keynote Address: Patuxent Day—November 5, 1983," p. 14.

27. Report prepared by Patuxent Institution Research Office at my request, untitled, undated, submitted 1988.

CHAPTER 4. JUDICIAL INTERVENTION: LESSONS OF THE PAST

1. *Banning v. Looney*, 213, F.2d 771,348 U.S. (1954).

2. This is not, however, to argue that conditions improved, or improved greatly, in each and every jurisdiction, or that the rate of progress was much the same throughout the country. Neither is it to suggest that there were no setbacks in any given jurisdiction. For one rich historical

account of the fits and starts of correctional reform and administrative change, see Paul W. Keve, *The History of Corrections in Virginia* (Charlottesville: University Press of Virginia, 1986).

3. Clair A. Cripe, "Courts, Corrections, and the Constitution: A Practitioner's View," in *Courts, Corrections, and the Constitution: The Impact of Judicial Intervention on Prisons and Jails*, ed. John J. DiIulio, Jr. (New York: Oxford University Press, 1990), chap. 10.

4. For an argument along these lines, see Nathan Glazer, "Should Courts Administer Social Services?" *The Public Interest* (Spring 1978): 64–80.

5. For examples, see DiIulio, *Courts, Corrections, and the Constitution*.

6. *Harris v. Flemming*, 839, F.2d 1232 (7th Cir. 1988).

7. Robert Bradley, "Judicial Appointment and Judicial Intervention: The Issuance of Structural Reform Decrees in Correctional Litigation," in DiIulio, *Courts, Corrections, and the Constitution*, chap. 9.

8. Kathleen Engel and Stanley Rothman, "Prison Violence and the Paradox of Reform," *The Public Interest* (Fall 1983): 97.

9. John J. DiIulio, Jr., *Governing Prisons: A Comparative Study of Correctional Management* (New York: Free Press, 1987); and Bert Useem and Peter Kimball, *States of Siege: U.S. Prison Riots, 1971–1986* (New York: Oxford University Press, 1989).

10. For example, see Malcolm Feeley and Roger Hanson, "The Impact of Judicial Intervention on Prisons and Jails: A Review of the Literature," in DiIulio, *Courts, Corrections, and the Constitution*, chap. 1.

11. This section of this chapter is based on several sources: interviews with several participants in the Alabama litigation; Philip J. Cooper, *Hard Judicial Choices: Federal Dis-*

trict Court Judges and State and Local Officials (New York: Oxford University Press, 1988), chaps. 7 and 8; Larry W. Yackle, *Reform and Regret: The Story of Federal Judicial Involvement in the Alabama Prison System* (New York: Oxford University Press, 1989); and national and local newspaper accounts.

12. This section of this chapter is based mainly on two sources: (1) my work as a consultant to the New York City Board of Corrections; (2) Ted Storey, "When Intervention Works: Judge Morris E. Lasker and New York City Jails," in DiIulio, *Courts, Corrections, and the Constitution*, chap. 6.

13. Quoted in Storey, "When Intervention Works," p. 152.

14. Quoted in Storey, ibid.

15. See Sheldon Ekland-Olson and Steve J. Martin, "*Ruiz*: A Struggle over Legitimacy," in DiIulio, *Courts, Corrections, and the Constitution*, chap. 3.

CHAPTER 5. PRIVATIZATION OR NATIONALIZATION?

1. In my opinion, the two best available sources on the subject are Charles H. Logan, *Private Prisons: Cons and Pros* (New York: Oxford University Press, 1990), and Douglas McDonald, ed., *Private Prisons and Public Policy* (Rutgers, NJ: Rutgers University Press, 1990). Both books reach pro-privatization conclusions, but both admit the tenuousness of those conclusions.

2. Alexis de Tocqueville and Gustave de Beaumont, *On the Penitentiary System in the United States and France*, trans. Francis Lieber (Philadelphia: Carey, Lea and Blanchard, 1833), p. 36.

3. For a fuller statement on these measures, see John J.

DiIulio, Jr., *Governing Prisons: A Comparative Study of Correctional Management* (New York: Free Press, 1987), chap. 2.

4. Dennis F. Thompson, "Moral Responsibility of Public Officials: The Problem of Many Hands," *American Political Science Review* (December 1980): 905–16.

5. See Logan, *Private Prisons*, and my review of it in *Commentary* (March 1990): 66–68.

6. John Locke, *Second Treatise of Government* (New York: Mentor, 1965), p. 308.

7. Herbert Kaufman, *Red Tape: Its Origins, Uses, and Abuses* (Washington, D.C.: Brookings Institution, 1977), p. 4.

8. Arthur C. Millspaugh, *Local Democracy and Crime Control* (Washington, D.C.: Brookings Institution, 1936).

CHAPTER 6. SOCIAL SCIENCE AND CORRECTIONS

1. Randall Collins, *Sociological Insight: An Introduction to Non-Obvious Sociology* (New York: Oxford University Press, 1982), p. vi.

2. Claude Lévi-Strauss, *The Bearer of Ashes* (Boston: Routledge & Kegan Paul, 1983), p. 27.

3. Alexis de Tocqueville, *Democracy in America,* vol. 2, ed. Phillips Bradley (New York: Vintage, 1945), p. 14.

4. The classic statement of this theory is Gresham M. Sykes, *The Society of Captives* (Princeton, NJ: Princeton University Press, 1958).

5. See Bert Useem and Peter Kimball, *States of Siege: U.S. Prison Riots, 1971–1986* (New York: Oxford University Press, 1989), and John J. DiIulio, Jr., *Governing Prisons: A Comparative Study of Correctional Management* (New York: Free Press, 1987), esp. chap. 1.

6. For this definition, I am indebted to James Q. Wilson, Collins Professor of Management, University of California at Los Angeles.

7. Gustave de Beaumont and Alexis de Tocqueville, *On the Penitentiary System in the United States and France*, trans. Francis Lieber (Philadelphia: Carey, Lea, and Blanchard), pp. 55, 58–59.

8. For one recent example, see Paul Johnson, *Intellectuals* (New York: Harper & Row, 1988).

9. Thomas Sowell, *Knowledge and Decisions* (New York: Basic Books, 1980).

10. Cited in Edward C. Banfield, "Policy Science as Metaphysical Madness," in *Bureaucrats, Policy Analysts, Statesmen: Who Leads?*, ed. Robert Goldwin (Washington, D.C.: American Enterprise Institute, 1980), pp. 1, 18.

11. Banfield treated me to this remark when I was in his "Political Economizing" class at Harvard University in the Fall of 1980.

12. Edward C. Banfield, "The Training of the Executive," excerpt of published essay, copied and circulated by the author, Harvard University, Fall 1980.

13. For this distinction and for the example I shall use to illustrate it, I am indebted to Professor Banfield, who shared it with me as a member of his "Political Economizing" class at Harvard University in the Fall of 1980.

14. I am indebted to my Princeton staff assistant, Valerie Kanka, for helping me to track down this rendering of the Rhodes criteria.

15. For a discussion that takes cognizance of this reality, see Joseph White and Aaron Wildavsky, "Fixing the Deficit—Really," *The Public Interest* (Winter 1989): 3–24; see also Aaron Wildavsky, *The Politics of the Budgetary Process* (Boston: Little, Brown, 1979), esp. pp. 190–221.

16. For a fuller statement along these lines, see Wildavsky,

Politics of the Budgetary Process; see also James Q. Wilson, ed., *The Politics of Regulation* (New York: Basic Books, 1980), chap. 10.

17. For a fuller argument along these lines, see Bernard Crick, *In Defense of Politics* (Chicago: University of Chicago Press, 1972).

18. For example, see McKinsey and Company, *Strengthening TDC's Management Effectiveness: Final Report* (Dallas, TX: May 14, 1984).

19. For a general discussion of Carlson's leadership, see John J. DiIulio, Jr., *Barbed Wire Bureaucracy: Leadership and Administration in the Federal Bureau of Prisons, 1930–1990* (New York: Oxford University Press, forthcoming).

20. For example, see National Institute of Justice, *Research Program Plan, Fiscal Year 1989* (Washington, D.C.: November 1988), p. 5: "Applicants bear the responsibility of demonstrating that the research proposed . . . could ultimately contribute to a practical application in law enforcement or criminal justice."

21. Robert M. Carter et al., eds., *Correctional Institutions*, 3rd ed. (New York: Harper & Row, 1985), pp. 473–513.

22. Charles Lindblom, "The Science of 'Muddling Through,' " in *Public Administration: Cases and Concepts*, ed. Richard J. Stillman II, 3rd ed. (Boston: Houghton Mifflin, 1983), pp. 238–49.

23. Ibid., p. 241.

24. See Crick, *In Defense of Politics*.

25. Lindblom, "The Science of 'Muddling Through,' " p. 247.

26. Ibid., p. 248.

27. See David Cohen and Charles Lindblom, *Usable Knowledge* (New Haven, CT: Yale University Press, 1976).

28. Robert Behn, "Management by Groping Along," *Journal of Policy Analysis and Management* (Fall 1988): 643–63; Thomas I. Miller, "Gut-Level Decisionmaking: Implica-

tions for Public Policy Analysis," *Journal of Policy Analysis and Management* (Winter 1989): 119–25.

29. Miller, "Gut-Level Decisionmaking," p. 124.

30. Ibid., p. 123.

31. Carol Weiss, as cited in Thomas J. Anton, "Social Science Research and Government: Comparative Essays on Britain and the United States," *Journal of Policy Analysis and Management* (Winter 1989): 143.

32. Mark H. Moore, "What Makes Public Ideas Powerful?" in *The Power of Public Ideas*, ed. Robert B. Reich (Cambridge, MA: Ballinger, 1987), p. 83.

33. Mark H. Moore, "Statesmanship in a World of Particular Substantive Choices," in Goldwin, *Bureaucrats, Policy Analysts, Statesmen*, p. 35.

34. Aaron Wildavsky, *Speaking Truth to Power* (Boston: Little, Brown, 1979); quotation from p. 19. I do not mean to imply, however, that I find nothing of value in this and other works by Professor Wildavsky. On the contrary, his views on this subject, as on many others, are powerful and engaging.

35. In this literature, officers are normally described as ill-educated racists. For example, see John Irwin, *Prisons in Turmoil* (Boston: Little, Brown, 1980).

36. Richard R. Nathan, *Social Science in Government: Uses and Misuses* (New York: Basic Books, 1988).

37. Ibid., p. 3.

38. Ibid., pp. 9–10.

39. Ibid., pp. 11–12.

40. Ibid., pp. 44–45.

41. Unless otherwise noted, my discussion of the key features of demonstration research is a simplified and abbreviated version of ibid., pp. 45–49.

42. Ibid., pp. 80–81.

43. Ibid., pp. 97–121.

44. For example, see Michael Novak et al., *The New Consensus on Family and Welfare* (Washington, D.C.: American Enterprise Institute, 1987).
45. Nathan, *Social Science in Government*, p. 121.
46. Ibid., p. 77.
47. Joel H. Garner and Christy A. Visher, "Policy Experiments Come of Age," *National Institute of Justice: NIJ Reports* (Washington, D.C.: September/October 1988), pp. 2–8, 7.

CHAPTER 7. CONCLUSION: THE AMERICAN PENAL CREDO

1. Though by no means authoritative, an argument in support of the Mosaic half of this connection can be found in Paul Johnson, *A History of the Jews* (New York: Harper & Row, 1987).
2. Gustave de Beaumont and Alexis de Tocqueville, *On the Penitentiary System in the United States and France*, trans. Francis Lieber (Philadelphia: Carey, Lea, and Blanchard, 1933), p. xviii.

Index

289